One Man's Judgment

An autobiography

The Rt Hon Lord Wheatley PC

Butterworths
London
1987

United Kingdom Butterworth & Co (Publishers) Ltd, 88 Kingsway, LONDON
WC2B 6AB and 61A North Castle Street, EDINBURGH EH2 3LJ

Australia   Butterworths Pty Ltd, SYDNEY, MELBOURNE, BRISBANE, ADELAIDE,
PERTH, CANBERRA and HOBART

Canada   Butterworths. A division of Reed Inc., TORONTO and VANCOUVER

New Zealand   Butterworths of New Zealand Ltd, WELLINGTON and AUCKLAND

Singapore   Butterworth & Co (Asia) Pte Ltd, SINGAPORE

South Africa   Butterworth Publishers (Pty) Ltd, DURBAN and PRETORIA

USA   Butterworths Legal Publishers, ST PAUL, Minnesota, SEATTLE,
Washington, BOSTON, Massachusetts, AUSTIN, Texas and D & S
Publishers, CLEARWATER, Florida

British Library Cataloguing in Publication Data

Wheatley, John Wheatley, Lord
One man's judgment: an autobiography.
1. Wheatley, John Wheatley, Lord
2. Judges—Scotland—Biography
344.11'0092'4   KDC313.W
ISBN 0 406 10019 5

Printed and bound in Great Britain by
Butler & Tanner Ltd, Frome and London

Dedication

To Nancy, without whose love, patience, understanding and help most of what I have achieved would not have been possible.

Foreword

Throughout my career I never had in contemplation that I would write my autobiography, and when I was asked by the publishers to write this one, I accepted with much misgiving. I had never kept a diary nor had I retained personal records of my various activities. Consequently I have no personal papers against which I can check what I have written, and such papers as I had retained all disappeared progressively in our three moves to new houses. There is nothing like a 'flitting' to get rid of old junk but you have to be ruthless. I know of judges who have kept copies of every judgment they delivered, other than the formal 'I concur' ones. That may be a wise course, because not only does it cut out a good deal of necessary research when composing a future judgment on the same or a similar topic, but it obviates the danger of issuing a contradictory opinion. I never engaged in the practice of dwelling over my opinions in reported cases which I had decided, unless they were relevant to the issue under consideration. The reason for this was that both at the Bar and on the Bench I took the view that when a case was finished it was finished. That stemmed from a piece of advice which my father gave to me on the day following my being called to the Bar in November 1932. I had gone back to Shettleston to spend the weekend with my family. My father, who was a quiet man whose advice was widely sought, said to me, 'I am only going to give you one piece of advice – do your best and then whistle.' I have tried to follow that advice throughout my career. The import of these terse words expands the more you consider them. Do all that you can to the best of your ability when doing the particular job. No one can ask for more: when you have finished it, whistle and get on with the next job. Don't spend the succeeding time wondering whether you have done the right thing or the wrong thing. Occupy that time in applying your mind to the job in hand. So, if I make mistakes in this autobiography I apologise in advance. I shall certainly try to be as accurate as possible.

In deciding on the format which the book should take I discarded the 'milestone approach' because of the danger of an omission. In this regard I had in mind the story told of F E Smith, Lord Birkenhead. When he had been installed as Lord Chancellor, his friends gave him a complimentary dinner. In the course of his speech the Chairman asked Birkenhead to recall the great milestones in his life. In his reply F E said: 'The first great milestone was the day I was called to the Bar. The second was the day I took silk. The third was the day when I was appointed Attorney-General. And the fourth was the day I took my seat on the Woolsack as the Lord High Chancellor of Great Britain.' At that point his wife, who was sitting next to him, pulled his coat tails and said to him 'What about our wedding day, my dear?', only to receive the reply 'The Chairman asked for milestones, not millstones.'

Instead of milestones I prefer to look at phases. When I look back on my life I realise that there was a short period on which my whole public life has hinged. The earlier phases of my life led up to it, and the subsequent phases stemmed from it. That period was the year 1947. In the space of seven months during that year at the age of 39, I took silk, was appointed Solicitor-General for Scotland, was appointed Lord Advocate, made a Privy Councillor, and elected to Parliament as the member for Edinburgh East. It seems logical to deal with the phases leading up to that vital point in their various aspects, and then deal with what flowed from it.

Wheatley

Contents

1 My family background

My father, Patrick Wheatley, was born in the village of
Bonmahon in County Waterford. His father brought his
wife and children to Scotland to obtain work in the Lanarkshire coalfield and thus get away from the terrible poverty
which blighted Ireland at the time. My mother's parents
were Irish too, but they came from Belfast in the north. Her
father, Peter Murphy, was a labourer who had also come to
Scotland to obtain employment. My mother was born after
the family came to Scotland, the family home being a
cottage on the south bank of the Monkland Canal north of
Shettleston. Adjacent to that cottage, which was demolished
when I was young, there was a large bing which was called
locally the 'Sugarally Mountain' because the deposit was the
colour of sugarally (liquorice). One of our local pursuits as
boys was to slide down the bing sitting on the lid of a large
biscuit tin.

I am led to understand that my father's parents had quite
a large family, but not all of them survived into my ken,
and I can only speak of those whom I came to know. From
hearsay I learned that the family lived in a small house in a
miners' row in the mining village of Braehead in conditions
which can only be described as deplorable. My Uncle John
who came through it all to become a Cabinet Minister in
the first Labour Government, and a successful one at that,
described these conditions in one of the many pamphlets
which he wrote, the true chronicler from bitter experience.
Despite the size of the family, harsh economic circumstances
made it necessary for lodgers to be taken in, an expedient

1

only made possible by resort to the shift system not only in the pit but in the use of the beds. It is not surprising that there was engendered a deep and bitter resentment in the breasts of the three sons, John, Thomas and Patrick, against a system which obliged human beings to live in such conditions. It produced an evangelism in all of them to get rid of the system and replace it with one based on Christian principles of social justice. Their sister Mary married a miner called Edward McDade and they lived in a miners' row in the village of Drunpark, near Bargeddie. They had a large family and had to live in similar cramped and primitive conditions. We used to visit them from time to time when I was young, and I was able to see for myself the conditions under which miners and their families were obliged to live. Yet the house was spotlessly clean inside and was beautifully kept. The same motivation seems to inspire people in entirely different walks of life. Just as officers of the British Empire stationed in remote and lonely outposts were said to change for dinner while dining alone just to keep up their morale and save themselves from going native, so wives of working people who were consigned to live in the most appalling conditions sought to make their homes a little palace and an oasis in the desert of social dereliction.

All three boys, John, Thomas and Patrick,·went into the pits at the early age of about eleven years. This was almost an inevitable migration for young boys in a mining village in those times. They were not obliged to stay on at school to a given age, and as soon as a job was available they left school and started work usually beginning at the pithead. Patrick, my father, very soon decided that mining was not for him, and left the pits to take employment as the odd-job boy in the village store. That must have whetted his liking for that kind of work because years later he opened a grocery shop in Shettleston, and his brother John joined him. Curiously enough, in due course that shop, which had been converted into a bank, was the locus of a daring bank-robbery which culminated in two separate trials over both of which I presided as the trial judge. To further the coincidence, that shop was exactly opposite the tenement in which

2

we lived for many years in Shettleston Road. After giving up the grocer's shop my father and my Uncle John went separately into the publishing business. They each started in a small way, but their businesses prospered. In 1918 my Uncle John converted his business into a limited company and my father joined the company taking his business with him. The company did well and a reasonable income was assured to both families. Accordingly, while we were never well-off we were comfortably established, and we were never exposed to the extreme hardships which were the lot of so many people who lived in our area. That, however, acted as a spur and not an opiate, and from my earliest recollection our family was involved in the political battle to get rid of the poverty and the injustices which existed all around us.

On my mother's side I have only personal knowledge of three uncles and two aunts. One of the uncles stayed in Shettleston with a large family. Another also lived in Glasgow, but we did not exchange visits and my recollection of him and his family stems from hearsay accounts. A third one emigrated to the United States, and he and his wife came back for a holiday in the early 1920s. They stayed with us for a while and then went for a nostalgic holiday to Saltcoats. They took my sister Nettie and me with them, and we enjoyed that holiday immensely. My mother's sister Nellie, was a spinster who stayed with us. She had a dairy business in Wellshot Road, Shettleston, and this was quite an asset to our domestic well-being. Another sister, Annie, married a man called James Foylan, and they went to live in Crieff where James was employed in the insurance business. He was killed in action during the later stages of World War I leaving a widow and four young children, but of this more anon.

Before her marriage my mother had been what was known at the time as a pupil teacher, and taught in St Michael's School in Parkhead. She and my father were married in St Paul's, Shettleston, in 1899. My sister Nettie was born in 1900, my brother Tommy in 1902 and I on 17 January 1908. We were a very happy family. Our house was

3

comfortable and warm, and while luxuries were limited we never lacked any of the necessities of life. Yet at the end of each quarter when the Co-operative dividend was paid out there was always extra money for some eagerly awaited extra item of clothing or household equipment. My mother was a very good cook and we were always well fed. Her 'cloutie dumplings' were unsurpassed and remain unsurpassable. In 1916 the happiness and tranquility of our home was shattered by the deaths of my Aunt Nellie in March and my brother Tommy in May at the age of fourteen. Tommy was suddenly struck down with appendicitis and was removed to the Royal Infirmary in Glasgow. When he arrived there it was discovered that peritonitis had set in and he died shortly after his admission. From what I was told by my sister Nettie, it appears that he had been suffering pain from the appendix for some time. He had kept this to himself since he was sitting 'Intermediate' exams at the time and was unwilling to say anything about the pain in case such a disclosure would result in him not getting to sit his exams. Unfortunately the disclosure was not made until he was leaving for the Infirmary when it was too late. Tommy had wanted to be a doctor, but it was not to be.

I doubt if my parents ever really got over Tommy's death. My father died in January 1937 at the age of 62. My mother died in in January 1951 at the age of 74. Nettie died in April 1972 just shortly before her 72nd birthday. My mother lived to see me become Solicitor-General, Lord Advocate and a Member of Parliament in 1947. Nettie, in addition, saw me appointed a Senator of the College of Justice in 1954, a life peer in 1970 but she died a few months before I was appointed Lord Justice-Clerk in 1972. My father did not live to see any of these offices being filled by his son, although he would probably have had the keenest appreciation of these honours which had befallen me. I am sure that he would have derived much satisfaction from the fact that the advice which he and my Uncle John had given me to go to the Bar had borne such rich fruit. He was a quiet, undemonstrative man with a cool and detached judgment, but I think that he would have allowed himself a quiet ironic

4

smile at the thought that one day his son would become Baron Wheatley of Shettleston and a peer of the realm. What I think would have pleased him more than the nature of the award was the stated reason for which it was given – for public services in Scotland.

Nancy, my wife, was born in 1906. Her parents were of Border stock, her father coming from Hawick and her mother from Selkirk; but their married life was spent in Glasgow. Her father was a joiner to trade, and was a stalwart in the Labour movement in its early days. As I shall recount later, he was my first, but fortunately not my last contact with the Nichol family. Nancy's mother died in 1917 leaving a young family of girls and a boy. Nancy was only eleven years of age at the time and three of her sisters were younger than she. It was under this great loss that the family grew up.

2 A boy in Shettleston

I was born in a tenement house at 231 Main Street, Shettleston. This is vouched by my birth certificate. I have no recollection of staying there, as we moved across the road to another house at 210 Main Street when I was two years old. I do not have the faculty of itemised recall of my very early years, a faculty enjoyed by my old friend Sir Compton (Monty) Mackenzie among his many characteristics. But I have very clear memories of the 13 years the family spent in the house at 210 Main Street. In my youth I ran up and down the common stair at No 231 to see if it brought back memories of my sojourn there, but to no avail. All that was established was that there was a common lavatory on each half-landing for the use of the occupants of the three houses on the landing above, but no bell was rung. I did note, however, that this compared unfavourably with the house at 210 Main Street, which had an inside bathroom with a wc, a bath and a washhand basin – but no hot water.

My earliest recollection is of walking down to mass at St Mark's Church on a Sunday morning with my parents, Nettie and Tommy. We had just passed the halfway point at Blair Street – a good 200 yards from the house – when I started to whinge and asked for, nay demanded, a carry. I remember my father saying: 'You're a big boy now and you don't need a carry' – I was three at the time – 'This is the last carry you'll get.' And it was, physically speaking, although my father carried me financially until I went to the Bar at the age of 24. This was the beginning of a consciousness of life in Shettleston during the early decades

6

of the present century. I have always thought of myself as having been born and bred in Glasgow, but that is not factually correct. Shettleston only became part of the City of Glasgow in 1912, having been a district of Lanarkshire prior to that. It had most of the unfortunate characteristics of too many of the Glasgow districts at that time – bad housing, poverty, low wages or unemployment, but, in the compensatory way which nature has, these were matched by a friendly neighbourly spirit, a ready helping hand in trouble or distress, and a ready wit and good humour which lightened even the darkest of times.

Shettleston had a mixed community, but the children from the diverse homes met on common ground at school. I went to the local school, St Mark's, Carntyne, at the age of five and remained there until I was nine, when I went to the junior department of St Aloysius College in Garnethill in the centre of Glasgow. While, as I have said, the community was a diverse one, the large majority of the children came from homes where the father was either unemployed or among the lowest strata of wage earners. This was reflected in the physical condition and appearance of the children, but it would be foolish to pretend that the significance of this was apparent to us children at the time. My memories of this remained clearly in my mind and the significance started to take shape in retrospect as my political awareness developed. This manifested itself in various experiences. There was no welfare state in those days, no National Health Service, and no vitamins for children who required them to offset their living conditions and the resultant threats to their physical welfare and ultimate well-being. Low wages, and particularly unemployment, created poverty in the direst sense of the word, and such remedial measures as were provided were pitifully inadequate for what was required to counter the consequences of the resultant social evils. These consequences inevitably were reflected in the children from such homes who became my schoolmates and my playmates. In those days the only form of public support for families in real need was indoor or outdoor relief provided by the parish council. However

7

well-intentioned that body might be, the level of public funds made available to it was woefully short of what was required. The parish council was known simply as 'the parish' and was one leg of the tripod of local government institutions in those days, the other two being the local town or county council and the local education authority, all of them being elected bodies. Resort to the 'parish' was a last resort because, however unjustifiably, it carried a certain social stigma. That, allied to a strong feeling of independence, which found its way into a refusal to take advantage of some of the provisions of the welfare state when it was introduced, was reflected in the oft-repeated phrase: 'I've never taken charity in my life, and I am no' starting it noo'. Later on I shall have something to say about the great social changes which the welfare state brought about, but the old parish relief was a different matter. The poverty and deprivation of the parents were evidenced in the children when they came to school. Looking back, I would hazard the guess that at least one-third of the children bore visible signs, although others must have been bearing the hidden consequences, such as the seeds of tuberculosis. But rickets, deficient eyesight, running ears, skinny bodies and lack of energy in playing games were evident.

What we could see was that they were children to be pitied, and it came as no surprise when these schoolmates were irregular in their attendances. Those of us who were more fortunate were too young to realise that these physical deficiencies were the result of malnutrition and bad housing conditions, and the one dramatic thing which brought a realisation that something serious was wrong was when we heard that Jimmy or Jeanie had been taken to hospital. It was not just the physical appearance of these unfortunate children which singled them out. If, perforce, their parents had to seek parish relief, so far as the children were concerned it took the form of a supply of clothing and footwear. The clothing was of a common brand and the type of footwear supplied was clogs, so that the children bore the stigmata of parish relief, and were readily identified thereby. Even at that early age I was conscious of how much more fortunate

8

I was in not having to carry such burdens, and my parents kept telling me that such handicaps were not the fault of the children or their parents, and that I should be kind to these less fortunate schoolmates. That advice must have been fairly general, as indeed it should have been in Christian homes, for there was no class distinction and certainly no apartheid in our games either in the school playground or outside. There is an old Scottish expression which many people would apply to that situation, namely that we were all Jock Tamson's bairns. I have always eschewed the use of that expression because of its doubtful factual accuracy which, as far as I know, Mrs Tamson has never been called upon to vouch. Nonetheless, we all sat together and played together at school, and, far from the 'parish' children being regarded as being inferior beings, they were in at least one respect the object of my envy. In the summertime when clogs were not in supply or possibly regarded as inappropriate for use, many of these children came to school in their bare feet or, as we called them, their 'berries'. This was a Glasgow adaptation of 'bare feet' and I had the great desire to come down to the school in my berries, but when I sought my mother's permission to do so I was met with a stern refusal. My mother was the soul of kindness, but I have a shrewd suspicion that her refusal stemmed as much from a desire not to be thought unable to provide me with boots or shoes as it did from concern over my tender feet. On a few occasions I compromised – chiefly myself – by taking off my shoes en route to school and walking the rest of the way on my 'berries', my shoes being hung round my neck by the laces. This demonstrated that I had shoes to wear if I wished. I particularly resorted to this devious expedient on hot summer days to allow me to follow the watering-cart which paraded the streets ejecting jets of water at the rear to lay the dust and clean the streets. The joy of paddling along getting my feet wet and cool was difficult to resist.

The children in Shettleston in those days had to make their own recreation and find places for it. Not for them were the expensive computer games and model trains which feature in so many homes today, often to the discomfiture of the fathers when they find that their sons of five and six can beat them at computer games. For games like football and rounders larger areas were required, and we were fortunate in having quite a number of open spaces in Shettleston. One particular pitch where I played hours and hours of football is now covered by the area of Shettleston Public Baths. The back courts of the tenements were the venue for games which could be played in more restricted spaces. The boys' games there were leap-frog and its developments, cut fit (foot) and guide and hunch-cuddy-hunch, and the various variations of 'bools' such as 'moshie' and 'plunkers'. Bools were marbles and plunkers round iron balls. The favourite games for girls were skipping ropes and peevers (hop-scotch). Skipping could take place in the back courts but peevers required 'beds' to be chalked out, and this ruled out the back courts which were grass or earth. Accordingly the 'beds' were chalked out on the pavements of the adjacent street and peevers were played there. Just after I went on to the Bench I noticed with mixed feelings of nostalgia and dismay, a bed chalked out for peevers on the hallowed surface of Parliament Square – outside the Courts. Skipping ropes were taboo for the boys, being looked upon as a sissy's game. How wrong we were, as we discovered later in life when skipping ropes became an integral part of our football training. The fact that access from one back court to another was usually readily available, particularly if you were good at climbing and jumping, supplied fertile ground for games which were a development of 'hide and seek'. In these games efforts were made by the hiding side to win the race to free the 'den' in which the other side had lodged captives. Such games were 'run-sheep-run' and 'leave-oh', and a more curtailed variation called 'kick the knacket (can)'.

Life seemed to be full of fun in those days. I was fortunate to be able to indulge in the recreations and relaxations which involved some financial expenditure, an advantage not enjoyed by many of my playmates. However, we shared what we had. If a ball had to be provided for football or a bat and ball for rounders, someone was always able to provide them. Our paid entertainment consisted principally

10

of going to the penny matinée at the cinema on a Saturday morning or buying one or other of the boys' papers or comics during the week. My mother was perhaps over-indulgent to me in this latter respect. The *Magnet*, the *Gem*, the *Boy's Friend*, and the *Penny Popular* were the boys' papers and *Comic Cuts, Chuckles* and the *Funny Wonder* were the comics which constituted my extra-curriculum reading. Talking of *Chuckles*, they had a scheme whereby on sending the editor a postal order for sixpence you were enrolled as a member of the Chuckles Club which entitled you to put the letters CC after your name. This was a distinction of which I availed myself for a few months after which the pomposity of it wore off, and I did not carry the privilege into adult life. As for the penny matinées, they were 'the *Jinkies*'. There we were enthralled by serial dramas like the *Exploits of Elaine* and the *Perils of Pauline*, where the heroine was left at the end of each episode on the verge of a fearful death, contrived in the most ingenious ways, and just as the almost certain death was about to occur, the picture would disappear to be replaced with the words 'To be continued'. Needless to say, we could hardly wait for the next Saturday to come along to see how the impossible was achieved and certain death averted. But my favourites were the cowboy films, an attraction which has never left me, or my wife for that matter, and the same applies to the Keystone Comedies and the Charlie Chaplin ones in particular. In those days the cowboys were always the goodies, and little did I know then that later in life, as a judge, I would have to deal, and deal severely, with 'cowboys' who were baddies.

There were three cinemas in Shettleston then, the Palaceum, the Premier, and one down the 'back road', the name of which I forget as I never went to it. The Palaceum was my favourite, and remained my favourite as I grew up. The film features in the Premier were not so good, the main attraction being a side-show, namely watching the rats running along the rafters overhead. The third picture house was one to which admission was obtained by presenting a penny or an empty jam jar.

The Palaceum enjoyed great popularity in its normal

twice-nightly shows. The films shown were probably the best in the area, and that for a very pragmatic reason. The programmes were changed every Monday and Thursday, each programme being scheduled to run for three nights. In the early days if the programme was a poor one, the people coming out of the first house would let that be known to the people queuing up outside for the second house. The result was that not only did the queue disappear, but the word spread like wildfire and the next two nights were disasters. So much so that substitute programmes often had to be shown on the succeeding nights, and in the result only the best of films were provided. However, in addition to the films the Palaceum also had variety turns, and these proved great attractions. Comedy sketches, singers, souffleurs, ventriloquists, magicians, contortionists and stand-up comics were among the 'turns' brought along, and they had to be good. If they were not, they were not left in any doubt about the audience reaction. It proved a good breaking-in ground for many people who went on to become national figures in the entertainment world, and a haven for former favourites who were on the way out. One very popular comedy-sketch company was James Houston and Company who did topical sketches such as 'The Washing House Key'. This was a regular subject of dispute in tenements where in the back court there was a common wash-house which had to serve possibly a dozen or so tenants, resulting in regular disputes about whose turn it was to have the use of the wash-house and possession of the key to it. The cast consisted of the father and mother and children of a local family called Gribben, but the company took the name of Houston which was Mrs Gribben's maiden name. Two of the daughters were at St Mark's School with me, the elder, Renée, being in my sister Nettie's class, and the younger, Cissie, being in my class. In due course they branched out on their own as The Houston Sisters and became national attractions. Cissie, who used Billie as her stage name in view of the role which she played in the partnership, was very much a tomboy at school, and preferred to play with the boys and held her own with them in the playground

12

games. I can still picture her with her little round face and fair hair, constantly wearing a wee red knitted coat. Cissie was quite versatile, and in addition to her stage career she wrote some mystery thrillers. The last time I saw her I was in my late teens. She boarded a tramcar in Shettleston Road, wearing a pair of trousers long before this became a woman's fashion; her hair was in an Eton crop which was part of her stage appearance; and she said in a deep baritone voice, 'Hello, John', leaving the people in the tramcar who did not know her wondering whether it was a he or a she. Poor Cissie died relatively young. This broke up the partnership act, but Renée went on to forge a new career for herself as a screen and TV star. I did not know her personally. She had been several years ahead of me in school at St Mark's. One evening, shortly before she died, she phoned me from London and expressed the wish for us to meet and talk about the old Shettleston days. I was a judge by this time and I suppose that she had seen my name in connection with some case or another and wanted a nostalgic journey down memory lane with another former Shettlestonian. That meeting, alas, never took place, much to my regret, as I am sure that it would have been a most interesting and entertaining one.

210 Main Street became 844 Shettleston Road when street names in Glasgow were rationalised to cut out the confusion caused through the same name being used for streets in different parts of the city. We stayed there until 1923, by which time I was fifteen and had gone to Mount St Mary's College as a boarder. Our house at 210 Main Street was a commodious two room and kitchen flat with a bathroom containing a bath, a washhand basin and a wc – but, as I have said before, no hot water. It was said that the owner had run out of money when building the property. There was a bed in an alcove in the kitchen, a reasonably sized double bedroom and a parlour, to give the name commonly applied to such a room in Shettleston. It was a sitting-room cum dining-room for use when visitors were having a meal with us, but our family meals were taken in the kitchen. The parlour had a large cupboard into which a bed could

13

be fitted, and this was the third area in normal use for sleeping purposes. There was a door to the cupboard which was kept closed when the bed was not in use, thus preserving the stateliness of the parlour when visitors were in the house. This bed was variously occupied according to the people to be accommodated for the time being. My parents always occupied the bed in the kitchen. The original arrangement was that I occupied the parlour bed with my brother Tommy, and my sister Nettie occupied the bedroom bed with my Aunt Nellie. The hot water necessary for ablutions was obtained in one of two ways. For minor ablutions a large kettle of water was boiled. For a bath, hot water had to be ferried in pails from the wash-house in the back court which served all six houses which comprised No 210.

Apart from the comparative luxury of a bathroom there was another peculiar feature attached to this house. There was a large area of ground beyond the common drying green in the back court, and this was divided into six to provide a garden for each of the six houses. This was a great joy to my father who had long yearned for a garden of his own. The house above us was occupied by a Mrs McGovern and her daughter Cissie. They did not wish to make use of their plot and kindly gave it over to my father for his use. He found great happiness in his garden during such leisure time as he had, and apart from providing us with a plentiful supply of vegetables and a little fruit from fruit bushes, he developed his love for roses which he maintained till his dying day. His activities were somewhat curtailed when he lost the McGovern patch. Mrs McGovern's son John, who had emigrated to Australia with his family, came back to Shettleston and stayed in his mother's house. Years later he became the MP for Shettleston on the death of my Uncle John. After a short while Mrs McGovern and Cissie left the house and John and his family remained in it. I never got to know how this came about, I only saw the result. Anyway, John reclaimed the patch allocated to the house, which he was entitled to do as the tenant of the house, and so my father had to make do with his own original plot. When in 1923 we moved up to a semi-detached house in the new Sandyhills

14

housing scheme, he had a garden large enough for all his needs, and too large for my liking. There his roses became a local showpiece.

One other feature of the house at 210 Main Street was that on the side of the road immediately opposite, there were three public houses in the space of fifty yards, and while I have no recollection of serious disturbances, the noise created as the patrons left at closing time in varying degrees of insobriety remains clearly in my memory. I have been a lifelong teetotaller, as was my father, and he never had drink in the house, nor do I. Many people have asked me whether it was those early experiences which made me a teetotaller. It would be easy for me to say 'Yes' to that, but frankly I think that the answer is that, at the best, they had only a peripheral influence. Basically, the reason why I do not touch alcohol is that I have had no desire to touch it. There is no virtue in not doing something that you have no desire to do. Whether that absence of desire has been due to the fact that alcohol has never played a part in our family life, or whether the outpourings from the pubs at closing time have had a psychological effect, or whether such an effect has resulted from my professional experience of seeing so many lives ruined and so much tragedy occasioned through the abuse of alcohol I know not, and I have never attempted to discover by self-psychoanalysis. All I do know is that I have no desire to drink alcohol in any shape or form, and that is a good enough reason for me.

By and large, I realise in retrospect that life in Shettleston was for me as a boy a very pleasant thing, although I recognise that many of my mates could not have had it so good. There were aspects of it which did not make much impression on me at the time, but fell into proper perspective as I grew older. For instance, I saw no inconsistency in the facts that as members of the Independent Labour Party my parents were opposed to World War I, and that if called up for military service my father would be a conscientious objector (although his very poor eyesight and his age might have exempted him), and the fact that our house was the base for my mother's nephews who had come from America to join the forces when they were granted leave, or the fact that for quite a period we took in a family of Belgian refugees until such time as they could be officially accommodated. During this period we had the experience of buying and cooking horse meat which our Belgian visitors wanted for their meals, a delicacy which we could never savour for ourselves. I also remember an old man who came to our house every Friday in time for lunch and stayed for tea. His name was Jimmy McCue and he lived in a hostel for old people which was run by an order of nuns in Garngad. I do not know how he came to be our visitor although I suspect that it was through the nuns. In any event he came to us for years during and after World War I. He had lost several fingers from his right hand, and I was fascinated watching him manipulate a knife with his stumps. There were many other visitors to our house, but they came via the political scene and I will deal with them in another chapter.

Tommy and Nettie were engaged by Aunt Nellie to deliver milk in cans to her dairy customers early in the morning, starting at seven o'clock, and I was clamant in my demands to join them. Eventually when I was seven years old I was allowed to do so on a limited basis, although my mother was not keen on the idea. However, as I occupied the same bed as Tommy in the parlour recess I was getting up along with him, and this fact carried the day for me. Nettie was eight years older and Tommy was six years older than I, and I had to accompany one or other of them and make my delivieries under their supervision. The highlight of the operation was on the return to the dairy when our rounds had been completed. There we were treated to a glass of milk and a sandwich consisting of a bar of cream chocolate between a couple of biscuits. As we had already had our breakfast before leaving the house, this was a most acceptable bonus. This short period of employment was brought to an end with Aunt Nellie's death in March 1916, after which the dairy was sold.

My widowed aunt, Annie Foylan, came down from Comrie to visit us on occasion, bringing her three sons and daughter with her. This rather stretched our sleeping

16

accommodation, but somehow we managed. It was great fun for her children who found in Shettleston advantages which were not available to them in Perthshire. These were particularly to be found in Marshall's Ice Cream Parlour, where the ice-cream and hot peas were devoured with relish, as were the chips in pokes from M and M – the finest fish and chip shop in the East End of Glasgow. These visits to our house were more than compensated for by the numerous visits which I made to their house in Comrie during the school holidays. There I played football regularly with the local boys and was actually incorporated into their local team. I also did a bit of caddying at the golf course, which provided me with some extra spending money. The countryside around Comrie is beautiful, and we had many delightful walks up the hills, along the banks of the River Earn and up the Lednock Valley. With the money from caddying we were able to hire bicycles by the day, and we often cycled up to Lochearnhead where we stopped and had a picnic before returning to Comrie. On one occasion my cousin Michael Foylan and I ventured further afield and cycled up to Killin. On our return journey we ran into a terrific rainstorm at the top of Glenogle and got thoroughly drenched. These visits to Comrie continued until my Aunt Annie left that delightful village to live in Dundee where her children, who had grown up, were centred.

My visits to Comrie were enriched by meeting there one of the most delightful characters I have ever encountered. His story is quite a remarkable one which I can only relate here in cameo. His name was Charles Williamson. As a young man he went to Italy to pursue his studies. While there he was converted to the Catholic faith, and in due course he studied for the priesthood and was ordained a priest. His father, who was a Presbyterian, was very annoyed at this turn of events, and not only did he disinherit him, but legend has it that he threatened to shoot his son on sight if he ever set eyes on him. Charles naturally stayed away from Comrie while his father was still alive. His father owned two estates in the area. The larger was Lawers and the smaller Tomperran. The estates had been entailed, and

Charles, who was an only child, fell heir to both on his father's death.

During his enforced exile from the family home Charles spent his time between Italy and Brompton Oratory in London where for several years he served as a priest. On his father's death he returned to Lawers to look after his mother, and was excused diocesan and parochial duties to tend to her and the estates. When his mother died in 1923 he was obliged to sell the Lawers estate for financial reasons, and he went to live in the smaller but delightful Tomperran which was nearer the village. In order to sell the Lawers estate he had to get the estates disentailed, but since he was the last in a line which was not going to be carried on, the legal process was carried through without difficulty. He had learned of the unfortunate position of my widowed Aunt Annie and her four children and offered her the occupancy of the West Lodge on the Lawers estate. My aunt gratefully accepted this kindness, and I spent a few holidays in that house, with the freedom of the Lawers estate to roam over. I was introduced to the mysteries of the country life which abounded by the two sons of the gamekeeper who lived in a cottage nearby. When the Lawers estate was sold my aunt had to vacate the West Lodge, but Father Williamson produced a solution which turned out to be a winner. On the Tomperran estate he had a large house called Coneyhill which had been used as a YMCA hostel during World War I and which had become vacant some time earlier. Another widow, a Mrs McGee, who had four sons and a daughter, had been installed as caretaker and had residential occupation of part of the house. The house was so large and so constructed that it was possible to divide it into three separate dwellings. Mrs McGee retained the part which she had occupied, my aunt was given one of the other parts, and in due course another widow called Mrs O'Keefe with a mixed family of sons and daughters was given the third.

The house bordered the first hole of the golf course on the north, the River Lednock on the west and Laggan Park, the local football and cricket ground, on the east. Its own grounds were well wooded, and all in all it was a country

18

paradise for a city boy on his many holidays there. Just south of the house and on the bank of the River Lednock, Father Williamson had converted a couple of cottages into a beautiful little church, and although he had not undertaken any parochial work officially, he was granted episcopal permission to have his own unofficial little parish of the three families at Coneyhill and a few other people who were in employment in some of the other estates in the area. He treated his little congregation to services which were a joy to attend. At mass on Sundays he would deliver a little homily which lasted no more than five minutes but which was so meaningful that its purport remained locked in one's memory. With years of experience behind me I can perhaps more fully appreciate the time which he must have taken to prepare these little homilies and to compress so much into so little.

He was a refined, gentle soul, whose kindnesses took many forms. He had us children along to Tomperran for tea and loved to show us his beautiful Italian garden. Another feature of Tomperran was that each room had the name of a flower which was depicted on the door. One of these was a watercress, whose initials were very appropriate for its use. Very early on in my association with Coneyhill he had arranged to take his local children for an outing to Loch Earn, and he kindly included me and my cousin John Patrick in the party. He hired a boat for a sail up Loch Earn and when we returned to St Fillans he took us into the hotel where we had a slap-up high tea. I was quite young at the time – not yet in my teens – and I was rather flush with money which I had earned through caddying. In my blissful ignorance of the propriety of such occasions I offered to pay Father Williamson for my share of the day's proceedings as I was a visitor and not one of his flock for whom the outing had been designed. He very quietly and kindly declined my 'Dutch' offer, but when we returned home and the incident was retailed to my aunt she was horrified in case Father Williamson was offended. She need not have worried, as he was too kind a soul to take offence for a juvenile indiscretion. He was quite amused, in fact, as she discovered later. His kindnesses to all his flock were legion, and it must have been a great delight to him when three of the boys followed him into the priesthood. They were Joseph McGee and my cousins Michael and Peter Foylan. How much greater would have been his earthly delight had he lived to see Joseph become the Bishop of Galloway and Michael the Bishop of Aberdeen. Unfortunately he died at the age of 93 before these latter events took place but I am sure that he looked down on them with a gentle and satisfied smile. His benefactions were not confined to his own flock. His kindnesses to all the children of the village of Comrie were widespread as were his gifts to the community as a whole. On his Diamond Jubilee in the priesthood, when he was 92, the villagers of Comrie, including the children, made presentations to him at a public function to commemorate the occasion – a signal tribute in the 1940s, long before the word 'ecumenical' had become part of our every day talk.

My recollections of these boyhood days in Comrie have been kept alive by my constant meetings with Denis McGee, a near neighbour of mine and a fellow parishioner at St Peter's Church in Edinburgh. From all this, and from what more I have to write, it should be quite plain that although the years of my boyhood in Shettleston were spent in times of a depression which manifested itself all around me I was cushioned by having caring parents, a good and comfortable home and freedom from the hardships which afflicted so many of my contemporaries. Boyhood for me was a happy time and I was not without ambitions which alas were not realised. In those early years I had no ambitions to become an advocate or a judge, but I did have the desire to become a Member of Parliament, as was evidenced in an entry which I made in my sister's autograph book which I signed 'John Wheatley, future Member of Parliament for Shettleston'.

My first ambition, however, was to become the 'tottie boy' in No 8 Grocery of the Shettleston Co-operative Society. I was there regularly for messages either with my mother or alone, and I was intrigued by the activities of the tottie boy. The potatoes were stored in a large box container and were extracted through a limited opening at the foot.

This was done by the tottie boy pushing a shovel through the hole and bringing potatoes out on the shovel. These were then placed in a large container on scales which were counter-balanced with heavy weights of differing sizes from a stone downwards. This to me was magic, but when I suggested to my mother that I should put my name down for the first vacancy, she pooh-poohed the idea and a potential Joseph Sainsbury was lost.

My next ambition was to become the soap boy in Jimmy Harton's barber shop. Most men went to the barber's shop for a shave, rather than shave themselves. This was before safety razors became popular and it was the era of shaving with an open razor, which was a delicate operation. There were not many of them in use in Shettleston in those days, since they were then single-purpose instruments. In later years when they were still in use in Glasgow, having them for shaving purposes was often just an excuse for having them in possession. Jimmy Harton employed a number of assistants and had about six or seven chairs in which the customers sat to be shaved. The soap boy's job was to go along the line and soap the face and neck of the customer for the oncoming barber. It was really a conveyor belt system. Perhaps I had seen too many Keystone comedies, but the idea of plastering men's faces and necks with soap from a massive soap brush seemed to me to be something that a boy should pay for and not be paid for doing. But again the maternal veto was exercised.

3 The budding politician

While I was fully engaged in the boyhood pursuits to which I have referred, there was another side of my boyhood which was not shared by many of the other boys. Just as I was born into a Catholic family, I was born into a Socialist family. I have always held the belief that the two ran in tandem and had a common philosophy in the attitude and duties one owed towards one's fellow men. This was a view which my father and my Uncle John had taken in the early years of the century. My Uncle John fought a public campaign against those within the Catholic Church, including some clergy, who took the view that the two philosophies were incompatible, and he won. He had a public debate with Hilaire Belloc, and according to reports he had a notable victory. Along with others, including my father, he founded the Catholic Socialist Society, which existed for a number of years until the battle was won. This removed what might have been a significant obstacle to the advance of the Labour cause in Scotland. In recent years there has been an upsurge in the interest about his impact on the Labour movement which has led to a number of university theses being written, and consequential pamphlets and newspaper articles. These usually deal in detail with this victory within the Church circles, and rather than repeat that history I merely refer to the issue and the result.

Apart from the basic issue, which was the main point, the important fact is that the Wheatley brothers, John and Patrick, and a number of others who took that stand fought the battle from within the Church and remained faithful

22

to their religious duties. This was not easy, as they, and particularly my Uncle John, became the target for personal abuse. Perhaps the most vociferous critic was the local parish priest, Father Andrew O'Brien. I can still remember the discomfort I felt as a young boy sitting in church and listening to his tirades against the Wheatley name from the pulpit. As his subsequent history indicated, he was somewhat unbalanced, but that only added to our discomfiture at the time. It became so bad that both of our families went to the adjacent church of St Michael's in Parkhead for our services, but after Father O'Brien left for pastures new, we resumed our attendances at St Mark's, and I have to record that thereafter we enjoyed the best of relations with the parish priests and curates who came to serve both St Mark's and St Paul's, the other Catholic church in Shettleston. There has always been a tendency, which is most marked today, for people who find themselves in disagreement with organisations of which they are members to opt out and fight the organisation from outside. Such people tend to become bitter against their former colleagues and their former beliefs, and spend more time attacking them than attacking their former opponents and their beliefs. On the other hand, those who think that their organisation has gone wrong but who remain inside and seek to put things right from there, can still adhere to their principles and philosophy and use them to effect the remedy.

The political vehicle for the Labour cause in Scotland during the early decades of the twentieth century was the Independent Labour Party (ILP). It had branches all over the place and was particularly strong in the cities. The Shettleston branch was probably a typical one, promoting not only political activity but social and cultural developments locally. My father became Secretary of the Shettleston branch (as well as being Chairman of the Glasgow ILP Federation), and one of his duties was to organise weekly political meetings which were held on a Sunday night. These took place all the year round apart from the summer months. This involved booking not only speakers well in advance but also singers. It was traditional to have two singers, usually but

23

not necessarily a man and a woman, to entertain the audience before the speaker gave his address and between the end of his address and questions. These meetings carried on during World War I, when the ILP as a pacifist organisation had taken a stand against the war. The political addresses, however, were more directed to the social and economic problems than to the war issue, which naturally could not be neglected. My Uncle John was a regular speaker at these meetings. He was a local councillor in the Glasgow Corporation and had already made a name for himself as a housing expert. He was the prospective candidate for the Shettleston Division for the first Parliamentary election after the war. Apart from the singing at meetings, which paid homage to the cultural side of the activities, there was a literature stall which provided material for political and educational development. As well as political weeklies such as the *Forward* and the *Labour Leader* (later the *New Leader*) there were pamphlets and books on all kinds of political topics. The stall was the responsibility of the literature salesman who at that time was Sam Nichol, Nancy's father. I became a sales boy along with Jimmy Nichol, Sam's son. Jimmy became a first-class footballer and for many years was a half-back with Portsmouth FC. He played in two English FA Cup Finals at Wembley, but alas Portsmouth lost both. Little did I think then that my future life would be bonded to yet another member of the Nichol family. I had a great success selling newspapers and pamphlets, which were cheap, but not so much success with the books which were much dearer. Yet it was interesting to see how many books were sold from the stall. Many of those who attended the meetings were serious-minded people who read widely. My Uncle John was a prolific pamphleteer and I did a roaring trade with his pamphlets. One in particular sold like hot cakes. It bore the title 'How the miners are robbed'. I paraded up and down the aisles of the Palaceum, where the meetings were, calling out in a shrill voice: 'How the miners are robbed by John Wheatley, for one penny'. I would like to think that it was my cunning salesmanship rather than my uncle's reputation for a meaty pamphlet which sold them, but I doubt that.

I enjoyed listening to the singers. The old ballads were great favourites and I find myself singing some of them still when I am in the security of isolation. Although I heard the speakers talking I do not pretend that in the early stages I comprehended all that was being said, but as I advanced into adolescence I began progressively to understand the attacks on poverty and ill-health and bad housing and the consequential evils that flowed from these things because I had seen and could still see these all around me. As an adult looking back, I recognised that if I had not been born into a Socialist family my experiences as a boy in Shettleston, and since, would have made me one – a rebel with a cause: the cause being the elimination of the slums and poverty and the consequential ill-health that had been imposed upon the more unfortunate members of our society.

In 1916 as a boy of eight, I was given honorary membership of the Shettleston ILP for services rendered. This must have been in respect of my success as a literature sales boy, because although I had many other political activities as a boy, this was my most outstanding contribution at that time. Of course it was a gimmick, manifestly unconstitutional, but very acceptable. I was probably the youngest person ever to be enrolled in the ILP. I must have been somewhat simple at that age, because about the same time my mother took me to a Co-operative Women's Guild Burns' Supper, and, having been prevailed upon to sing, I sang 'Mother Machree' which is not usually part of a Burns' repertoire. As I have said, the ILP sought to develop cultural pursuits, and we had both a choir and a dramatic society. The choir had as its conductor 'Wee' Willie Hamilton, who had a beautiful tenor voice. He sang as first tenor in the Glasgow Cathedral Choir and was much in demand for the concert platform. I was drafted in as a boy soprano and managed to survive for over a year, after which I was drummed out unceremoniously. During practice Willie discovered me passing sticky sweets (which we called Cheugh Jeans) round the sopranos, and this was not deemed to be an effective contribution to their part in the singing. Willie

25

dubbed me a subversive influence and expelled me.

This was not the only outlet for my singing. I was by then attending the junior department at St Aloysius College, and we had singing tests there. I am sure that being drummed out of the Shettleston ILP choir affected my confidence and so, too, my voice, to such an extent that it allowed a young fellow called Sidney McEwan to come out on top. The fact that Sidney became a priest and an internationally famous concert singer with a most beautiful tenor voice that charmed thousands in concert halls in three continents and still lives on to our delight in his gramophone records, was obviously just a side effect of my ignominious expulsion from the ILP Choir, but for which I might have been that international concert-hall genius. Perhaps I should have slipped Sidney a Cheugh Jean because my voice was not so hot.

Uncle John, in addition to his prolific political pamphleteering, also wrote plays with a political theme for the Shettleston ILP Dramatic Society. The two which I recollect most clearly, and which were the most popular, were *The Fear of the Factor* and the topical post-World War I *What Tommy Fought For* – an exposé of the hollowness of Lloyd George's wartime promise of Homes Fit for Heroes to Live In. The scripts were cleverly written and the characters drawn from everyday life in Shettleston. In the result it was not difficult for the members of the party who were assigned the characters in the cast to fit into their roles, because the language was their everyday language, the topics were the current topics, and the characters were like people whom they knew, or even themselves. Uncle John's son, John Patrick, and I were given minor roles in children's parts, which was my introduction into amateur theatricals. These plays were very successful and were much in demand in other parts of Glasgow and the West of Scotland.

My cultural development was not confined to singing and dramatics. At a much earlier stage I had been sent to a dancing class but that only lasted for one season. The reason for that curtailment was that I disgraced myself at the end-of-season public display attended by the fond mothers if not by the fond fathers. During an Irish jig one of the other boys

26

knocked my hat off my head and danced away. I broke ranks and followed him. On catching up with him I gave him a retaliatory tap on the head with my shillelagh and danced away. My mother was 'fair affronted' at this, and said that this was me finished with the dancing class. I was also sent to piano lessons but these, too, were discontinued when it was discovered that I was 'plunking' them to go and play football. There was, however, one cultural activity which I took to with relish. Uncle John arranged for John Patrick and me to get boxing lessons from a local amateur, Bobby Russell. These I thoroughly enjoyed, even if at times to the discomfiture of John Patrick. My boxing lessons did come in handy during one of the election campaigns when I was delivering literature to a rather swell tenement in Wellshot Road. A boy, who obviously thought that this was a form of contamination, tried to pluck my stock of literature from me. I threw it down and started to use straight lefts as Bobby Russell had taught me. I was allowed to carry on with my distribution.

Running in tandem with these extra-scholastic activities were my involvements in the political field. I have referred to the Sunday-night political meetings, and I now turn to their aftermath. The speaker was always invited to our house for a meal after the meeting, and the family were included in the meal. Politics were discussed at length and at large, particularly if Uncle John was not fulfilling a speaker's engagement elsewhere and was present. These were occasions when the parlour was put to its proper use, and it was there that I met politicians at first hand many of whom in due course became Members of Parliament, such as Jimmy Maxton, Geordie Buchanan, Campbell Stephen, Johnny Muir, George Hardie, Duncan Graham, Joe Sullivan, the Rev James Barr and Neil McLean. Davie Kirkwood lived just down the road from us. I knew him well apart from hearing him speak at meetings and I was very friendly with his sons. If he knew that my Uncle John was to be there he would come along, because he laid great store by his acumen. Here again I do not pretend that I was able to follow all the political discussions, but I suppose that some of it percolated through, particularly as the years rolled by and I got older and the practice carried on.

My first election experience was the 1918 'Khaki' Parliamentary Election. Uncle John, who had been a local councillor for a goodly number of years and had served as a bailie, was confidently expected to win. My role was to deliver election literature to the houses in Shettleston, most of which were in three-storey tenements, and youthful legs were appropriate for such work. Our confident hopes of success were dashed when the Conservative candidate, Rear-Admiral Adair, a director of Beardmore's big works at Parkhead Forge, was returned with a majority of 72. Jingoism had overcome appreciation of years of faithful service. While my uncle was naturally disappointed at the result, it could have been a blessing in disguise. The only Labour candidate in Glasgow who was elected was Neil McLean in Govan, and if my uncle had been elected then he might have been somewhat dispirited by his comparative isolation and the weakness of the Labour representation in the House of Commons, whereas when he was elected in the 1922 election he went down to Westminster in the euphoria of the Labour successes in Glasgow and the West of Scotland, the better representation of the Labour party in the House, and the comfort of having so many of his old colleagues around him.

My next election experiences were the municipal election in 1919 which Uncle John won, and the General Municipal Election in Glasgow in 1920. This was a post-war necessity as elections had been in suspense during the war and a full new council fell to be elected. Three councillors were required for each ward, and the order in which they were elected determined the order in which they would have to stand for re-election in the next three succeeding years. My role in the campaign was now twofold. Once again I had to climb the tenement stairs delivering literature, but by then my legs were even more attuned to the climbing. Then, as a hardy veteran of twelve and an experienced campaigner, I was given the task of chalking the streets advertising the times and places of election meetings. We were sufficiently

28

civic-minded to confine our chalking to the macadam road-
ways or the asphalt pavements. We were expressly instructed
not to deface property. The result of the election was very
gratifying for us in Shettleston. Our three candidates, Uncle
John, David Kirkwood and Jimmy Marshall, were all
returned in that order, and Shettleston has remained ILP
or Labour ever since, in both national and local electoral
spheres.

I continued this kind of election activity during the succeeding municipal and parliamentary elections until I went
to boarding school at Mount St Mary's in 1923, when
distance and not lack of inclination proved the barrier.
However, I was able to play a part in the 1922 General
Election campaign when the majority of the Glasgow seats
fell to the ILP-Labour candidates. My uncle won the Shettleston seat, Jimmy Maxton won Bridgeton, Campbell
Stephen Dennistoun, Georgie Buchanan Gorbals, and for
good measure Davie Kirkwood won the adjacent seat of
Clydebank and Dumbarton Burghs. The tremendous send-
off to the victors in St Enoch Square, Glasgow, en route for
London and the House of Commons is history now. My
uncle made an immediate impact on the House. He was a
debater more than an orator, and a most effective debater
he was. He was so seriously immersed in the political battle
that humour seldom found its way into his speeches,
although irony often did. Nonetheless, he had a flashing
wit which broke through on occasions. During an election
meeting in 1922 a heckler called out to him: 'I wouldn't vote
for you if you were the Angel Gabriel'. Quick as a flash
came the retort: 'If I were the Angel Gabriel you wouldn't
be in my constituency'. His ability obliged Ramsay Macdonald – grudgingly I may say – to take him into his Cabinet
as Minister of Health in the first-ever Labour administration
in this country, and it is said that he was the only real success
as a Minister in that administration. When Labour lost the
next election and went into opposition he was a stern critic
of the path which Macdonald was taking, which was indicative of how Macdonald's mind was working and where it
was leading him to, and in fact did lead him to, so that when

Macdonald was again called upon to form a government after the 1929 election, he left out the one man who had been an outstanding success in the previous one, and who had left behind him monuments to his vision in the form of the thousands of local authority houses all over the country which had been built as a result of his inspired Housing Act of 1924.

He died just shortly before his sixty-first birthday in 1930, and his death was a great loss to the British Labour Movement of his day. There has been much speculation about the line which the Independent Labour Party would have followed if he had survived and what part he would have played in it, but speculation of that nature is fruitless. There is, however, one thing of which I feel sure. Although he was entirely opposed to the Macdonald line, he would have fought the battle from within the party, as he had done in a previous battle, and would not have been in favour of the ILP disaffiliating from the Labour Party to fight it from the outside. That too, however, is speculation. I have always had the greatest respect, affection and regard for him. Like so many others of his vintage he brought himself up against the odds without the benefits which are available today. With all the advantages which I have had, any success which has come my way pales into significance when compared to what he achieved against those odds.

Our family's involvement in the struggles of the times was not confined to the political field. In the 1921 and 1926 miners' strikes my mother was in charge of the soup kitchens which provided hot soup to the families of the striking miners who came along with large jugs for their quota. This was their main form of sustenance during the strike and it was much appreciated. In these strikes my father was involved in raising money to help the miners, and during the first of them he organised a Pit Pony Derby to be run at a local greyhound racing track. It was hoped that it would be a big moneyspinner but it came to a catastrophic end when the pit ponies, which had been brought up from the pits, ran straight on when they came to the first bend because of failing or failed eyesight.

30

The miners really had it tough in those days. Their slogan 'Not a minute on the day, not a penny off the pay' crystallised the issue and showed the conditions which the owners were seeking to impose upon the miners. Their working conditions were often not just deplorable, they were dangerous. These were starkly described in the poem 'The Image of God' written by the miner poet and playwright, Joe Corrie, which was an indictment of the private coal-owners who put quick profits as their first priority at the expense of the health, safety and indeed lives of their workforces. Joe's poem was written in the vernacular and ran thus:

> Crawling about like a snail in the mud
> Covered with clammy blae,
> Me, made after the image of God
> Jings but it's laughable tae.
>
> Howking awa' neath a mountain o' stane
> Gasping for want o' air
> And the sweat pouring doon my bare back bane
> And my knees are hacked and sair.
>
> Straining and cursing the whole shift through
> Half-blind, half-starved, half-mad,
> And the gaffer he says – 'less dirt frae you
> Or you'll go up the pit, my lad'.
>
> So I give my life to the Nimmo squad
> For six and eight pence a day
> Me, made after the image of God,
> Jings but its laughable tae.

With the collapse of the General Strike the miners were left to fight alone, and with the benefit of a very good summer they stuck it out for several months. The odds were stacked against them, however, and eventually they had to give in. It was a travesty of social justice. As a young boy I had an insight into the hard lot of the miners and the dangers they ran. My Uncle Tommy lost a leg in a pit accident when he was a boy. There was no Workman's Compensation then, and all he got was an artificial leg. When that had to be replaced he had to make his own. He was gifted with his hands and made a good job of it. He came to live with us

31

after he had left the pits and obtained a job in Glasgow. Nettie had to vacate the bedroom and use the parlour bed, while I shared the bed in the bedroom with him. On the first night I was in bed sleeping when I was wakened with the gas being put on. It was Uncle Tommy preparing to go to bed. He sat down on a chair, took off his trousers and underpants and then proceeded to take off his leg. I was not frightened only fascinated. I was then told the grim story of how it all came about.

The other sphere in which our family was involved in positive action was in the landlord and tenant conflict. World War I had not produced Lloyd-George's promised Homes Fit for Heroes, and unemployment and low wages were compounded by rent increases. This led to rent strikes and the slogan 'Rent Strike Against Increases. We are not Removing' was carried on placards which I as a boy helped to distribute, and which were displayed in most of the windows in the tenements of Shettleston. This was one battle which was won. A landlord and his factor raised an action against a tenant in the Small Debt Court of the Dumbarton Sheriff Court for payment of rent arrears alleged to be due as a result of increase of rent in respect of which notices had been served on tenants, including the defender. The tenant, who had the benefit of legal advice and representation, took two preliminary pleas, one a general plea to the relevancy and the other a plea that in view of the provisions of the Act founded upon, the Increase of Rent and Mortgage Restrictions Act 1920, the landlord did not qualify to make the increases which he had done. It being obviously a test case, it was transferred to the Ordinary Roll of the Sheriff Court and in due course it came before the Sheriff, the Sheriff Principal, the First Division of the Court of Session and the House of Lords (*Kerr v Bryde* 1923 SC (HL) 12). At each of these stages the tenant's pleas were sustained. This was a resounding victory for the tenants because it meant that all the increases which had been imposed in similar circumstances were illegal. This in turn meant that tenants had paid rent at an excessive rate, yet if they fell into arrears with current rent they were being served with a Small Debt

32

summons for rent alleged to be due, despite the fact that the increased rent claimed was illegal and the tenant might well be in credit as a result of the earlier overpayments which were a legitimate set-off. Nevertheless summonses were still being served for arrears which were not due, with the threat of eviction on non-payment, and some tenants, who had no legal advice, were just paying up. In Glasgow Sheriff Court at least the system was such that if they turned up at the Small Debt Court to dispute the summons the case might have been called without them being aware that it had, and decree passed against them in their complete ignorance.

My father started a campaign designed to inform tenants of their rights under the determined legal decision and to get them to come along with their rent books to clinics which were set up in the Shettleston ILP Hall and elsewhere to allow them to be checked by persons who were trained to do such work. My father did a great deal of the checking himself, and if the checking disclosed that the tenant was not in arrears but in credit, a letter was provided to be taken to the Court explaining the true position if no legal representation had been obtained. This was tiresome and long-drawn-out work for the checkers but they gladly undertook it as a counter to the injustice which had been perpetrated and was being further pursued.

Although tenants throughout Glasgow did not usually have lawyers acting for them, purely for financial reasons, they had a friend in court. Geordie Buchanan made a point of being in attendance in Court and would speak up for them. This annoyed solicitors, particularly those appearing for the proprietor or his factor, and they maintained that under the rules of court only a qualified lawyer or a party appearing for himself had the right of audience before the Court. This was perfectly true, but Geordie was as cute as they come. He knew that many solicitors sent unqualified members of their staff, sometimes office girls, to the Court on formal matters although they had no right of audience. This was also perfectly true and Geordie threatened to take the matter up with the Sheriff Principal to have this practice stopped unless the objection to his appearance was withdrawn. The practice was of great practical advantage to many solicitors, particularly if they operated a one-qualified-man business, and not surprisingly the objection was withdrawn and Geordie, who had become an expert in the matter, as he became an expert on social insurance matters, became an institution.

My going to the Jesuit boarding school of Mount St Mary's, near Sheffield, naturally cut off my Shettleston activities, but when I left that school and returned home to start my career as a student at Glasgow University I resumed my various political pursuits but in a more mature way. The ILP had an organisation called the Guild of Youth to cater for young people who were keen on politics. A branch of this organisation was opened in Shettleston and I joined it. Its activities were numerous and interesting. We met every Friday evening and on every fourth Friday we had a dance. The other Fridays were taken up with lectures and discussions. We were fortunate in having a large variety of interesting speakers locally on whom we could draw, and the political interest was surprisingly keen, considering the youthful ages of the members. We had a debate with the local Young Liberals and I represented. our organisation along with Davie Gibson. Davie was of a slightly older vintage and in due course became a local councillor in the Glasgow Corporation, of which he was eventually appointed Housing Convener. One of our Liberal opponents, who did not impress me greatly, became a Labour MP as a result of the 1945 election, and I had many a quiet smile when I heard him addressing our weekly Parliamentary Labour Party meeting in the House of Commons and telling us how and where we were going wrong and how we should be proceeding if we were real Socialists. Our Guild of Youth branch used to give yeoman service at elections which we regarded as the most important part of our political activities. Our monthly dances were very popular and attracted a lot of non-members. We viewed this as a way of getting such people interested enough in our political activities to join the branch but we soon discovered that if they were not

34

politically interested anyway the dancing was not going to lead them into political evangelism.

We also had a Dramatic Club, confining ourselves to one-act plays of Joe Corrie, such as *The Shilling a Week Man*. I was also a member of the St Mark's Church Dramatic Club which specialised in Sean O'Casey's plays. All in all I had quite an apprenticeship in amateur dramatics.

We also had a successful football team which won the Glasgow Federation Guild of Youth Football League in the two years of its existence (1925–6; 1926–7), and the Wheatley Cup which was presented by my Uncle John for a knockout competition. Yet our greatest success was in a friendly game in the close season of 1926. We played a challenge match against habitués of Simpson's Billiard Room in Shettleston, whose team contained many mature players compared to our adolescent brigade. They had two ex-senior players, one from Celtic and one from Third Lanark, two current seniors with English clubs, Bradford City and Brentford, and a number of ex-junior players. Yet we won 5–2. One of our local junior clubs, Shettleston Celtic, wanted to sign five of our team after the game, but we declined as this would have broken up our team completely. Our reason was vindicated by the success which our team had in the following season, after which the Guild of Youth League was disbanded for a reason which I cannot now recollect. Had the Monopoly Commission been in existence at the time, our success over the two seasons might have been referred to it in the first place.

Another form of outdoor recreation was a ramble every Sunday during the months from late April through to late September. We used to meet at noon to allow churchgoers to attend their services and avoid clashing. Rambles had been a feature of my younger days when the parent Shettleton ILP branch had also organised such outings. The format in both cases was much the same, although our younger membership in the Guild of Youth resulted in longer walks being undertaken. For many years the Glasgow tramway system operated on a maximum 2d fare irrespective of the distance. In fact one could travel about 20 miles for

2d. The idea was to get right out of the town and as far into the country as possible. A tramcar was taken to its appropriate terminus and the trek started from there. A large 'dixie' had to be carried in which tea was brewed, and teams of two took turns in carrying the dixie. Other impedimenta included a ball (a blether) for football, a bat and ball for rounders and skipping ropes for the girls. Some of the girls were among our most enthusiastic political members, and none more so than Nancy Nichol, one of the daughters of Sam Nichol who had been my boss on the literature stall. Our association was quite a casual one to begin with, and I did not realise that this was going to lead to the greatest thing that has befallen me. It was some considerable time before we started to go out together, but when we did and got to know each other our regard for each other grew and grew. As I shall explain in detail later I had decided on the Bar as a career when still at school, and my projected career of University and then the Bar took early marriage out of the question, but Nancy fully appreciated and accepted the position. Of course we married in due course. All in all it seems clear that my early days in Shettleston were happy and carefree, blighted only by isolated events, such as the tragic death of my brother Tommy in 1916.

In recounting these early days I have so far omitted to make any specific referral to my actual schooling and my time at the University. I have done so deliberately as I feel that they each warrant a chapter of their own.

4 Schooldays

I went to St Mark's Primary School at the age of five and remained there until the age of nine. My recollection of the actual content of that schooling is hazy and episodic. My most vivid recollection is the sing-song repetitive way of learning things, such as spelling, the multiplication tables and the catechism. This form of teaching may not conform to modern ideas, but the results were effective in that the basics were imprinted in our minds and provided a platform from which our future education sprang. At least we could read and write and count, and could produce answers from our brains without recourse to the modern aids without which so many shop assistants today are helpless.

The headmaster was Thomas Connolly, a kindly, gentle man, who had a wholly female staff under his charge. Of these I was mostly taught by Miss Convery and Miss Trainor. The latter and her sisters were friends of my parents, and the two families regularly exchanged visits. Marion Convery's chief occupation was releasing my arm which I regularly got stuck between the back of my seat and the front of the desk behind me. I had another teacher named Miss Diamond, who had the reputation of being a strict disciplinarian. The standard method of punishment was to be caned on the hand, and rumour had it that she went through canes at a remarkable rate. I can vouch for this in a rather curious way. One day she gave me some money and told me to go down to the local hardware shop and buy three new canes for her. This I did with pleasure since I was let out of school while the rest of my classmates were left in the classroom. My pleasure was shortlived because when I returned with the canes she tried each one of them out on me. I could not think of anything I had done currently which merited punishment of that nature, but then I may have chalked up a substantial debit balance. On reflection it seems to me that the efficient Miss Diamond was simply testing my efficiency as a buyer.

In 1917 at the age of nine I left St Mark's School and joined the junior department of St Aloysius College, a Jesuit school in Garnethill, Glasgow, just a hundred yards up from Sauchiehall Street. The junior department was staffed by lay teachers, female and male, while the senior or secondary school was staffed mostly by Jesuits, with one or two laymen particularly in the fields of science and art. My first teachers were Mr McAllister in Junior II and Mr Evans in Junior I. The latter was courting a young lady who worked in an Admiralty office in Cadogen Street, and once again I was used as a message boy, although this time I was cast in the role of Eros. Regularly I was given a letter to be taken to the young lady, sometimes with the instruction that I had to wait and bring back a reply. I had no idea of the contents of the letters, although even in those days I had a shrewd suspicion that they were not weather reports. I am happy to say that my intercession proved fruitful and the nuptials duly took place. It might appear that I was something of a teacher's pet. I trust that Miss Diamond's technique adequately gives the lie to that, and so far as Mr Evans was concerned he arranged for me to take the letters during the morning or the lunchtime breaks when all my pals were in the playground playing football, as I would have liked to have been doing.

In due course I migrated from the junior school to the senior one. The classes there started at Form 2 and went up to Form 6. In the first year there were three classes, newcomers to the school going into 2A or 2C, while the pupils who came up from the junior department went into 2B. In the next two years there were only two classes, 3A and 3B and 4A and 4B. That took the pupils up to the Intermediate Certificate examinations, and in the following two years

38

Forms 5 and 6 led into the 'Highers', the examinations which provided the entrée to the universities or other tertiary educational establishments. The headmaster was Father Eric Hanson, a leading educationalist of his day. When he took over the post in the early years of the twentieth century, the College was in danger of collapsing through lack of support from the Catholic community in the West of Scotland. In those days, and for many years thereafter, the only two Catholic secondary schools in Glasgow and the West of Scotland were the College and St Mungo's Academy which was run by the Marist Brothers, in the Townhead district of Glasgow. The collapse of the College would have been a disaster, and such a disaster was averted by Father Hanson through his prowess as an educationalist and his strong personality. He gave the College the kiss of life and transformed the ailing school into a first-class educational establishment with a record of achievement which has lasted through several generations and which stands high among its contemporaries at the present time. It is an independent school and still attracts pupils from areas well beyond the boundaries of Glasgow. In my day I had classmates who travelled from as far apart as Bo'ness and Kilmarnock. This was not simply because there were no secondary Catholic schools in their area in those days. There was the added reason that their parents, like mine, wanted their sons to have a Jesuit-oriented education. The Jesuits have a variety of vocational functions, and traditionally education is one of them. Alas, decreasing numbers in vocations over the last few decades have caused this aspect of their work to be restricted in the interest of missionary work in the various forms in which the Society of Jesus is involved. Both spiritually and educationally, I owe so much to my days under Jesuit tutelage, first at St Aloysius and later at Mount St Mary's, that I cannot allow the opportunity to pass without acknowledging with the deepest gratitude the benefits I received from the teachings of such people as Fathers Wilson, Corrigan, Ambrose and Bullen at St Aloysius, and Father John Manning at Mount St Mary's. Father Manning probably had the greatest influence of all on my development,

39

taking place as it did during the last stages of my scholastic career and in conditions where teacher and pupils were closely drawn together.

At St Aloysius the day started with morning mass at 8.55 am in the adjacent parish Church of St Aloysius. Except for a good reason, we were all expected to attend the mass, and classes started at 9.25 am. Each written exercise was headed by a dedication in the form of the letters AMDG – Ad Majorem Dei Gloriam – to the greater glory of God – and finished with the letters LDS – Laus Deo Semper – praise to God always. This is the practice in all Jesuit schools and binds closely the temporal side of our lives with the spiritual spirit in which it should be carried out. All in all I feel that I can echo the words of an old Aloysian, Thomas Corcoran, better known to hundreds of thousands as Tommy Lorne, arguably the best Scottish comedian of his time, who, when proposing the toast of 'The College' at an Old Aloysian dinner, said in his own whimsical way and in his own broad Glasgow accent: 'I owe a lot to the Jesuits. I was teached by the Jesuits.'

I had the great privilege of being asked to propose the toast of 'The College' at the Centenary Dinner of the College in 1959. I doubt if any greater honour can be conferred on a past pupil than that of proposing the toast of the School at a Centenary dinner, and I am very conscious of it. I only hope that I was able to do passing justice to my commission. Out of that dinner came an inspired idea. The size of the gathering in the Banqueting Hall of the Glasgow City Chambers was such that it was impossible to make personal contact with one's classmates and contemporaries. A few of us, therefore, later decided to have a little dinner annually, restricted to people who had been in or about our class at the College, with no speeches but ample opportunity for reminiscing. The first of these was held in 1960 and it has carried on ever since. Someone suggested that we should have a name for the group, and so the name 'The Hanson Club' was devised. This was a tribute to the headmaster to whom we all owed so much if only for the preservation of the school, but for much more as well. We had over thirty members to begin with, and the successive dinners have been a great success. Unfortunately, but inevitably, time has taken its toll of the original members but we have extended qualification of the membership to people who were at the College while Father Hanson was headmaster. This seems to us to be a fair compromise to allow the dinner to be carried on meaningfully among people who had a common interest in their education under Father Hanson without appearing to be setting up a dinner in competition with the annual dinner of the much broader Old Aloysian Association.

After six years in the junior and secondary departments of St Aloysius I went to Mount St Mary's College, a Jesuit boarding school in Derbyshire, only some eight miles from Sheffield. Uncle John had a son John Patrick who was some eight months older than I. We had been together at St Mark's and St Aloysius and both of us had passed the old Intermediate examination in 1922. At St Aloysius he was called John Patrick and I was called Jack. This was designed to distinguish us. Uncle John thought that a period at a boarding school would do John Patrick a great deal of good and John P went to the Mount in 1922 while I remained at St Aloysius. He brought back very good reports from the Mount, both in relation to life at the school and scholastic achievements. This so impressed my parents that they decided to send me there and so I became a pupil at the Mount in 1923. Whether it was the change in the régime or just a change in the process of my growing up or the beneficial influence and guidance of Father John Manning SJ who was my form master during the two years I was there, I know not, but in that period I blossomed. My one big disappointment was that the official football game was rugby, whereas at St Aloysius it had been soccer. I had managed to get my place at outside left in the College First Eleven, but that was no passport into a rugby XV. At the Mount we played soccer in the playground attached to the school buildings (as distinct from playing fields for rugby and cricket which were some distance away). This we did during our morning break from classes and at the lunch-break, and my soccer skills such as they were served me in good stead when I began to play rugby. In my first year I concentrated on learning the game and made the second XV, which was the best I could hope for since my contemporaries had been playing the game for years, but in my second year I was promoted to the first XV in the position of hooker with the responsibility for taking the place kicks. My soccer came in handy in leading forward rushes in the well-known Scottish fashion although the traditional cry of 'Feet, Scotland, feet' was then unknown to me as I had never previously been at a rugby match and TV rugby lay years ahead.

We had a voluntary boxing class at the Mount organised by the gym teacher, ex-Sergeant-Major Cole. I joined it and this lead me to near-fame or near-disaster – which of them was never established. There was a lay brother at the Mount by name of Brother Redmond, a dear old soul who had spent many years at the Jesuit Retreat House at Craighead in Lanarkshire. While there he had made firm friends with Tommy Milligan who became the welter-weight boxing champion of Great Britain. Tommy had gone to Italy to fight Bruno Frattini for the welter-weight championship of Europe. He returned to Britain as the new European Welter-Weight Champion and on his way up north to his home in Lanarkshire he stopped at the Mount to see his old friend. There was great excitement among the boys and Tommy kindly ageed to stage an exhibition match to let the boys see a champion in action. An opponent – some people would say a stooge – had to be found, and Sergeant-Major Cole organised a boxing competition to find the fall guy – no doubt in more ways than one. I emerged as that person and I found myself in the gym, bedecked in a singlet and pants with the boxing gloves which I had worn during the competition still on my hands. The gym was crowded but there was no sign of Tommy. I wondered if something had gone wrong. Suddenly the ranks broke and Tommy emerged dressed in his everyday clothing. He came up to me and shook hands. He then said in a kindly voice: 'Do you mind if I don't go on with the exhibition? You see, I respond

42

instinctively, and if you were to land a punch on me I might counter automatically and hit you so hard that I might do you an injury. I would not want that to happen.' I could not argue with that, even if I thought that the chances of me landing a punch on him were remote, and I appreciated the kindness and thoughtfulness which had prompted it. Tommy said that he realised that this would be a great disappointment to the boys who had wanted to see him in action. It was a bit of a disappointment to me too, although I had mixed feelings on the point. Taking an objective view, I suppose that the removal of risk rather than fleeting fame was the wiser choice.

It was in the confines of the classroom and Father Manning's private room that I feel that the greatest impact was made on my academic and spiritual development. Father Manning was an excellent teacher who seemed to be able to get to the roots of a pupil's problems, explain away difficulties in simple terms, and in his homespun way psychoanalyse the pupil and iron things out for him. Here again it might be thought that this appreciation was formed in retrospect, but at sixteen and seventeen instant appreciation can have developed, and without appearing to be precocious I must admit that at the time I was very conscious and appreciative of the assistance and guidance I received from that mentor of mine. He had a great love of the arts, and was intensely fond of music and drama. Every year he produced a play and the range of plays he produced was quite amazing. In this field, too, he showed great insight in the choice of players for characters and coached them with unfailing patience. In my first year he put on W W Jacobs' *The Mate's Promotion*, and when I was given the title role my friends suggested that I had been typecast as the tough, aggressive mate. The same suggestion could not be made in relation to the part I was given to play during my second year in the production of *The Upper Room*. The play is centred in an upper room of a house on the way to Calvary. The occupants are the Virgin Mary and the apostles of Jesus, including Judas who arrives just after the great betrayal. Nothing was shown of the journey along the Via Dolorosa but the incidents were

43

revealed in reports which were given by the various characters and by off-stage incidents which were heard but not
seen. The part of the Virgin Mary was originally assigned
to Cuthbert Dignam, an oustanding actor even as a school-
boy, who in due course became a well-known stage, screen
and TV performer, having changed his name from Cuthbert
to Basil. His brother Mark Dignam was perhaps an even
more prominent actor. While the script made the role a
silent one, it also provided for the Virgin Mother to speak
the Epilogue. Father Manning took the view that this was a
mistake since it rested uncomfortably with the sorrowful but
meaningful and impressive silence with which she reacted to
the reports of the events as they were revealed to her. As
this silence had to be maintained throughout the play itself,
it seemed an anticlimax that it should be broken to speak
the Epilogue. Cuthbert Dignam was accordingly withdrawn
from the role and given a major speaking part where his fine
voice could be used to advantage, and the Epilogue was
assigned to another boy. It was then that I was brought in
to do the non-speaking part which did, however, call for
some acting and I am happy and proud to say that, according
to Father Manning and the school magazine, I managed to
do it rather well.

Another aspect of these formative days was the amount
of time we spent in Father Manning's room discussing all
kinds of matters. It was a custom at the Mount that in the
evening after night studies the pupils could go up to the
master's room and discuss with him any problems which they
had, or just engage in general conversation. We discussed a
whole variety of themes and problems, spiritual, economic
and social, and while in the social and economic fields we
boys found a great deal of common ground in identifying
the problems and the injustices in our social system we were
not always at one in devising the answers to them. It was
here that Father Manning came in, trying to hold the balance
and seeking to appraise the strengths and weaknesses of
the arguments. He was, however, always very patient and
understanding with me when I must have appeared if not
to him, at least to some of my colleagues, a young firebrand.

But then, they did not come from the Shettlestons of this world. In my first year at Glasgow University (1925–6) I was studying amongst other subjects Political Economy, and I wrote Father Manning a long letter explaining how I would go about solving the problems which beset the country at the time. I think that he must have thought that I was on the point of leading the youth of the country on to the barricades and was liable to be shot, because he sent me a characteristically kindly and understanding reply praising me for my concern but urging me to proceed with caution and not to overreach myself. As I have already said, I owe much to that kindly and saintly man.

The classes at the Mount were not identified by such terms as First Year, Second Year, etc. Instead they were progressively Preparatory, Elements, Figures, Rudiments, Grammar, Syntax, Poetry and Rhetoric. I joined in Syntax, and in Poetry I sat the Oxford and Cambridge School Certificate examinations and managed to pass with distinction in all subjects which gave me a certified entrance to Cambridge University. Father Manning wanted me to go back to the Mount for another year in Rhetoric and study for a scholarship to Cambridge or Oxford. This was coupled with a guarantee that I would be made a school captain, of which there were several, and an obvious and secure place in the first rugby XV. However, I felt that although the fees at the Mount were reasonable I had already put my parents to a bit of a financial strain to keep me there, and the sooner I started with my university career at Glasgow the better. The same considerations equally applied to all the alternatives, so I decided that I should stay at home and go to Glasgow University to which my certificates also gave me entry, and eschew an Oxbridge career. Although I spent only two years at the Mount they were highly profitable ones in my development and I conceived a great regard for that school, just as I had for St Aloysius and my affection for both persists to this day.

As at St Aloysius, the day began with morning mass and our religious education was deeply developed. If any problem arose there was always Father Manning's room to go to in order to thrash it out. In all these circumstances it is not surprising that I developed and still have a deep and abiding regard for the Society of Jesus and its members. This is reflected in the fact that while my four sons, John, Patrick, Anthony and Michael, all had their primary education at Holy Cross Academy in Edinburgh, I decided that I wanted them to have the benefit of a Jesuit education. St Aloysius is the only Jesuit school in Scotland, and as it is a day school with no provision for boarders the Mount was the obvious choice and to the Mount they all went. I wish to make it clear that my decision to send them there in no way casts any reflection on the standard of education provided at Holy Cross (now St Augustine's). To me the determining factor was the Jesuit dimension. If, as is the position now, the Mount had at the relevant time made provision for girl pupils my daughter Kathleen would have gone there too. Instead she was convent-educated, first in Edinburgh as a day pupil and then at the Sacred Heart Convent School in Aberdeen as a boarder. The Jesuit connection was sustained as a result of Anthony's decision to join the Society of Jesus on leaving the Mount.

Before I left school I had decided that, if possible, I would make the Bar my career. Uncle John had always taken a great interest in me and his view that I should do so was wholeheartedly endorsed by my father. I just accepted that advice and never considered any alternative. This absolved me from the very difficult decision which young poeple nowadays are called upon to make, often too early in their careers, when there are several options with relative attractions open to them for decision. In my young days the options, due to a variety of circumstances, were very limited. Today the disciplines from which the choice has to be made are much more extensive, and there are often subdivisions within a discipline which only complicate the problem of choice. In an age when the attainment of the qualification is no guarantee of employment, the problem is exacerbated. I feel very sorry for the youngsters of today who are faced with these problems. For my part, with tunnel vision I just made for the Bar.

5 University days

Membership of the Faculty of Advocates is a prerequisite to the right to plead as an advocate before the High Court of Justiciary, the Court of Session and their respective appeal courts. Of course, a party litigant can appear on his own behalf and plead his own case, and an English barrister can appear and plead in a Scottish appeal in the House of Lords, where appeals from Scotland are restricted to civil cases. Entry to the Faculty can be obtained through passing the requisite Bar examinations or their equivalent in university degrees. The latter is the usual way followed by the prospective advocate. The system was designed to secure that he had satisfactory standards in general education and in law. In my time at Glasgow University, the first was normally secured by obtaining a Master of Arts degree, or a Bachelor of Science degree, although occasionally both were taken. Thereafter a Bachelor of Laws degree (LL B) was taken to satisfy the requirement in law. The LL B course was stiff in that the pass mark was 70 per cent and you had to pass subjects two at a time to get a pass in each. A pass in one and a failure in one meant a failure in both. In the Law and Arts Faculties the system was solely one of lectures. The only exception to that in my experience, so far as an Ordinary MA degree was concerned, was in the Logic Class where something akin to tutorials took place.

Some of the classes were very large and passes could depend not on an understanding of the lectures but on the ability of the student to take accurate notes of the lectures and reproduce them as required at examinations. Fortunately in many cases the drawbacks of that system were more than compensated for by the excellence of the teaching staff. In the Latin class we had as our professor, John Philimore, regarded by many as the finest classical scholar of his day. His quick mind and mastery of his subject not only made him a first-class teacher but enabled him to indulge in repartee in Latin when an aspiring but rash student tried to score off him. If a student came in late and left the door into the lecture room open, he was greeted with cries of 'Shut that door', and as he made his way to his seat feet of other students were stamped in unison with his measured tread. The same treatment was afforded to professors and lecturers. This all happened one morning to Professor Philimore. When he reached the rostrum the tramping ceased, and at that point a bright young spark, obviously anxious to show that he had learned some Latin, shouted out: 'Claude ostium' – shut the door. Quick as a flash Philimore turned to him and said: 'Claude ostium' – close your mouth. The rampant appreciation of the students lasted for several minutes. Philimore's right-hand man was Dr Paddy McGlynn, himself a first-class Latin scholar whose Silver Latin Book became a standard textbook and whose teaching ability was of the highest standard. In the English department Professor McNeill Dickson was perhaps pre-eminent in his field in Britain and beyond. There was one lecturer in the department who, in his very first lecture, stressed the importance of listening to what was being said and trying to grasp its significance, only using our notebooks to enter aide-mémoires to what had been said. I found this advice most refreshing, because I regarded the regurgitation process as most unacceptable.

On the other side of the coin I had a most unpleasant yet salutary experience during my first term at the University in the class of Political Economy. In our first term examination the Professor set a question which involved mining royalties. I had written a full answer which I considered to be a reasoned one and in which I recommended the nationalisation of mining royalties as a solution to the problem. When my examination paper was returned to me

48

I discovered that I had been given a zero mark for my answer. This was somewhat of a shattering blow to a youngster of seventeen in his first term at the University. I realised that my answer in its result had not been acceptable to the Professor whose political views were not only well-known but were made evident in his lectures. In my juvenile ignorance I thought that the fact that I had analysed the position and had come up with an answer would have indicated some knowledge of the subject and merited at least a few marks. The moral was obvious. There were some examiners who did not want independence of thought but only a regurgitation of what they themselves had issued. Several years later I noted with satisfaction that the Coal Act 1938, which was put through Parliament by a government of the Professor's political persuasion, had enacted that a Coal Commission, which was set up by the Act, should acquire the fee simple in all coal and mines of coal together with property and rights annexed thereto. I felt inclined to send him a copy of that Act with my compliments, but I did not know whether by that time he was alive or dead.

In the Faculty of Law we had many outstanding teachers. In Scots Law we had Professor Gloag, who with his equally distinguished counterpart Professor Candlish Henderson of Edinburgh University, had produced the standard treatise on Scots Law. During the course of all his lectures I only once saw him refer to a note, and that was when he extracted a crumpled piece of paper from a waistcoat pocket and gave us the reference to a case which he had mentioned earlier. He was literally a walking encyclopaedia of Scots Law. Then there was Professor John Glaister in Forensic Medicine of whom I have something to say elsewhere; John Muirhead, a soldier with a distinguished war record was an eminent solicitor and teacher of Civil Law; Roderick Nicol lectured in both Private and Public International Law; Harold McIntosh in Jurisprudence; and John Boyd in Mercantile Law. In Conveyancing we had Professor Girvan, an experienced practitioner who had the faculty of making clear the mysteries of his abstruse subject. At least they were mysteries to students like myself who had virtually no practical office

49

experience of conveyancing beyond drafting a testing clause. In those days apprenticeship had to be done in parallel with classes which were in the early morning or late afternoon. I managed to do quite a good paper in the conveyancing degree examination and the external examiner told me that in the circumstances there were no questions he wished to put to me. As I was walking on air towards the door he said, 'By the way, the answer which you gave to the practical question was rejected by the Appeal Court in the case of "Blank" ' (I have long since forgotten its name and reference). This brought me down to earth with a thump. I paused in my tracks and turned round. He went on to say: 'You'll be interested to know that it was only a majority decision and that the judge, Lord X, who dissented, took the same line as you did.' This reinflated my ego, but when I came to have first-hand experience of Lord X when I was at the Bar I realised that there was a hole in the balloon which I had sought to reinflate. Incidentally, the external examiner was a Mr Hill Watson, who in due course became a very distinguished judge and whose early death was a great loss to the Scottish Bench.

With my success in conveyancing and in jurisprudence, I had notched up the number of subjects required for my LL B graduation. I had graduated MA in 1928 and now in April 1930 I graduated LL B. I could have arranged to start my year's devilling there and then, but I had just turned 22 and I felt that there was time enough to do so. In any event, I had started an apprenticeship as a solicitor, and it had almost eighteen months to run. I had adopted this course because I felt that an apprenticeship with a firm which did a great deal of court work would be helpful to me when I went to the Bar, and it gave me cover against the possibility of something unexpectedly happening which would prevent me from going to the Bar, in which case I could practise as a solicitor. I occupied the intervening period making full use of the opportunities I had to get familiar with the various aspects of court work. At the same time I decided to take those classes in the Law Faculty which I had not already taken and had not required to take in my law degree. I accordingly finished up by taking and passing all the eleven subjects which were taught in the Law Faculty at that time, namely Scots Law, Conveyancing, Civil Law, Jurisprudence, Forensic Medicine, Evidence and Procedure, Political Economy, Constitutional Law, Mercantile Law, Private International Law and Public International Law. I was fortunate in serving my apprenticeship in the office of Shaughnessy and McColl. Colonel Shaughnessy, the senior partner, took a kindly paternal interest in me. I spent most of my time working with John W McColl, who had the merited reputation of being one of the three best pleaders in the Glasgow Sheriff Court. I learned a lot from him. He was friendly with Craigie Aitchison whom he regularly employed as Counsel when Craigie was at the Bar, and Craigie had recommended the firm to my Uncle John as a good training ground, which indeed it was. Little did I think, or have reason to think, in those days that years later I would fall into the line of successors to Craigie as Lord Advocate and, in due course, Lord Justice-Clerk.

During my years at the University I never took any active part in student politics or games. On my return home from Mount St Mary's I had become deeply involved in the Shettleston Guild of Youth and found the outlets for my interest in both there. I regarded the politics in which we were there engaged to be the politics of the real world in which we lived and the issues on which we fought were the issues affecting the people we lived among. From what I could gather politics at the University were rather frolicsome affairs. In saying that I do not wish to convey the view that none of the students in the University societies was interested in and occupied with the real social and economic problems of the times, but there was a lightheartedness about the proceedings which suggested that fun and games were the essence of the confrontations and not the basic philosophies or issues. While there were students who were keenly interested in the fundamental matters, they were overshadowed by the people who looked on the political scene as a platform for frivolity. This was clearly demonstrated during the General Strike of 1926, in my first year at the University.

51

Since I believed in the justness of the miners' cause and approved of the support which the trade unions were providing in calling a general strike, I took my turn on the picket lines at the St Rollox railway works in Glasgow. At the same time scores of my student contemporaries were volunteering to drive cars, buses and even railway engines in order to break the strike. No doubt some of them did so simply as a matter of principle or political conviction, but there were many of them who, judging by the stories they kept recounting, were primarily motivated by the fun they got out of their strike-breaking experiences. Nothing persuaded me more than this to confine myself to local activities in Shettleston.

I do recall, however, one political meeting which I attended at the University. It was organised by the Conservative Club and was addressed by Walter Elliot, who probably had the widest ministerial experience of any Scottish Member of Parliament. He was then in the earlier stages of his career which became a long and honourable one, and which was only blighted by the wholly unjustifiable way that he was kept out of office by Winston Churchill on the two occasions when he became Prime Minister. That is by the way. In any event at the University meeting I tackled Walter with seeming success on figures which he had used in connection with local authority houses which had been built in Scotland under the Conservative Government. I asked rather naively how many of these had been built and had been made possible as a result of the Labour Government's Housing Act of 1924. He replied rather laconically, 'None'. On a supplementary question I was able to put substantial figures to establish the opposite based on housing schemes in Glasgow which were generally known. The Act of 1924 had been put through parliament by my Uncle John when he was Minister of Health, and I was very interested in the results which it had produced. Walter gave an equivocal and unsatisfactory reply which brought howls of derision not just from Labour supporters present but from a strong contingent of Scottish Nationalists led by 'King' John McCormack, and an even larger body of the unaligned.

52

After the meeting I had various approaches made to me from different sources to become more actively involved in party politics at the University but I turned these down because I still felt that such services as I could render were more needed in the wider arena outside, preferably in my native Shettleston. Many years later I found myself again opposed to Walter Elliot, this time in the House of Commons and in particular in the Scottish Grand Committee. Despite our political differences, Walter and I became good personal friends. This is a feature of life in the House of Commons which many people outside the House have difficulty in understanding but it is simply a matter of recognising personal integrity despite differing political views. Curiously enough, in the early 1950s just before I left Parliament but after I had demitted office as Lord Advocate following the 1951 General Election, I found myself teamed with Walter in what I think was the first TV debate on Scottish Nationalism. Our opponents were 'King' John McCormack and Dr Robert McIntyre representing the Scottish Nationalists. I got to know Bob McIntyre very well in later years when we were both members of the University Court of the University of Stirling, and once again I found myself developing a personal friendship with a person when our political views were diametrically opposed on the subject of the debate which we had earlier held. This friendship was further extended because Mrs McIntyre took an active interest in the work of the Royal Scottish Society for the Prevention of Cruelty to Children when I was Chairman of the Executive Committee of that estimable body. In retrospect I think that I made the right decision in confining my activities at the University to my academic pursuits and my leisure time to local political activity.

6 The road to the Bar

When I finished my apprenticeship with Shaughnessy and McColl, I was ready to take the first steps in my progress towards the Bar. This involved making arrangements to 'devil' to a practising advocate during the 'year of leisure' when the prospective advocate had to devote himself to learning his trade and was not allowed to get involved in lucrative employment, which could interfere with that purpose. The 'devil-master' had to be a junior counsel, and it was deemed desirable to get attached to one with a good allround practice. I was fortunate in that the junior counsel normally employed by Shaughnessy and McColl in their cases was John (Jock) Cameron – now the Honourable Lord Cameron, KT – and arrangements were made for me to go to Edinburgh to see him. And so one September day in 1931 I went through to Edinburgh to a flat in Dublin Street where I met the man who was to be my mentor. I was warmly greeted and was introduced to Mrs Cameron who in turn introduced me to the young baby whom she was holding in her arms. I tenderly shook the hand of the baby who, 54 years later, was to become one of my several successors as Lord Advocate, namely Kenny John, Lord Cameron of Lochbroom. To my delight I was accepted as a 'devil' and it was arranged that I should start devilling in the winter term of the court. Thus began an association and friendship which have extended for over fifty years, over thirty of which were on the Bench as fellow judges.

The importance of the 'devil' getting proper guidance and instruction from his devil-master cannot be overstressed.

54

The more widely based the practice of the devil-master, the more experience and guidance the embryo advocate obtains. Unlike some other countries such as England where there are separate courts for different types of cases, with a consequential tendency towards specialisation, the courts in Scotland are divided into two, civil and criminal, and even then it is the same judges who function in both. Counsel in Scotland therefore tend to be general practitioners and not to specialise on any exclusive basis, and their training should be oriented accordingly. To 'devil' to a counsel whose practice is narrowly confined could be a distinct disadvantage and should be avoided. It may be that some counsel tend to be briefed in one type of case rather than others, but to keep one's practice as widely based as possible is highly desirable, since among other things it provides a good background for future advancement. In recent years there has been a tendency among some counsel to concentrate wholly on practice in the criminal courts. There may be some short-term advantages in that, but there are definite long-term disadvantages, and the precarious nature of the short-term advantages should not be overlooked. There are already ominous signs that these short-term advantages are at risk. My advice to young people coming to the Bar is – do not plump for the soft easy option but prepare yourself to be ready to cope with any situation which is reasonably foreseeable.

I was extremely fortunate with my devil-master. Although not yet eight years at the Bar he had acquired a wide civil practice and was an advocate-depute. This provided me with a broadly based experience on both fronts. In addition, I was advised by my master to seek experience by spending such spare time as I had in going into the various courts and studying how counsel conducted cases, whether well or badly. While I was kept fairly busy with the work farmed out to me to devil up for him, I tried to get into the courts as often as I could to carry out this aspect of my training. I naturally gravitated to those cases in which Jock was appearing, but not exclusively so. As he was an advocate-depute I went through to the Glasgow circuit to see how things were carried on there, and so started a connection which lasted for many years during which I appeared as defence counsel, advocate-depute and judge.

Going through to the Glasgow High Court to study the techniques of criminal pleading had the built-in advantage of allowing me to stay at home during the circuit. The earliest trial I attended was that of *HM Advocate v Peter Queen*. It was packed full of interest for me. Not only was Jock prosecuting but the defence was in the hands of a very able and experienced silk, Macgregor Mitchell, KC. To add to the piquancy of the drama – because drama it was – Professor John Glaister (Primus) was to be the expert pathologist for the Crown and his defence counterpart was the well-known English expert of the day, Sir Bernard Spillsbury. Each had a great reputation, and there was great public interest in how they would fare against each other.

Queen was charged with the murder of the woman with whom he had been living for some time. She had been found strangled in a bed in the house which they were occupying, the instrument of strangulation being a piece of rope which had been cut from a clothes pulley in the house. According to the police evidence, Queen had gone to the local police station and had thrown a set of house keys on to the counter saying: 'I think I've killed my wife.' The police witnesses who spoke to this had made no note of what had been said, and this opened the door to the suggestion, astutely deployed in cross-examination by Magregor Mitchell, that they were mistaken in what Queen had said, and that what he did say was: 'Don't think I've killed my wife.' This was the lead in to the forensic evidence for which Spillsbury was briefed. Queen's father was a well-known and successful bookmaker in Glasgow who could afford the expense of bringing Spillsbury up from London to Glasgow as an expert witness. Such a witness is entitled to sit in court and listen to the evidence in the case other than the expert evidence led from other witnesses, and Spillsbury sat all through the lay evidence. Of course, he was not allowed to sit in court while Glaister gave his evidence but it was legitimate to put to him the evidence which Glaister had given and invite his comments on it. Briefly, Glaister's evidence was that the

56

strangulation could not have been self-inflicted. The defence case, apart from the challenge about what Queen had said at the police station, was that the death had been self-inflicted. This was the tenor of Spillsbury's evidence and he gave detailed reasons for that view, just as Glaister had given detailed reasons in support of the opposite view. Spillsbury gave his evidence in an imperial manner, designed to carry great conviction which it no doubt did in certain quarters. For my part I had found Glaister's matter-of-fact and down-to-earth reasoning much more acceptable, and I took the view of Spillsbury's evidence in chief that when you blew the froth away there was little of substance left. I realised that it might be presumptuous of me at that early stage of my career to form such a critical view of a witness of such reputed eminence, but as I listened to Jock Cameron's devastating cross-examination and demolition of the Spillsbury theory I felt somewhat reassured.

In the result the jury found Queen guilty of murder by a majority. Although by custom the details of a majority verdict are not announced in open court, I learned through the grapevine that it was a narrow one. I felt that this reflected the impact of the manner of Spillsbury's evidence rather than the content of it. On my score-card Glaister had a clear points victory if not a technical KO. But for all I know, the majority of the jury may have proceeded on something else, namely the non-acceptability of the police evidence that Queen had said: 'I think I've killed my wife.' Be that as it may, Glaister's reputation has survived to a much greater extent than Spillsbury's.

My period of devilling was interesting but quiet. At the suggestion of old Mr John Cameron, Jock's father, who was a member, and at one time President, of the legal body styled the Solicitors in the Supreme Court (the SSC Society), I spent my working time in Parliament House in the SSC Library and not in the corridor leading to the Advocates' Reading Room where most devils do their work. Not only was it quieter in the SSC Library but there I came under the guidance of Dr Malcolm, arguably the best law librarian of all time in Scotland who eventually transferred to the WS

Library. He was a gentle and kindly soul, and a huge reservoir of knowledge, who took an interest in me and taught me a great deal on the subject of how to go about finding the legal authority you are looking for. John Cameron senior also took a paternal interest in me, both during my period of devilling and thereafter during my career at the Bar, and I was indeed fortunate in having such kindly advisers in those early days when I was very much a stranger in Parliament House.

There was an element of loneliness, too, in the evenings when I had no work to do. I had obtained very comfortable 'digs' in Falcon Avenue, adjacent to St Peter's Church, but I did not savour the idea of sitting in night after night listening to the radio. I was a signed player for Shettleston FC and hopefully playing for them on a Saturday afternoon, but I was getting no team training with them, which was a disadvantage. I sought to remedy this by attending a PT class in Boroughmuir School on two evenings a week and by going out running on the other nights, but it was not satisfactory. I went home to Glasgow at weekends, getting the 4 pm train on a Friday and returning with the last train on the following Monday evening. This I was able to do because the Court of Session, which deals with the Civil business, does not sit on a Monday. I carried this on until the end of the term when I decided to commute from Glasgow during the court sittings for the rest of my devilling period. This solved my training problem and made life more pleasant. Nothing very spectacular took place during the rest of my devilling period and in the first week of November 1932 I was called to the Bar.

7 Early days at the Bar

There were four of us called to the Bar at the same time. The others were Jim Shaw, who in due course became Dean of the Faculty of Advocates, a Senator of the College of Justice with the title of Lord Kilbrandon, the first Chairman of the Scottish Law Commission to which he was seconded from his judicial duties, and eventually a Lord of Appeal in Ordinary in the House of Lords; James Leechman, who filled the posts of Clerk of Justiciary and Solicitor-General before being appointed a Senator of the College of Justice; and Edward Keith, who became a distinguished sheriff in the Edinburgh Sheriff Court. In those days it behoved an advocate to have chambers in the 'advocates' quarters', an area in the New Town lying immediately north of Queen Street and bounded by Queensferry Street on the west and Broughton Street on the east. Most advocates had their chambers in the house where they lived, although a few who could afford it lived outside the area and had separate chambers within it. Newly-called people like myself who had not much money to play with, had to find somewhere to live and at the same time have 'chambers' to which hopefully papers from solicitors could be delivered. Fortunately at that time there were quite a number of ladies who specialised in letting out rooms in their houses to young and not-so-young advocates and catering for them. James Leechman and I teamed up and obtained accommodation in the house of an elderly lady, a Miss Walton, who for many years had provided such accommodation at 72 Northumberland Street. We each had a bedroom and shared a sitting-cum-dining-room and a bathroom. We used the sitting-room for working purposes in the evening, and for such few consultations as we might have at that early stage of our careers if we could not arrange to have them in Parliament House. The young advocates were very fortunate in that there was a library called the Juridical Library in Charlotte Square to which we had access in the evenings and at the weekends. It was jointly operated by the Faculty of Advocates and the Writers to the Signet, and members of both bodies had the right to use it. There was a caretaker who lived on the premises, and entry could be obtained up until 11 pm simply by ringing a bell. No entry was obtainable after 11 pm, but once in you could stay inside as late as you liked, the only obligation imposed being to see that the lights were put out if you were last to leave and to ensure that the main door was properly closed when you left. This was a godsend, because it was a very complete library to be available to young counsel who might only be able to afford a few textbooks.

James and I stayed at Miss Walton's for about a year and then moved to similar but slightly more commodious accommodation in the house of a Miss Mathie at 66 Great King Street. We remained there together until the Easter vacation in 1935 when James was married. I remained on until the end of the summer term, when I followed his good example and left to get married and go into a house of my own which was a flat at No 8 Dundas Street in Edinburgh. Even when I had my own house and had started to build up my own library in a room which I used exclusively as a study, I still had frequent recourse to the Juridical Library for access to the many books which I did not personally have. Nowadays the system has considerably changed. Many of the advocates, and particularly the young ones, have their 'chambers' in Parliament House. There is access to the Advocates Library at all times and there are rooms available for consultations. Papers can be delivered to them by being placed in the advocate's box, the rows of which line the corridors of Parliament House. This system has the twin benefits of having 'chambers' in the place of work with an

60

extensive advocate's library to hand, and the option to live wherever the advocate chooses, free from the restriction to the expensive New Town area. As I have had no personal experience of this new system I cannot express any view on how it compares with the one in which I grew up at the Bar.

I was very fortunate at the Bar. Although I had no connection with the law before I was called, apart from my somewhat tenuous one as a young apprentice attending the Glasgow Sheriff Court and its adjacent coffee-houses, I started to pick up a practice fairly quickly, a practice which I am pleased to say kept increasing as the years rolled by. What I found most satisfactory was the fact that it was spread over a fairly wide area on the civil side and had an extensive criminal side to it as well. One thing I sought to do was to return work sent to me by solicitors as quickly as I possibly could, even if it meant sitting up late to achieve that result. I know that this was very much appreciated by busy court solicitors, and I discovered many years later an endorsement of that. A judicial colleague and personal friend told me that when he first came to the Bar a solicitor who had regularly briefed me mentioned this to him and advised him to follow the same practice. Knowing what a beaver for work my friend was, I think that the advice was superfluous, but he was good enough to say to me that he had followed it.

Within a very short time of my call to the Bar, I was instructed in a criminal case which had quite an impact on me. I was to act as junior to Macgregor Mitchell, K C, in the defence of a professional man who was charged in the Sheriff Court at Ayr on an indictment which libelled a contravention of section 5(1) of the Criminal Law Amendment Act 1885 in that he had carnal knowledge of, i e intercourse with, a young girl who was over the age of thirteen and under the age of sixteen. This was a very important case for our client, a married man, whose professional career as well as his good name and family relationships were at stake, and it was a charge which he vehemently denied. The case was set down for trial before a jury to be presided over by Sheriff-Principal Lyon-Mackenzie, K C.

61

The prosecution was in the hands of the Sheriff Court Advocate-Depute (an office which has not been filled for many years) who at that time was James Guy, M P. My senior, who was affectionately known as 'Grigor', was a wily old bird, whose homespun approach in a broad Scottish tongue went down well with juries. He said to me at the consultation before the trial: 'Wheatley, we're going down to the land of Burns, and there are several quotations from Burns which I think are appropriate in a case like this. Here's a list of them – have them in court for me.' So in due course I followed him into court carrying not a pile of law books but a large edition of the Works of Robert Burns with appropriate pages dog-eared. As the evidence unfolded I was forming the impression that we would win the case even without the help of Rabbie.

The complainer was a girl of fifteen years of age. She had been engaged from time to time by the accused and his wife to act as what we call nowadays a babysitter, and she was a frequent visitor to the house. Her account of the alleged offence was so exaggerated as to be unbelievable. To put it bluntly, it was a physical impossibility. That clearly pointed to a 'not guilty' verdict. Jim Guy, who addressed the jury just before lunch, did what he could, which was not much, with the bad job with which he had been saddled. That left for the afternoon session Grigor's speech for the defence, the judge's charge to the jury and the jury's verdict. After lunch Grigor started his speech to the jury and built it up beautifully to the point where he would hit them with Rabbie's words of wisdom. I was sitting with my book at the alert, ready to hand it to him. At that very point a lady juror in the front row of the jury box elected to be sick right in front of Grigor. The cause of that eruption is a matter of speculation, but its effect was undisputed. I need hardly say that nothing is more calculated to stem a flow of oratory than the member of the audience closest to the orator being sick all over the place. The court was adjourned for half an hour to allow the jury box and the unfortunate juror to be cleaned up. In the interval Grigor said to me: 'Wheatley, we'd better cut out the reference to Burns and get the speech over as soon as possible.' This he proceeded to do. Lyon-Mackenzie delivered a commendable short charge to the jury, commendable in the circumstances for its brevity rather than for its content, and after a fairly protracted period of deliberation the jury returned to the court and, to our amazement, delivered a majority verdict of 'not proven'. According to custom the jury's figures were not disclosed, and so the nature of the majority verdict was not made known. There being three possible verdicts – guilty, not guilty and not proven – the bare announcement and recording of a verdict of 'not proven by the majority' could leave the answer open to a whole variety of possibilities. All fifteen could have been in favour of an acquittal but were divided on the form which the verdict should take, or seven could have been in favour of guilty and eight for 'not proven', yet the same verdict would have been returned. As it stood the accused was left in the situation where it might be surmised that he had just scraped through to an acquittal by the skin of his teeth. In any circumstances that is bad enough, but in a charge of that nature where the evidence was so clearly indicative of a 'not guilty' verdict it was a grievous injustice.

I shall deal with the question of the 'not proven' verdict elsewhere in this book, but from that very early point in my career I have been firmly of the view that a jury's exact figures should be announced, particularly when the complication of three possible verdicts persists. It is only in recent years that, because of this, it has been laid down that the trial judge has to advise the jury that before a verdict of guilty can be returned at least eight of the jury of fifteen must be in favour of such a verdict. Even so, that does not clear up this situation completely, and, apart from the consideration to which I have referred in the Ayr case, there are other possible complications which the announcement of the actual voting figures would counteract. That change, in my view, should take place forthwith. I have never heard a satisfactory or convincing explanation for the existence or retention of the present practice.

Going back in the train to Glasgow from Ayr after the trial, my experience of life at the Bar was extensively widened. The Sheriff-Principal, the Advocate-Depute, Grigor and I were seated in the dining car having tea. Suddenly Jim Guy leant forward and said to Grigor: 'Grigor, you're a wonderful man with a jury. I've seen you make them laugh. Aye, I've seen you make them cry. But that's the first time I've seen you make them spew.' We all laughed, but I was somewhat puzzled. This was the sort of remark which would not have surprised me coming home from a football match in Glasgow, but I did not expect to hear it in the company of what I then regarded as Olympian figures of the Bar. However, I put it down to being part of my growing-up process in my new environment. I soon learned that the characteristics ascribed to Jock Tamson's bairns and Judy O'Grady know no social barriers.

When I came to the Bar certain hitherto lucrative aspects of civil work had gone into decline. Shipping cases and commercial cases had tended to find their way to the English courts if jurisdiction there could be established. Fortunately for members of the Bar and their grocers, butchers and other tradesmen, reparation cases continued to abound. These mainly related to damages claimed for injuries sustained at work, in road accidents, on faulty stairs and defective foot-pavements. Only rarely did such cases not go to jury trial, and the art of advocacy flourished in the civil jury courts. Alas, nowadays most civil actions for damages go not to jury trial but to proof, and that great training ground for advocacy is fast becoming barren land. Indeed I wonder how many of the present-day junior counsel have been briefed to prepare a Bill of Exceptions and how many senior counsel have addressed the appeal court on such a Bill.

Even so, reparation actions were subject to some severe restrictions in those early days. Contributory negligence to any extent, if causally connected with the accident, was a complete defence. In industrial accident cases the doctrine of common employment made the fault of a fellow servant a complete defence for the employer. No action at common law could be laid against an employer for an accident to an employee caused by the fault and negligence of a fellow employee. The Law Reform (Contributory Negligence)

Act of 1945 rectified the law of contributory negligence and limited it to a *pro rata* deduction from any award of damages. By the Law Reform (Personal Injuries) Act 1948 the defence of common employment was abolished with the consequential repeal of the Employers' Liability Act 1880 which had provided a very limited way round the common employment doctrine. About the same time, in consequence of new and widespread social legislation Workmen's Compensation was taken off the statute books for future cases.

These were substantial changes and upheavals in my early days at the Bar. Workmen's Compensation had been introduced towards the end of the nineteenth century to provide a simple code of compensation for accidents arising out of and in the course of employment. I doubt if any single field of legislation, which was designed to find a simple formula for compensation, gave rise to so much litigation right up to the House of Lords. All kinds of refinements were sought out of the successive Acts of Parliament which were passed, and the simple solution became a legal jungle and a lawyer's paradise. On the whole the changes, referred to in the previous paragraph, led to more work for the courts and the Jeremiahs were confounded. Even so, the number of reparation actions which would have come to court would have been fractional had it not been for the fact that there were solicitors and counsel who were prepared to undertake them on a speculative basis. At first these 'spec' actions were frowned on in certain quarters but the critics began to realise that without them there would be no need for solicitors and counsel to be instructed for the defence, and a lucrative source of business would be lost. Such actions did not take the form of 'spec' actions in some other countries where the lawyer acts on the basis that he gets a specified percentage of any sum recovered by way of his fees from his client. In Scotland, solicitors and counsel gave their services on the basis that, if the action succeeded and expenses were awarded to the client, the lawyers would get their fees as recovered from the other side under the expenses award, and the solicitors would likewise recover any outlays which they had paid on behalf of their clients. If the action were lost

65

solicitors got nothing for their services or outlays and so were out of pocket. Counsel only suffered to the extent of not getting any fees, while the principal beneficiaries under this system were the clients most of whom could not have afforded to fund their actions out of their own pockets and might not qualify for legal assistance under the old Poor Roll. The lawyers fared very well on the law of averages, but there was a financial sanction in this system which tended to secure a high standard of care and professionalism in the preparation and presentation of the 'spec' case.

I built up a substantial reparation practice and was regularly employed in civil jury trials. In contrast to criminal jury trials in Scotland where there are no opening speeches junior counsel are called upon in civil jury trials to make opening speeches to the jury for the pursuer and defender respectively before the evidence for the party is adduced. Broadly speaking, the purpose of the opening speech is to explain the circumstances and the nature of the client's case and the evidence which will be adduced in support of it. The experienced senior counsel of my young days at the Bar laid great store in the opening speech by their juniors, trusting that it would contain all that it should, and they laid stress on its presentation as well as on its contents. Although I did a fair amount of work for defenders, in fact I had a general retainer for a large employers' insurance company, the bulk of my work was for pursuers. In this I tended to be instructed along with certain senior counsel on the basis that we formed a good team. The two silks with whom I was most regularly teamed were Arthur Paterson Duffes and James Paton. While the junior counsel opened the case to the jury, the senior handled the witnesses and made the final speech for his side to the jury. This was, of course, flexible so far as the handling of witnesses was concerned, and the junior was sometimes asked by his senior to take certain witnesses in chief or in cross-examination. For instance, Duffes used to ask me to handle the medical witnesses on both sides. I early on realised that particularly in industrial accident cases terms of a technical nature would be used in the written pleadings or in the precognition of witnesses or in experts'

66

reports, and, if repeated in court, such technical terms might be foreign to the ordinary juror. I accordingly deemed it advisable to make myself familiar with the setting in which the accident took place and the manner in which machinery worked so that I could explain it to myself in terms which I, and hopefully jurors, could understand. Accordingly I went down pits, into factories and into the holds of ships, and so got to know what the technical terms meant. Sometimes photographs can facilitate this process, but at other times and in other conditions they cannot. For instance, down a pit the miners may be talking about the pavement and the ceiling and what lies in between. A juror who has never been down a pit can get a mental picture of a space where the ceiling is the height of his sitting-room at home, when in fact it may only be one-tenth of that height. I had to use this technique with Arthur Duffes at consultations in order to get the proper mental picture into his mind. He could not readily picture anything which went beyond one dimension. I had accordingly to try to build up a representation of the locus on his study floor using his books to construct the other dimensions and present a mock-up of the actual layout. This apparent weakness was paradoxically one of his great strengths with a jury. He presented to the jury the simple picture which he had built up in his own mind from the mock-up whereas other counsel who regarded themselves as fully knowledgeable about technical matters would use technical jargon which most jurors would not understand, and would get involved in incomprehensible technical arguments with experts. Duffes kept his communings with the jury on his own – and their – simple levels. The success of this technique was proved in the large number of wins we chalked up in our jury trial forays. Of course we had our failures, but these I was able to weather more philosophically than APD, who tended to regard a jury's adverse verdict as a personal affront. He was a great character of complete integrity and mental honesty, who was bitterly disappointed in not achieving a judgeship in the Court of Session, although he did become a part-time Sheriff-Principal. He fought some Parliamentary elections unsuccessfully as a Conservative candidate, and I am sure that his failure was in part owing to the fact that he would not compromise his principles, even to please his own party supporters. This was the position in one election which he lost by a handful of votes, having refused to give certain assurances to members of the licensing trade.

James Paton was a quiet man with a plain matter-of-fact approach to things. He had a shrewd mind and a pleasant delivery which seemed to appeal to juries, and he finished up with a good track record in the jury trial stakes. He did more criminal work than Duffes, and he and I were paired in quite a number of murder trials. From these two experienced counsel I learned that if you score a bull point in cross-examination, leave the point right away, preferably by sitting down. The latter tactic can have a most telling effect. Many a time the telling effect of a bull point has been eroded by the cross-examiner seeking to gild the lily, only to give the witness the opportunity to cover up his flawed answer.

James Paton had a country cottage in Midlothian, and from time to time he and his wife would invite Nancy and me out for tea on a Sunday afternoon. This was brought back to my mind when, on my recent retirement, I received a letter from the daughter of Mrs Mary Donnelly who had been the Paton's housekeeper. She wrote to say that her mother had told her that just after we had left the cottage on one occasion James Paton said to her: 'Mrs Donnelly, I may not be alive to see that young man reach the top of his profession, but mark my words, he will go far.' He did not live to see the advancement which came my way, but I like to think that I justified the confidence which he had in me. That personal relationship was also reflected in something which Mrs Paton said to Nancy during one of our visits: 'I do like it when your husband goes on circuit with James. They get on so well together and your husband looks after him so well.'

Undefended divorce cases were pot-boilers for young advocates, and while the fees were not large, it was surprising how much the money from them mounted up when you

were given a fair number of them. In my early days, undefended divorces were heard only on Saturday mornings, and
so did not conflict with other work in the practice. They
were the only cases put out for a Saturday morning, but as
the number of divorces multiplied other days of the week
had to be allocated to this purpose.

I was called to the Bar just in time to see in operation some
of the archaic practices in the civil courts which were swept
away by the Administration of Justice (Scotland) Act 1933.
Up until then a person appointed to be a judge of the Court
of Session had to sit a trial or examination of his qualification
for the office in terms of the Provisions of the Court of
Session Act 1723 and of the Acts of Parliament of Scotland
therein referred to. The appointee was given a case to try –
usually, but not necessarily, on a preliminary point of
relevancy – and he had to report his decision to one of the
Divisions whose members would review it. I have been
unable to find a case where the appointee failed to pass
the test and was ploughed, but in the very early centuries
anything was liable to happen. Lord Wark was the last judge
to be called upon to sit the test, which he did in February
1933, and Lord Carmont was the first judge not to be
subjected to the indignity, being installed without trial in
May 1934. The Bill Chamber was also abolished, its functions
being transferred to the Outer House. From the practical
point of view the most fundamental change was the abolition
of the right of a party to choose the Lord Ordinary and the
Division before whom his case would be heard. This was a
right exercisable by the party initiating the cause by
summons or petition. It was done by marking on the principal document the Division and the Lord Ordinary selected.
While in theory it should not matter which Lord Ordinary
or which Division of the Appeal Court heard the case, it
became the practice for solicitors, especially in reparation
actions, to mark the summons to a Lord Ordinary whom
they considered was more likely to give a fairer deal to a
pursuer than one or other of his colleagues. By the same
process of reasoning they would take out an insurance for
the future of the case by nominating the more favoured

69

Division. This was not only invidious but it could also be counter-productive. If a judge was regarded as being favourably disposed to pursuers he was inundated with cases marked to him, whereas a 'defender's' judge got very few, if any. In those days each judge kept his own rolls, and if too many cases were marked to him, his rolls had to be pruned by transferring some of the cases to another judge who was liable to be the judge whom most people avoided. In the result, since there were only five Outer House judges, to avoid being hoist with their own petard, some solicitors opted for the 'middle of the road-ers'. This tactic was not open so far as the Divisions were concerned. It was, as I have said, all very invidious, and there was much relief, at least in judicial circles, when the law was altered.

I have always found the criminal side of the law to be most interesting. Over the centuries both branches of the legal profession have provided legal representation to 'poor' people both in the civil and criminal courts. Annually, the respective legal bodies appointed from their members counsel for the poor and agents for the poor. Their services were provided free, and the only hope the lawyers had of obtaining remuneration lay in a successful civil action where expenses were granted against and recovered from the other side. In criminal cases the return for services to a 'poor' client was nil. In my one year as counsel for the poor in civil causes my remuneration was one guinea, my share of expenses recovered from the co-defender in a successful divorce action. During the first three years of his membership of the Faculty of Advocates an advocate was supposed to make himself available in the Glasgow High Court for instructions from an agent for the poor in connection with the Glasgow circuits. The instructions often consisted of being handed a copy of the indictment by the agent for the poor on entering the Court precincts, and there was usually little time to see the client down in the cells to get his story and line of defence before the case was called. While this provided experience to the fledgling advocate, it was doing scant justice to the client. All the cases were not like this, however. If the accused could raise some money either by himself or through relatives or friends, the solicitor would prepare the defence in varying degrees of efficiency, and might even find sufficient to pay counsel a small fee which might hopefully cover his train fare from Edinburgh. The solicitor's best chance of a sizeable fee was to get the client out on a substantial money bail and take the bail bond in his own name. If the bail bond was in the solicitor's name, he and he alone was entitled to recover the bail money when his client surrendered to the bail.

I did a good deal of criminal work, particularly on the Glasgow circuit, both as junior to a senior in serious cases, such as murder, and perhaps more often on my own in non-murder cases. In those days, when capital punishment was still the only penalty for murder, a senior counsel had to lead in a murder trial, and the Dean of Faculty could nominate a senior to act if one could not be engaged privately. The tradition of the Bar was such that if for any reason a senior counsel was not available to take on the defence, the Dean of Faculty himself would take it on. This slipshod and often unsatisfactory way of instructing counsel and generally preparing the defence was in itself an argument in favour of the introduction of a legal aid system. On the law of averages there are always likely to be more convictions than acquittals in criminal trials and so a young counsel should not be unduly despondent if his points table for victories, home or away, is not very impressive. From the professional point of view it is not so much the result that impresses instructing solicitors as the manner in which the counsel has comported himself. Success is usually a very satisfactory thing, but professional advancement and acceptability will normally depend not so much on the number of scores notched up as on the manner in which they were achieved. Paradoxically, the more advanced a counsel becomes, the more cases he is liable to lose, because he is often instructed just because of the difficulty of presenting a winning case. On the other hand, I have known counsel having a good score of success without having any of the real attributes of an advocate. Gimmicks, clever or otherwise, are regularly associated with jury trials in the minds of spectators. This is possibly because

71

of trial scenes which they have seen on television or in a play or in a film, most probably in an American court, and they seem to expect such tactics as the norm in any court. It is a practice which does not get much or any encouragement in our courts unless it is a strategy which is warranted in the circumstances. I remember one raw counsel almost bringing the building of the Glasgow High Court down upon our heads through his gimmicks and antics. I was prosecuting in the trial as the advocate-depute and the novice counsel was defending. When he came to cross-examine the principal witness for the Crown he started to execute mannerisms which he had seen on the screen. He marched up and down the well of the Court and when his back was to the witness he would suddenly wheel round, point his finger dramatically at him and say: 'I put it to you that you are wrong when you say – so and so.' This happened several times interlaced with pregnant pauses, and I saw the signs of gathering storms creeping over the face of the judge who operated on a short fuse. I was in a quandary. I wanted to warn the cross-examiner to stop his antics as the Vesuvius on the Bench was about to erupt, but I did not want to appear to be inter-rupting and possibly interfering with my opponent. My quandary was solved by Vesuvius erupting. I thought that the roof was going to cave in on us when I heard the baying voice of the judge shouting at the unfortunate counsel telling him to cut out his antics and get on with the cross-exam-ination. The point seems to be that if you wish to get away with a gimmick don't let the judge see it. This was the tactic of a wily old jury practitioner before my time, who, if he felt that he was going to get an adverse charge to the jury from the trial judge, would stand facing the jury with his back towards the Bench. He held his gown wide apart with his extended hands, and as he reminded the jury that they had come away from their lawful pursuits to act as jurors and that they and they alone were the judges of the facts, he would drop the arm furthest away from the judge, but still shielding it from the sight of the judge with his other hand by holding out his gown, and adding 'And it doesn't matter what anyone else may say', the whiles pointing a vigorous finger which the jury could see but the judge could not, in the direction of the judge.

Personally, I always tried to avoid gimmicks, but on occasions I could not refrain from using quotations which I thought appropriate to the occasion. Whether this stemmed from my early experience of Macgregor Mitchell wanting to quote Burns to an Ayrshire jury or from my interest in English literature both at school and university I know not. Sometimes it has a telling effect – sometimes it backfires. In my very young days at the Bar I had an experience which I related to my old friend from our university days, the late Harald Leslie (Lord Birsay) and which Harald never tired of recounting. In my speech to the jury I had, as I thought, analysed the facts in such a way as to demonstrate not only that the Crown had not proved its case but that my client was innocent beyond a peradventure. So in my peroration I reminded the jury that they and they alone were the judges of the facts and that the facts were as I had presented them. I then proceeded to remind them of Rabbie's own words, which I had first heard uttered in broad Scots by Davie Kirkwood at a political meeting when I was a boy: 'But facts are chiels that winna ding and downa be disputed.' This certainly impressed the jury who had clearly grasped the import of my adjuration and gave effect to it. They convicted my client, and to add insult to injury they did so unanimously! On the other side of the coin, when I was defending a businessman in a fraud case, where a conviction would have ruined his personal and business reputation, I finished my address to the jury by reminding them of this and recalled to their minds the passage from Othello: 'Good name in man and woman, dear my lord, is the immediate jewel of their souls: who steals my purse steals trash; 'tis something, nothing. 'Twas mine, 'tis his, and has been slave to thousands. But he who filches from me my good name, robs me of that which not enriches him and makes me poor indeed.' On this occasion the jury went with me and acquitted my client. I have since wondered what the verdict would have been if some juror had remembered that these words were spoken by that two-timing arch-villain Iago.

73

Perhaps the most curious experience I had in my criminal practice as a defence counsel was when I was asked to accept a general retainer from the leader of a gang of confidence tricksters to cover the defence of any member of the gang who found himself in court on a criminal charge. This gentleman had been convicted of one of his tricks in a sheriff and jury trial and had marked an appeal on the advice of his solicitor. When I received the papers for the appeal I noted from the sheriff's charge to the jury that they had been advised that corroboration of the victim's evidence could be found in a statement made by the accused in evidence which contained a denial which other evidence in the case indicated was false. I immediately arranged for a new ground of appeal to be added on the basis that this constituted a misdirection in law. At the appeal I submitted that this was introducing corroboration by false denial into criminal law which was erroneous, since that doctrine had only a very limited appli-cation which was confined to a certain form of civil action. As this was the only evidence on which the Crown could establish corroboration, I had little difficulty in persuading the Appeal Court to quash the conviction despite the efforts of the Solicitor-General, J S C Reid, to hold it. My client, who had been facing a stretch of imprisonment and who did not understand a word of the technical legal argument which I had advanced, was dumbfounded at the result. He clearly thought that I had manufactured a confidence trick which was beyond his ken and which was certainly not in his manual. It was then that he asked my instructing solicitor if he could retain me to defend any of his gang who were caught, and was greatly surprised, so the solicitor told me, when he was informed that while I would accept a brief from an individual charged with a crime if I were free from other commitments, I could not look at a general retainer of that nature.

By 1939 I had acquired a substantial all-round junior practice, but the advent of the war posed a problem for me. The ILP with which I had been associated personally and through my family had always been a pacifist organisation. I found myself with a strong conviction that the fascism of

74

Hitler and Mussolini was posing a very real threat to the democratic nations of Europe, including Britain. I realised that I had to choose between adhering to the pacifist attitude of the ILP or departing from it. So when Hitler threw down the gauntlet and Britain picked it up, I resigned from ILP, which had disaffiliated from the Labour Party in 1932, and aligned myself with the Labour Party which was supporting the war. When the Labour Party joined in the formation of the National Government in 1940 there were changes in the Crown office team. George Thomson was appointed a full advocate-depute and I was appointed advocate-depute in the Sheriff Court – an appointment which has now been in abeyance for a long time. When this appointment was made, Lord Advocate Cooper asked me if I wanted to be reserved from military service and I said: 'No.' He then pointed out to me that there was a big Sheriff Court trial in the offing, arising out of a mining disaster in Fife, in which the coal company, its directors and its manager were the accused, and he wanted me to undertake the prosecution. I said I would wait until I got my calling-up papers and would go then. I was thus able to carry through the Sheriff Court criminal trial. Moreover, I was able to appear as the leading counsel for the pursuer and respondent in a House of Lords appeal, although I had been less than nine years at the Bar. It happened, as so many things happen, through a series of strange events.

The action was a claim of damages for personal injuries sustained by a man who was off-loading cargo from the hold of a ship which was berthed at the port of Fremantle, in Australia. There were two defenders in the action, the ship owner and the stevedores. The action was raised in the Court of Session where jurisdiction had been established. Each defender blamed the other and following a proof the pursuer was awarded damages against the stevedores, who appealed unsuccessfully to the appeal court in the Inner House. A further appeal was then taken to the House of Lords. There had been a rapid change of senior counsel on our side. One senior had taken the proof but he was not available for the appeal to the Inner House and so another

75

senior counsel was brought in. This one was not available for the appeal to the House of Lords so a third senior was brought in. Just before the House of Lords appeal was due to take place, the third senior raised a technical point to which he said he could not find the answer, and which he could not argue against if it was raised in the House of Lords. He accordingly returned his papers. The instructing solicitor, Thomas J Addly SSC, was so fed up with this that he said to me that he was not inclined to instruct a fourth silk, and asked me if I would lead in the Lords if he got another junior to cover me. I told him that it was not normal for a junior counsel to lead in the Lords, and that while I was willing to undertake the responsibility I would only do so if I obtained the approval of the Dean of Faculty. Approval was obtained and the appeal to the House of Lords proceeded with my old stable-mate Arthur Duffes appearing for the appellant defenders, my friend George Thomson for the respondent defenders and myself with Gordon Stott as my junior for the pursuer and respondent. In opening the appeal Duffes had a very stormy time, but curiously enough the point which had deterred by senior no 3 was raised by Lord Macmillan, and I was asked to deal with it after Duffes had made his submission on it but before he had concluded his full speech. I had been unable to find any authority on the point but I had prepared an argument on it which I delivered. Their Lordships listened to it patiently and when I finished Duffes was asked to resume his speech. That was the last we heard of the point for it was never mentioned again even in their Lordships' speeches when judgment was being delivered. Neither George Thomson nor I was asked to answer the other submissions made by Duffes on the merits of the appeal which was dismissed out of hand. But for the record, as a junior counsel leading for a party in a House of Lords appeal, I did have my say.

There was one further incident during this period which was noteworthy, but which was indeed a sad one. I was in Glasgow Sheriff Court conducting a civil case when word came through that Lord Justice-Clerk Aitchison had died. This was a great blow to me, as I had always felt that he had been to some extent instrumental in my coming to the Bar with the advice he had given my Uncle John on that subject. But, indeed, it was a great blow to all who had the privilege of knowing him and to many who had only known him by repute. At the Bar he was the leading criminal counsel of his day and figured as defence counsel in virtually every prominent criminal trial in Scotland at that time. His successes had made his name a legend in Scotland – a fame which had percolated to England as will be seen from a story which I am about to recount. From time to time, Craigie Aitchison went to Harrogate to take the waters at the spa for health reasons. On one such occasion he was sitting in the lounge of the hotel having afternoon tea, when a man at an adjoining table called over to him: 'There's no point in each of us sitting alone. Do you mind if I join you?' As they were the only two people in the lounge Craigie invited him over to his table. During some trite conversation the man said: 'What line are you in?' and Craigie replied: 'I'm in the law.' 'Where do you live?' was the next question. 'Edinburgh' was the reply. 'That's interesting', said the man, 'a great friend of mine lives in Edinburgh and he's in the law. I wonder if you know him?' 'I might', said Craigie, 'what's his name?' 'Craigie Aitchison' was the reply. 'I've heard of him,' quoth Craigie and changed the conversation. A little later he asked to be excused for a few minutes as he had an important phone call to make. He went to the telephone and informed the police about what had taken place. He was advised to return to the lounge and keep the man in conversation. He did so, and about ten minutes later two detectives came into the lounge, took one look at the unlucky 'con' man, and said: 'Oh, it's you, Jimmy' and took him away.

Craigie's life story is a most interesting one. He was already a legend when in 1929 he was appointed Lord Advocate in the Labour Government's second period of office. He had been a Liberal but had joined the Labour Party some years before. His change from poacher to gamekeeper was noted by the old Glasgow newspaper, *The Bulletin*, in his appearance in their series of 'Great Scots'. A caricature of him, bewigged and begowned had the following doggerel under-neath:

The Labour chiels may toast their tawse
And vow to skelp the loon,
But murder's no the trade it was
Since Craigie's for the Croon.

He had a broad kindly streak in him, and a great sense of humour. On one occasion when he was sitting in court to deal with a man who had been remitted to the High Court for sentence, the whole proceedings were held up for more than half an hour due to the non-appearance of counsel. The counsel in question was quite a character in himself, of whom many stories could be told. He originated from Dundee and had never lost his Dundee accent. When everyone else was in a flurry he walked calmly into court and sat down. Craigie did nothing at that stage but allowed the case to proceed. It was only after the accused had been sentenced and taken down to the cells that Craigie took public notice of the earlier delay. Referring to the counsel by name he said: 'Why did you keep the court waiting for over half an hour?' Counsel looked up at him and said: 'My breakfast wisnae ready.' Craigie burst out laughing and walked off the Bench. Normally he would have anticipated a long and detailed explanation of unexpected circumstances beyond counsel's control followed by obsequious apologies. The refreshing candour in relation to a very ordinary domestic situation carried the day, but it was not all Lord Justice-Clerks who would have accepted the explanation with such good humour.

It was not long after Craigie died that I got my calling-up papers and went into the army. This placed more and more responsibilities on Nancy's shoulders. In late 1937, just after Kathleen's birth, we had moved to a much larger house at 15 Drummond Place, Edinburgh. We decided that when I left to go into the army the family would stay on in this house and not rent it out for the duration of my service and go to live in smaller and cheaper accommodation. This was a procedure which many people adopted since there was bound to be a substantial drop in income, and in many cases it was not a matter of choice but a matter of necessity. We worked it out that with careful housekeeping and the cushion of savings which we had managed to accumulate from my practice we could stay on in our own house. By this time we had a second child, John, and during the remaining period of the war following intermittent leaves, Patrick and Anthony duly arrived. Without any significant intrusion into our reserve savings Nancy managed to eke things out. How she managed to do it I never could quite understand, but an inherent determination always to live within the income available to her without sacrificing the interests of her family has been the keynote of her financial policy all through our married life. At some point or another I feel that I must introduce our own family, and this seems as convenient a point as any.

8   Our own family

Family life is a very personal thing and in my view it is not something to be paraded before the public, even when relations have been as harmonious as fortunately they have been with us. Nancy and I were married on 5 August 1935 in St Joseph's Church, Glasgow, the officiating priest being Father Michael McCarthy. The wedding reception was held in the old Grosvenor Restaurant in Glasgow, opposite the Central Station. Everything went swimmingly until it came to the cutting of the cake. The head waiter said to me: 'Will you get Mrs Wheatley to cut the cake?' I turned and said: 'Mother, will you cut the cake?' That was enough to kill any marriage from the start, but Nancy took it in her stride. She vows that it caused a transformation in my mother who up to that point had been weepy at the thought that she was losing her son, and that the tears vanished to be replaced by a radiant smile which remained with her for the remainder of the proceedings, even when I got Nancy to cut the cake. Fortunately, Nancy has a great sense of humour as well as a forgiving nature, and the incident has been relegated to the storehouse of amusing incidents which have studded our married life.

In due course we were blessed with five children, Kathleen, John, Patrick, Anthony and Michael in that order. I am sure that it is their wish as much as ours that I should confine my record of them to basic statistics. Kathleen was convent-educated and obtained an honours degree in history at Edinburgh University. Prior to her marriage she was a history teacher, first in St Augustine's School in Glasgow and then in James Gillespie's School for Girls in Edinburgh. She married Tam Dalyell MP and lives an altogether too-busy life at the Binns, the Dalyell family home in West Lothian. Life as the wife and secretary of a busy MP is a full-time occupation in itself, but when it is conjoined with all the other things which she does the wonder is that she finds time for them all. Tam may be a controversial figure at times on matters about which he feels strongly, but no one can gainsay his conscientious attention to his Parliamentary duties, the tenacity with which he keeps burrowing until facts which have been buried are brought into the light of day, and the personal service which he gives to his constituents and their problems in a wide-scattered and large constituency.

Tam's mother gave the Binns over to the National Trust for Scotland in 1944, but the family have the right to continual living there. As a National Trust property the house is open to the public from May to September inclusive, and Kathleen acts as the Trust representative on a voluntary basis, with the responsibility of organising the place and seeing to its availability to visitors. She has also to run the family home in the private part of the house, and look after the needs of Tam and their two children, Gordon and Moira, who are currently at Edinburgh University studying Law and Arts respectively. She is a member of a number of committees, some local, some national, such as the Historic Buildings Committee and some offshoots of that.

John took a law degree at Edinburgh University and in due course he was called to the Bar. After practising for a number of years he was appointed a sheriff, and is at present Sheriff of Perth. While at the Bar he twice stood for Parliament as a Labour candidate for the constituency of Dumfries, and while not winning on either occasion he comported himself well on both. He married Bronwyn Fraser and they

81

have two sons, John Nichol and Mathew. They live in a very pleasant country house in Drum in Kinross-shire. They have some 19 acres of land attached to the house on which they operate a miniature farm with over 40 sheep, some horses, poultry and a large kitchen garden.

Patrick also took a law degree at Edinburgh University and is a partner in a large SSC firm in the city. He married Sheena Lawrie and they have three sons, Patrick David, Giles and Martin. They live only a mile away from us in Edinburgh, and they are our nearest contacts.

Anthony, as I have already said, became a Jesuit priest, who took a Master of Arts degree in Economics at Fordham University in New York during his training. He was ordained in the Sacred Heart Church, Edinburgh, on 29 June 1974 having spent eleven years in preparation for it. The Jesuits believe in an extensive and intensive period of preparation for the priesthood. It used to be fifteen years, but is now about twelve, since a further year of theology takes place after ordination. Even at that, the final vows are only taken years later, after spells of priestly duties have been carried out. He spent periods of service in Mexico and Guyana as a result of which his health was seriously impaired, and he was returned to Britain for medical treatment. He still requires medication but he has been given different assignments in recent years. As I write this he is serving as a Chaplain at the University of Manchester and three other tertiary educational establishments nearby, but his future movements are undecided.

Our youngest son, Michael, has set up in business for himself as a freight service company, transporting goods in containers all over the globe. He married Ann Barry and they have three children, Richard, Jennifer and Angela. They live in Old Philpstoun in West Lothian, about a mile from the Binns.

Our children all live within easy reach of us and we see them and their families regularly. Nancy has a bracelet with discs attached, each one containing the name and date of birth of one of the ten grandchildren. It is a very convenient aide-mémoire when birthdays come along. Apart from Gordon and Moira all the grandchildren are still at school. Although John and Patrick followed me into law, they did so entirely by their own choice and without any inducement from me. I simply mention this because I am not a believer in parental vocations although parental consultation and guidance should always be available.

The whole family congregated to celebrate our Golden Wedding which was marked with a mass of thanksgiving in our local parish church of St Peter's in Edinburgh. The mass was concelebrated by our parish priest, Father (now Monsignor) McNally, his curate, Father Holuka, both very good friends of ours, and our son Anthony.

The occasion held for us a most pleasant surprise. We had wanted the mass to be a purely family affair with only the children, their spouses and our grandchildren there with us. When the procession emerged from the sacristy it contained to our surprise our newly ordained archbishop, the Most Reverend Keith Patrick O'Brien, Cardinal Gray's successor. He explained his presence thus. His episcopal ordination had taken place on the previous day, 5 August. It had been followed by a reception in Craiglockhart Convent. He had learned that Nancy and I, who had been invited to both, had decided to postpone for one day our Golden Wedding mass and family celebrations to enable us to attend his celebrations. Accordingly, he said, the least he could do was to come to ours. It was a kindly and generous gesture which we all very much appreciated, and the occasion was enhanced by that pleasant surprise. We have been blessed with a happy married life.

After I had drafted this book in manuscript, Anthony informed Nancy and me that he had resigned from the Society of Jesus and had asked to be relieved of his priestly duties. This came as a great surprise and disappointment to us as he had spent 23 years of his young life in the Society from noviceship to priesthood, and we thought that he was firmly entrenched. We realise that the decision was his and had to be his alone, and must have been reached after careful thought and consideration.

9 Life in the Army

My first experience of army life was in a Royal Artillery training regiment at Marske-on-Sea in North Yorkshire. Despite the marked change in living conditions I soon adjusted to the life. Although I had to sleep on a palliasse on the floor, the food was good and plentiful, and I managed to wangle frequent showers in the ablutions. Between square bashing, football and running I soon found myself in good physical shape. After a series of rather elementary IQ tests I was included in a class of 'specialists' where we were taught the technical side of gunnery. This stood me in good stead when I went to the Officer Cadet Training Unit and, more importantly, when I was posted to a regiment after I had passed out from OCTU. I could write much of this early period, but I shall confine myself to two incidents, one home, one away.

The first occurred during my first spell of army leave. I went up to Parliament House to see how things were going in court and to chat with old colleagues who were still there. I was dressed in civvies, and as I was standing at one of the empty fireplaces in Parliament Hall I was approached by Jimmy Cooper WS, a brother of Lord Cooper, who had regularly instructed me in the past. He found out how long my leave lasted, whereupon he said he would like me to appear in an appeal before the Division on the following week if I wanted to take it. It was a case which I had started before I left and which we had won in the Outer House. I was no stranger to the case and he no doubt thought that it would provide me with a fee which would be acceptable in my new straitened circumstances. I agreed to take the case, but on reflection I realised that it could be a brutum fulmen or white elephant, call it what you will. The tradition was that during the war serving members of the Faculty of Advocates could appear in court in their service dress instead of their wig and gown. Traditionally members of Faculty so appearing were officers of rank, and as far as I knew no non-commissioned officer had ever appeared, not even a regimental sergeant-major let alone a local unpaid lance-bombardier. On the other hand if I donned my wig and gown I would have to pay a year's Faculty dues. This would have involved me paying out my fee for appearing plus half as much again. That did not appear to me to make sense, and it seemed reasonable to assume that the principle of a serving member of Faculty being allowed to appear in court in appropriate uniform in lieu of wig and gown should apply irrespective of rank. So I turned up in court in my battledress with its single stripe and my big army issue boots which clattered loudly with every step I took. The story has followed me through the years as if it had been part of a one man crusade to democratise the army or the Faculty, I know not which, when it was purely an exercise in common sense and parity of reasoning. For good measure, I was successful in the appeal.

The second incident took place during the early stages of my army life when I was in the training regiment. I had a colleague called Tom who was quite a character. In civvy street he was the managing director of a brewery. There were over 1000 recruits in this training regiment, and he arranged for a bottle of beer for each one of them for the Christmas day dinner, with some soft drinks for 'odd bods' like me who were TT. He also supplied the officers' mess and the sergeants' mess. He was obviously *persona grata*, but he never took advantage of this at the expense of the other bods. One day a large Daimler car drove into the camp, and after some directional enquiries had been made it stopped outside the hut where Tom was ensconced. It so happened that he was barrack-room orderly that day, and he had managed to 'win' a pot of paint and a brush. So there he was, dressed in his denims, vigorously slapping paint on to the hut when the car drove up. It was explained to him that an important contract had cropped up and because of its importance the directors did not want to make a decision without the managing director being present. So Tom invited the board members and the secretary into the hut and sat them round the table. The meeting had been duly constituted and the secretary had started to drone out the terms of the proposed contract: 'Whereas the party of the first part and the party of the second part, etc' when the bombardier came into the hut with the troops to change into PT kit. He was an experienced soldier who had been to a number of different courses, but he had never been taught how to cope with a board of directors meeting in a barrack-room. He was nonplussed but Tom just waved an airy hand and said: 'Carry on, bombardier, we won't be too long.' So to the intonation of a battery of legal phrases the boys of the young brigade changed into vests and running shorts. The proceedings were brought to an abrupt halt by the advent of the Battery Major who had been advised that a strange-looking vehicle had entered the camp and its occupants had been off-loaded into a barrack-room. With that urbanity which characterised all his conversations he said to Tom: 'What the hell is going on here?' Once again Tom stepped into the breach. 'We are just holding an important and urgent board meeting, sir. May I introduce my colleagues, Mr A, Mr B, etc.' Before he had completed the roll-call the Major had managed to gather sufficient breath to splutter: 'Get to hell out of here. Take a 48 hours' leave and conduct your business where it should be conducted.' Tom muttered a grateful thanks, managed a hurried salute, and, without waiting to change out of his denims, made a dive for the door and the Daimler before the order could be countermanded, leaving behind him yet one further page in the history of the British Army. After I left Marske for OCTU I never saw Tom again, something which I regret as I would like to have heard what further inroads he had made into the standardised routine of army life. But I will say this for him. The cognoscenti said that his beer was the best they had ever tasted.

In due course I was put up to interview for admission to the OCTU at Catterick. I was led to believe that such interviews took different forms. Mine consisted of appearing first of all before two War Office Blimps who asked a few innocuous questions before passing me on to the real interview which was conducted by a former commandant of the OCTU who really knew his stuff. He started off by asking me if I would like to sit down and pointed to an armchair. I thought that this was most civilised, thanked him and sat down, taking off my forage cap in the process for politeness. After a few technical questions he said to me: 'I see that you were born and brought up in Glasgow. What do you think the economic situation will be like in Glasgow after the war?' I could not have thought of a better question myself. I proceeded on the assumption that we would win the war, and expanded on the economic situation I hoped we would see. After about five minutes of uninterrupted exposition on my part he held up his hand and said: 'That's enough. We'll get you into OCTU right away.' That was good news, and when the sergeant came in to conduct me out of the room I decided that I would show them that I could do more than talk; that I had learned something in this man's army during my months with the training regiment. I sprang to my feet, placed my forage cap on at what I conceived to be the correct angle, gave a smart salute, did an about turn, and marched out behind the sergeant in the approved style of the barrack square. When we got outside the sergeant turned to me and said in a broad Glasgow accent: 'Hey, Mac, don't you think that you should put your cap on the right way roond?' I took it off and looked at it. He was right. I had been wearing it with the badge to the back.

In a few weeks I was in the bleak wastes of Catterick Camp at the RA OCTU where I went through training for the next five months. I do not know whether the course was deliberately designed to test how the cadet would react to adversity, but it certainly seemed that there was a deliberate attempt to undermine such self-confidence as one had acquired. I somehow managed to survive the ordeal, although not without incident. Among other things, an artillery officer was supposed to be able to ride a motor-bike. I had never ridden a motor-bike in my life, and I had to be taught. My tuition consisted on day one of being told the basic operation of the machine and how to ride it, followed by an instruction to get on to it, start it up and drive it twice round the parade ground. Somehow or another I managed to do this and was quite chuffed with myself. On day two we had to go out on our bikes in convoy over the moors. I lost count of the number of times I fell off, had to pick up the bike and myself and get started again. I do remember hitting a tree and the bike climbing several feet up the trunk. How I got the contraption back to barracks I shall never know, but back to barracks I rode it. Curiously enough it all came right in the end. When in due course I had to go out on exercises with my regiment, the order was that officers had to ride up and down the columns on motor-cycles to keep a constant check on the guns and vehicles, and I found that I could handle the machine passably well. But then we were on roads. I shudder to think what might have happened if the convoy had been obliged to go over moors.

However, I passed out of OCTU in due course. It was a gamble to which regiment one would be sent and where it was stationed. I was posted to 484 Battery of 119 Field Regiment RA which was part of the 61st Division stationed in Northern Ireland. 484 Battery was located in Ballymoney in County Antrim. As a unit we were merely marking time although we went on occasional firing exercises in the Sperrin Mountains, but there was an air of unreality and lack of involvement in it all. There was, of course, a complete black-out in Antrim but the lights were still shining brightly on the other side of the border, which only tended to pinpoint Ulster. However, we never saw or heard anything of enemy aircraft. After I had been about five months there the regiment was posted to Holland-on-Sea on the east coast of England where the fact that we were at war took on a more realistic aspect. We had various visits from German bombers, and while bombs were dropped around us we had only one near miss. Our exercises became more intensive and we frequently had to take the guns up to the south bank of the Wash for gunnery practice. There was a great plus in these exercises because going to and fro on a motor-cycle I saw a lot of lovely parts of England which I had never seen before. In due course we were transferred to a camp on the outskirts of St Albans and things started to get hotted up there. Rumours were rife that our training had to be stepped up and that we were to form part of one of the assault divisions when the invasion of Europe took place in the autumn of 1943. Certainly our training was stepped up and we had reached the point where we were ready to move off at a moment's notice. But autumn came and went and no invasion took place. Instead there was an anticlimax. The regiment which had its origins in a territorial unit in the midlands of England, was virtually stood-down and we became what was to all intents and purposes a posting station with veterans being posted to us from the Middle East and our own personnel being posted away in dribbles to other units. Our Colonel, Vivien Hill, who was a regular soldier, was shattered by this turn of events. All our training and all the expertise which we had acquired seemed to become history overnight. The Colonel came to me one day and said: 'They have made a nonsense of the regiment, and as things are now you are being wasted here. You should be doing work for which your professional training has equipped you' – I had acquired a good track record as a defending officer in courts-martial – 'You should apply for a posting to the Judge Advocate-General's Department.' I said that I would be quite happy to stay with the regiment, but he said that if I did not make the application he would do so. I didn't and he did. Within not much more than a week I received word that I had to report to the Judge Advocate-General, Brigadier Shapcott, at JAG Headquarters in London. I had hardly time to say goodbye to my troop before I was on my way. This was towards the end of 1943. When I had my interview with Brigadier Shapcott (he was

90

called Shappy throughout the JAG régime, but not to his face) he set out to impress upon me the reputation which he had as a tough guy. We were all members of a team and there was no room for ambitious officers seeking quick promotion. Promotion would be strictly by seniority. I replied that this was all right by me. After a two months' training period at HQ I was posted to the Northern Command branch of JAG at York, where I remained for about a year. The CO when I arrived was a Colonel Halse for whom I had no regard at all, but he was soon replaced by Colonel Max Turner, a member of the English Bar, who was very much on top of his job and for whom I had a great respect. I found that my experience in criminal cases at the Bar stood me in good stead when adjusting myself to the work, and I built up quite a reputation. So much so, that when the second-in-command was posted away Max Turner asked Shappy to appoint me to the post. Shappy stuck to his declared policy and said that I was well down the list in seniority and it was not my turn. I think that Max was more disappointed than I was. I had been told that this was the policy and had accepted it. In any event, when the appointee arrived in the person of Major Clifford White he and I became good friends and spent most of our recreational time together playing tennis, cycling and horse-riding at local stables.

Towards the end of 1944, out of the blue I received a posting to, of all places, Scottish Command in Edinburgh. I had not asked for such a posting, but I accepted it with relish. As members of the JAG staff had normally to find living accommodation in the area where they were functioning, this meant that I could stay at home. The work there was not so intensive as it had been in York, with one notable exception. A case of suspected murder at a Prisoner of War camp for German officers had been engaging the attention of the authorities for some time. A protracted dispute had taken place on whether the matter should be dealt with by the civil authorities or by the army authorities. The Lord Advocate carried the day but he was unable to make any headway because of the lack of corroboration

91

which the law of Scotland requires for a conviction, and there was only one witness forthcoming to speak to murder as opposed to suicide, which the death had been made to look like. The case fell back to the army authorities and the JAG took over. Shappy sent word to my CO, Colonel Hallis (not Halse), that he wanted me to take over the investigation. I did so, and with immense help from an interpreter who was seconded to me I picked up bit after bit of evidence which *in cumulo* provided all that was required to involve a number of the deceased's co-prisoners of war in a murder charge. I sent all the statements which I had obtained with relevant documents to London where they were gratefully received. In the event several convictions were obtained on the murder charge. Colonel Hallis informed me that Shappy was very pleased with my work in the case. Not very long after this I was granted three weeks' leave of absence to contest the 1945 Parliamentary General Election as the Labour candidate in the North Ayrshire and Bute constituency, of which I have more to recount in the next chapter. Thereafter I returned to duty, and in August 1945 I was told that I was wanted on the 'phone. It was Max Turner who had left Northern Command some time before to take over a joint Eastern-Southern Command of the JAG Department. He explained to me that he was about to enter hospital for a major operation and would not be returning to duty; that Shappy wanted me to come south right away and take charge of the Eastern Command branch. I told him that there was a difficulty about my doing that and that I had better speak to the boss himself about it. Shappy must have been at his elbow because he came on to the 'phone right away and in peremptory manner said to me: 'Put up your major's crown and come down and take over right away.' I explained the difficulty. The General Election had come and gone and a Labour Government had been formed. George Thomson had been appointed Lord Advocate, and he had been in touch with me to say that he had put in a requisition for my immediate demobilisation as he wanted me to be one of his advocates-depute. I explained all this to Shappy and said that I did not think it fair to sit on this

92

information and carry out his instructions, only for him to discover within a short period that I was being demobilised. He took the point and told me to treat his instructions as cancelled. He then rang off, and, as I then thought (erroneously), went out of my life. My prognostication of the situation was proved right, because within a week my demob came through. By then I had begun to wonder what had happened to the principle of promotion strictly by seniority. I had carried the rank of Captain during my whole period in JAG. I had never acted as second-in-command at any of my stations. There must have been many officers of equal or higher rank who were senior to me in the department. Yet I had been offered this very important post. There were certain explanations which passed through my mind but I decided that there was no profit in speculation. What mattered was that I was satisfied that I had taken the right course in putting all the facts to Shappy.

Some five years later Shappy's path crossed mine again. By that time I had been elected to Parliament and was Lord Advocate and he was still the Judge Advocate-General. The Government were proposing to introduce a Bill which in due course became the Courts-Martial (Appeals) Act 1951, and a provisional draft Bill had been prepared. A meeting was arranged to consider the draft proposals, and representatives of the services concerned along with the appropriate departmental ministers were called to it. I was deputed to attend that meeting as a senior law officer and to preside over the proceedings. I was sitting at the table flanked by my ministerial colleagues when the service representatives and the departmental officials came trooping in. In view of my experience in JAG it did not surprise me that they came in strictly in order of seniority. Bringing up the rear was Brigadier Shapcott. There were certain clauses in the draft Bill dealing with the office of the Judge Advocate-General. During the whole of the proceedings Shappy never let his eyes rest on me. As there was no controversy in relation to the provisions dealing with his office, he had no occasion to speak. When the very successful meeting concluded the service representatives and the departmental officials left, again in strict order of seniority. When Shappy came to the door he turned, looked at me straight in the face, gave me the slightest of winks, turned and went out of the door and out of my life.

10 The post-war Bar and parliamentary elections

On being demobbed I returned to the Bar and once again I very soon picked up a busy practice. The position was complicated by the fact that I was an advocate-depute. This meant that, apart from going on circuit to conduct prosecutions on behalf of the Crown, I had a good deal of paper work to do in the Crown Office. Being fairly regularly in court with my private civil practice and criminal and justiciary appeals, I could only keep abreast of the paper work by going up to the Crown Office when I had finished in court and working there until I had completed what had to be done before going home to deal with the work which had to be attended to in connection with my civil practice or in anticipation of an impending circuit or criminal or justiciary appeals. While the work passing through the Crown Office was then not so voluminous as it is at present owing to the great upsurge in crime, there were only four advocates-depute and the work load was quite burdensome. There was, however, an extra-advocate-depute for the Glasgow circuit who operated in the South Court, where by custom all the below-the-belt cases were dealt with. Other cases were also taken in that court, but all murder cases were taken in the North Court. The post of Extra-Advocate-Depute was not a salaried one, the incumbent being paid quite a small and inadequate *ad hoc* fee for the whole circuit. In my young days at the Bar it was amazing how many reduced pleas of guilty the South Court Depute was prepared to accept!

The post of Solicitor-General had only been a part-time

one in that the holder of the office was allowed to take part in private civil practice, which in view of his status tended to be a busy one. Our Solicitor-General was Danny Blades, KC (who was appointed on a non-political basis) but Lord Advocate George Thomson altered that system in 1945 and made the post of Solicitor-General a full-time salaried one at £3,000 per annum, replacing the old part-time salary of £2,000 per annum. This additional £1,000 was scant recompense for the loss of the right to engage in private practice in civil causes, but it had the carrot of being a stepping stone to ultimate judicial preferment, which in Danny's case was not long delayed. However, it gave the Solicitor-General more time to attend to Crown Office business. The Lord Advocate's salary was then £5,000 per annum which was on a par with the salary of the Lord Justice-General and was £200 per annum more than the Lord Justice-Clerk's, while all the other judges were at £3,600 per annum. These salaries were fixed by section 45 of the Criminal Procedure (Scotland) Act 1887, and it is worthy of note that despite the fall in the value of money after two world wars, the figures were not increased for 67 years when by the Judges' Remuneration Act 1954 they were increased by £3,000 per annum. This did not fully compensate for the loss of money value in the interval, and although these figures have steadily increased since then, such increases were usually in arrears of the upward trend in the cost of living and the downward trend in the value of money, but the intervals were not of the order of 67 years. It would be an interesting exercise to work out what would have to be paid nowadays to give the purchasing power of those basic 1887 salaries, having regard to the changing value of money and the rate of taxation. I personally have no grievance. I consider that judges do relatively well. But our gross salaries are public knowledge. They appear in almanacs and every time there are increases they are blazoned in the press, while people in private business get salaries which can be several times as large, but the public never get to know what they are except, perhaps, by chance.

The salary for advocates-depute was £800 per annum,

with supplementary *ad hoc* fees for appearing for the Crown
in justiciary appeals, that is criminal appeals from the courts
of summary jurisdiction. No extra fees were paid for appearing in criminal appeals, that is from cases which were
based on indictment and taken before a jury. I never quite
understood the reason for this, or the justification for that
matter, but ours was not to reason why. In those days,
counsel who appeared at the trial normally appeared in the
appeal. This was a great advantage to the Appeal Court
when matters were being discussed relative to what had
happened at the trial and no record of the proceedings was
available at that stage. As things have developed, the calls
on the time of advocate-deputes are such that they are liable
to be away on circuit when the appeal calls and counsel who
acted for the defence are likely to be engaged elsewhere in
the more lucrative activity of a criminal trial.

I found the work of prosecuting much more exacting
than the work of defending. When defending, you can play
along by ear to a certain extent, although not all along the
line as some people do, and if you make a technical slip it
may not matter at the end of the day. A prosecutor has to
be careful in the questions he asks and how he asks them.
He has to take care that questions are put which evoke
answers which are essential to the proving of the Crown
case. If he errs on such matters, his error may result in a
failure to obtain a conviction, or open the door to the
quashing of a conviction on appeal. The traditional fairness
of the prosecutor in our criminal system is something which
I trust will be observed and preserved.

While on circuit I found my evenings fully occupied in
preparing lines of cross-examination, in collating the evidence which had been given in court, and in preparing my
speech to the jury. When I became a judge I found myself
following almost the same exercise, but to a more intense
degree, although excluding preparation of lines of cross-
examination. As an advocate-depute I found the forensic
battle in court stimulating, particularly when faced with a
formidable adversary, such as my old devil-master, with
whom I had to cross swords from time to time. The one

97

part of the job which I disliked was in moving for sentence in a murder case when the only sentence prescribed by law was death by hanging. While I realised that I was only a cog in the machine doing his duty I still disliked it, and had a feeling of sympathy for the poor judge who had willy-nilly to pronounce such a sentence, little thinking that one day I, too, would have that unenviable job.

Despite my busy practice, I found myself becoming more and more involved in the political field. My adoption as Labour candidate for North Ayrshire and Bute while I was still in the army was the starting point of what became a hectic period of political activity on a much wider canvas than my Shettleston activity had been. Subsequent to being adopted for North Ayrshire and Bute, which was not a seat which Labour could expect to win since the sitting member, Charles Macandrew, had a five-figure majority, I was approached by representatives from the Labour Party in Dundee to allow my name to go forward for adoption for the Dundee Constituency which at that time was a two-member seat. John Strachey had already been adopted and a second candidate had to be found. This was an attractive offer as Labour was confidently expected to return two members, which in fact occurred. I told them that as I had already been adopted for North Ayrshire and Bute, it would not be fair to drop out and force them to find another candidate so close to the election just because a better option had come my way. Of course I might not have been chosen for Dundee at the selection conference but I was assured that there was strong support for me there. I realised that I bore a name which was much respected in the Labour movement, but I did not wish to play on it as I wanted to be my own man. So regretfully I refused the invitation. Curiously enough, I was then approached by representatives of the Shettleston Labour Party to stand as the Labour candidate against the sitting ILP member, John McGovern. This was an even more tempting apple. It would give me the opportunity of fulfilling the prophesy I had written into my sister's autograph book. I was assured that there would be no difficulty in my being selected as the candidate. I had the

98

feeling that this was all as much a desire to oust McGovern (which in view of the history of his getting the seat in the first place I could well understand) as to put me into Parliament. The big stumbling block, however, was the same as it had been in the case of Dundee. I thought over it long and hard. I had a long talk with our old doctor and family friend, ex-Councillor Dr James Dunlop, and finally I said 'No'. I sometimes wonder what would have happened if I had said 'Yes'. The Labour party selected as their candidate a local lad, Stewart Dallas, who was a young solicitor. I had known him since he was a boy. He lived just a few doors down the road from us in Grampian Crescent in Sandyhills. He had won a good MC in World War II, but had no political background. Yet he ran McGovern close at the election with the Tory a bad third. I have wondered whether my various connections with Shettleston – family, political and football – might have swung the election in favour of the Labour party, but who knows? In the event I was given my three weeks' leave from the army and went through to Ayrshire to woo the constituency of my choice in the short time available to me.

Although this was my first experience as a candidate, I had plenty of experience of the nitty-gritty work of electioneering. In the 1929 General Election Jennie Lee, who was contesting the adjacent North Lanarkshire seat, came to Shettleston to speak for my Uncle John. Her constituency was an extensive one and involved many meetings in the villages which studded that area. As a result she lost her voice after addressing the meeting in Shettleston. This was just on the eve of the run-in to the election, and she had planned doing what the Americans call a whistle stop tour of her constituency. Being without a voice was a serious handicap, and some form of substitute had to be found. Having lost her voice speaking for one John Wheatley she decided that another John Wheatley would have to act as her substitute voice. And so, during the final days of the campaign I toured North Lanark with Jennie in a car. Her presence was an indication of her anxiety to be with her people, and I was there to explain why she could not speak to them and why

99

they had to put up with me as her mouthpiece. It all turned out satisfactorily, because she was returned with a substantial majority.

It was obvious that I had a very hard fight on my hands in the North Ayrshire and Bute constituency. It was unlikely that Labour would make much impact on places like Bute, Arran and Cumbrae where feudalism still held sway, and in the northern reaches of Ayrshire which were in the constituency. While not neglecting these areas the tactics were obviously to concentrate on the various towns on the mainland. This we did with telling effect, to such an extent that when the votes were ultimately being counted the piles of votes for myself and Charles Macandrew at the first sorting-out stage were level pegging. It was only when the island boxes were emptied and sorted out that the count swung in favour of my opponent who finally had a majority of about 2,000. I cannot say that I was surprised, but I was disappointed at not winning. However, on any realistic prognostication this was a safe Tory seat with a well-established and highly respected sitting member. Of course the prognosticators had not foreseen the landslide towards Labour which took place when even safer seats changed hands. What did cause me a great deal of sorrow was the intense disappointment of my band of workers, especially on the mainland, who had toiled hard and had the scent of victory in their nostrils. It is very easy to get a wrong impression of the probable total vote from the canvass responses in an immediate area on which one's efforts have been directed, and there were quite a number of areas on the mainland where we were doing exceptionally well. Unfortunately there were other areas where the position was just the reverse, and there were too many of these for our benefit. However, our opponents were generous enough to say that we had given them the hardest fight and biggest fright that they had ever had. I got great consolation from the many friends which I made during the campaign.

My election agent was Jimmy Forde, who was a councillor for the landward area of Stevenson in the Ayrshire County Council and who was the first Provost of Stevenson when it became a burgh. He knew the Ayrshire scene like the back of his hand. I stayed with the Fordes during the whole of the campaign and I cannot pay a sufficiently high tribute to the care and attention I received from Nellie Forde and her family of three daughters and two sons. I must have been one big nuisance for the upset which I made to their sleeping and domestic arrangements, because I was given a bedroom to myself and was fed like a fighting cock, although meals were taken at the most irregular hours. Jimmy was an astute and efficient election agent and a shrewd politician. I could not have been better served. Space does not permit me to go through the legions of worthy characters throughout the constituency with whom friendships were forged, but I must mention the Lambies of Saltcoats. Bob and his wife Beenie were both remarkable characters. They were of the old school who devoted their whole lives to their political cause. Both were councillors in the Saltcoats Town Council and both held the office of Provost in due course. Their son Davie is the Member of Parliament for what is now called Cunninghame South. In those days Saltcoats was part of the constituency of Ayr Burghs, and Saltcoats and Ardrossan formed an island in the sea of the North Ayrshire constituency. Saltcoats was a Labour stronghold and well-organised, and in the result the Lambies were able to muster a strong workforce to help me in the adjacent area of my constituency. This was done in such a way as not to weaken the turn-out of the Labour vote in Saltcoats and Ardrossan, which was a great relief to me because the Labour candidate in Ayr Burghs was a young man who became and still is a great personal friend of mine as well as a Parliamentary colleague. His name was Willie Ross, and although he failed by less than a thousand votes to win that election, he was in the House of Commons in about a year, having won a by-election at Kilmarnock. He went from strength to strength as a House of Commons man, and when Labour won the 1964 election he became Secretary of State for Scotland. He filled that office with great distinction, and although he was out for a period during the Tory administration of 1970–1974, he returned to it in 1974 and served *in cumulo* as

101

Secretary of State for Scotland for a longer period than any other holder of the office. To add to his lustre he was appointed Lord High Commissioner of the Church of Scotland in 1978, an office which he and Elma carried through with equal distinction and acceptability. He is now in the House of Lords, and as I have retired and have more time to attend that august body, we often have meals or tea together and swap reminiscences that go back to 1945 and the meetings which we jointly addressed on the Low Green in Ayr.

During that election I had three experiences which I feel are worth recounting. We had been given the use for a couple of days of a large van belonging to the Scottish Co-operative Wholesale Society, which was well equipped with a loudspeaker apparatus. We decided to use it to tour Arran and took it over on the service steamer. We went round the island and stopped at strategic places where I made full use of the loudspeaker. I noticed that while people appeared to be listening to what I was saying, no one came near the van, even when I invited them to discuss with me any problems which they had. This was explained to me at Lamlash by the one person there who was openly supporting the Labour candidate. Feudalism was still rife and no one wished to be seen identifying with the bogeyman. Even when I assured them that they could come forward in safety as I had passed the Duke heading for Brodick as I came down to Lamlash they still hung back. The end of a hectic day was a meeting in a hall at Brodick which was reasonably well attended, although not necessarily by my supporters. Just before the meeting started I had a telephone message from Jimmy Forde in Stevenson that a storm had blown up on the Firth of Clyde and that all regular shipping services were cancelled. That meant that the van was marooned for the time being. I would not have been able to get a scheduled steamer trip back in any event, because of the lateness of the evening meeting in Brodick and arrangements were to be made to get private marine transport. The message from Jimmy was that control at Greenock had decreed that in view of the weather conditions nothing under 30 feet would be allowed

102

out in the Firth of Clyde that evening, but there was nothing to worry about because he had managed to get a craft which measured 30 feet 9 inches which would be at Brodick pier for me at 10.00 p m. I managed to finish the meeting in time to be on Brodick pier at the appointed hour. There was still some light but the boat was less than 30 feet from the pier before I saw it because of the height of the waves. There was only one person aboard apart from the skipper – at least I assumed that he was the skipper because I recognised the other person as a committee member from Stevenson. Apparently Jimmy Forde had decided that he could not risk both the candidate and the election agent in the one naval disaster, so he had sent the committee member in his place. I was being given ample proof of his ability as an organiser. When I got on board and was able to get a proper look at the committee man, one look was sufficient for me. His face was a distinctly green shade. The skipper must have seen a fleeting look of apprehension cross my face because he assured me that we would manage all right. My loyal committee man was making violent but unsuccessful attempts to be sick, but I had no such inhibition. Before long I was proving my loyalty to our cause by giving up all I had for the movement. At least I thought it was my all, but I discovered that I had some in reserve for further displays of loyalty. My condition was not improved by the repeated assurances from the skipper that my magnanimity would do my stomach good. It was in fact giving me hell. My poor friend was not so well off. He could not match me. Curiously, when I put my foot on dry land at Montgomery Pier, Ardrossan, my discomfiture ceased. My colleague had made a dive for the car, but it had only proceeded about 50 yards when he asked for it to be stopped. He jumped out and proceeded to do with vigour on land what he had been unable to do on water. His loyalty to the movement having been established, we brought him back to the car and took him home. I have always felt indebted to him because he undertook that journey in my interest and suffered greatly for it. Jimmy Forde had met us at Montgomery Pier with a large smile on his face. Whether this was due to a recognition

103

that the poor creature who emerged from the boat might have been himself or was simply a sign of relief that he still had a candidate, I never got to know.

On the following day I was out all forenoon canvassing and making short addresses whenever a crowd could be mustered. Head Office in Glasgow had sent down a woman speaker who was an excellent propagandist to help with my campaign. She joined me in my tour of the mainland and we became so engrossed that we overran lunch time and had nothing to eat. A meeting had been arranged in the Pier Pavilion at Rothesay on the following afternoon and I wanted to get there early to meet the local committee and discuss with them the plan of campaign in Bute. Accordingly, I cut short my mainland visits and decided that we should have a meal before embarking for Rothesay. In view of the time – it was 4.00 pm on a Wednesday – there was only one type of meal that would fit the bill – a good oldfashioned high tea. To get that sort of meal there was only one place to look for – a baker's shop with a tearoom upstairs. We found one but the tearoom had a separate entrance. We went upstairs and had a first-class high tea. When we had finished my lady companion asked the waitress where the lady's room was. The girl replied: 'Come with me and I'll show you.' I wanted to ask the same question – well not quite the same, but a corresponding one, but being acutely aware of the sensitivity of the matter and not daring to invite the same reply as had been given to my companion, I tried to be discreet and said: 'And where is the counterpart?' She replied: 'Oh, the counter part closed at one o'clock today.' I wondered which of us was to blame. I felt that we were perhaps both at fault.

Anyway we got to Rothesay and met the local committee. It was surprisingly large and very enthusiastic. It was by far the best island reception I had received. We discussed a plan of campaign which they might carry out in my absence and then came to a delicate matter. They had been appraised of the fact that there would be a lady speaker coming with me, and as we had to stay overnight the question was which member of the committee would provide hospitality for the

104

candidate and which for the lady speaker. That could have produced an embarrassment or even a dispute, but there was an abundance of good sense and a satisfactory answer was found which was acceptable to all the locals and to us. There was, however, another problem. I had the following morning free and I thought it would be a good idea if I could hire a loudspeaker set with which to tour the island. The SCWS van was no longer available to us. Enquiries from shops drew a blank response. The lady propagandist from Glasgow came up with an idea. She knew the man who was running the summer show and she offered to contact him and see if he had a set which he would lend to us. I had no great hope that this would be a likely source of support for a Labour candidate, but on the following morning she and I went to the theatre to see her acquaintance. We were very politely greeted but again we drew a blank. He did have a set but he needed it for the show and he did not want to dismantle it. He was full of regrets and then said: 'Look here, you can have the use of the hall for an afternoon meeting for the cost of the lighting and cleaning.' I jumped at this and booked the hall for the afternoon of the day before the election. When I thanked him most cordially he replied: 'I've made the same offer to Sir Charles Mac-andrew and he has taken it for another afternoon. I like to be equally fair to both sides. You see, I'm non–political. I'm a Communist.' Our efforts were all in vain from the point of view of the ultimate result, but it was a heartwarming experience in terms of human relationships with my Bute committee.

The following year we took a house at Saltcoats for a month, principally to meet again the friends I had made in the area and allow Nancy to meet them. To her great regret she had been unable to come through and play her full part in the election since Anthony was not quite 15 months old and Patrick was but $2\frac{1}{2}$ years old. We had been in Saltcoats for scarcely a week when word came from Glasgow that they wanted me to stand as the Labour candidate in the Bridgeton by-election which had been occasioned by the lamented death of Jimmy Maxton. This was quite a problem

105

for me. I had known Jimmy since I was a boy. He had frequently been in our house after addressing meetings in Shettleston, and he had been a great personal friend and political ally of my Uncle John. At ILP socials in pre-war days Nancy and I, like so many others, had been regaled with the antics of that wonderful comedy duo – Jimmy Maxton and Paddy Dollan. I knew that Jimmy Carmichael had been groomed by the ILP to step into the shoes of the ailing Maxton when the situation arose. He lived not very far from my parental home in Sandyhills and I had known him and his family personally for many years. For some considerable time he had been a town councillor in the Bridgeton area and clearly had a lot going for him. Yet the ILP, which had disaffiliated from the Labour Party in the early 1930s, had stood apart from the Labour Party not only during the war but after the Party had formed the Government in 1945. The depleted number of ILP Members of Parliament constituted a separate party in Parliament. Old-time members of it like Davie Kirkwood and Geordie Buchanan had stayed with the Labour Party when dis-affiliation took place. Campbell Stephen left it after the 1945 election and there were rumours that others were about to follow suit. The Labour Government had already set about the gigantic task of structuring the social services into what became known as the Welfare State and had a heavy legis-lative programme ahead of it. Clearly my legal qualifications and experience as well as my political background could be an advantage in the carrying out of such a programme. It presented an uphill task because Bridgeton had voted solidly ILP for many years and I would have to endeavour to change these voters over to the Labour Party despite Jimmy Carmichael's strong position. The Labour Party had never fared well when opposing the ILP in elections in Bridgeton because of the personal magnetism of and affection for Jimmy Maxton. There were five candidates, Carmichael (ILP), Warren (Tory), Wendy Wood (Scottish Nationalist), Guy Aldred (Anti-Parliamentarian) and myself (Labour). It was always a two-horse race between Jimmy Carmichael and me. In the event he beat me by about 1,100 votes. I had

106

the feeling that given another week's campaigning I would have won. As the campaign proceeded more and more traditional ILP votes were coming my way according to reports. What might have happened if time had not run out on us is pure speculation, and it is votes cast and not speculation which counts. Not long afterwards Jimmy Carmichael joined the Labour Party and took the Labour whip, so the voting power in the House did not suffer.

Just over a year later, George Thomson became Lord Justice-Clerk following the death of Lord Moncrieff and perforce he had to vacate two offices. He had to resign as Lord Advocate and as the Member of Parliament for East Edinburgh. I had been appointed Solicitor-General in March 1947 when Danny Blades demitted office on being appointed to the Bench, and despite my comparative youth – I was still only 39 – I was appointed Lord Advocate. There was no natural progression in the filling of his seat as MP for East Edinburgh. I had to find favour both with the Divisional Labour Party and the electorate. Fortunately, I had worked hard and spoken often during George Thomson's election campaign in the autumn of 1945 and had become well known to the party members. And, despite my defeats in the previous two years, I had shown that I was prepared to take on difficult contests and was not just looking for an easy one. Anyway, I was chosen as the candidate and had a comfortable victory. It was a good Labour seat, and it has remained one ever since despite boundary changes. My immediate successor was my old friend George Willis. I had been the Chairman of North Edinburgh Labour Party when he was the Member of Parliament for that constituency following the 1945 election, at which he had won that traditional Tory seat. He had lost it at the subsequent election, but found favour again in East Edinburgh at the by-election following my retiral and gave excellent service to that constituency until he too retired in 1970. During the Labour administration in the late 1960s he was appointed Minister of State at the Scottish Office and was made a Privy Councillor. He in turn was succeeded by Dr Gavin Strang who has represented East Edinburgh ever since. In the Labour

107

Government of the 1970s, Dr Strang was appointed Parliamentary Secretary at the Ministries of Energy and Agriculture, thus maintaining the record of every Labour MP for East Edinburgh, starting with Pethwick Lawrence, having held ministerial office.

Reverting, however, to my by-election campaign in 1947, I had a first-class organisation spearheaded by Jimmy Boyle of West Lothian and Willie Marshall from Scottish Labour Party HQ. The campaign went like a bomb. I settled well into the constituency and, with Nancy's help in the sharing of the work, I built up good relationships throughout its various territorial divisions. Although there were boundary changes which brought in Craigmillar and Newcraighall for the loss of the Holyrood ward, I held the seat in the 1950 General Election and again in the 1951 election. Thus in the space of six years I fought five Parliamentary elections, winning three and losing two.

It was very important that an MP should keep in touch with his constituents. This I did by having regular 'interviews' (now called surgeries) at which constituents could consult me about their problems. As we lived adjacent to the constituency many who did not trouble to come to the interviews would turn up at our door, and if I was not in Nancy would deal with them, take notes and report to me on my return home at the weekend. She was a tower of strength too in many other ways. She attended meetings and functions on my behalf when my enforced absence prevented me from being present, and at weekends we both attended functions of which there appeared to be an abundance. Each of the four areas in the constituency – Musselburgh, Portobello, Craigentinny and Craigmillar (including Newcraighall) – had their own separate functions, and within each area there were numerous organisations which expected us to be with them on their social occasions. Nancy has a wonderful capacity for friendship, and among the women she knew many more people personally and by name than ever I could aspire to. When we went to some of the socials together, I found her doing dances, such as the Mississippi Dip, which were foreign to me. She had learned much in

108

my absence at her women's socials. Just as she was a great help to me in my public life, she was a wonderful wife and mother in our family life. Without her love, patience, understanding and help much of what I may have achieved would not have been possible.

I enjoyed my election campaigns. They were stimulating and they engendered friendships. I never attacked my opponents personally. I took the view that it was policies which mattered, not personalities. If a candidate resorts to personalities it is because he is weak on policy. In fact, I only once referred to an opponent by name and that was to exonerate him from a criticism which had been levelled against him unfairly. I have only one deep and abiding regret. An offer of a judgeship is something which has to be treated with the utmost confidentiality. When the offer came to me the only person in whom I confided was Nancy because her future was involved and she was entitled to have a voice in the decision. And she naturally kept it to herself. I did not even tell my sister Nettie. This obligation of confidentiality which I was in honour bound to observe prevented me from disclosing to my constituency party the offer and my decision on it, with all its consequences for them. They had been very good and loyal friends and had worked hard for me. Yet the first they got to know of it was when it was announced publicly in the media. They were perfectly entitled to feel that they had been shabbily treated, yet I could do nothing about it. I trust that even at this remote point of time when many of them are dead and gone, those who survive will accept both my explanation and my apologies and regrets for any sorrow or annoyance they may have experienced.

11 My life in Parliament

To be a Member of Parliament is an unforgettable experience. You have the feeling that you are at the very heart of politics and are involved in the making of important, sometimes momentous, decisions. It has its dull periods and its exhausting periods, but over the piece it is an experience I would not have wished to miss. When I entered the House in October 1947 I did so as Lord Advocate and had to sit on the Government Front Bench. On the face of it this was not unduly onerous because as a law officer I was only liable to be called on to speak on questions involving Scots Law which were being discussed. The same applied to Bills which were passing through their committee stage, when they are subjected to critical examination line by line and even word by word and consideration is given to amendments from any quarter. The committee stage of important Bills are sometimes taken on the floor of the House, the others are taken in the committee rooms upstairs. This is the real nitty-gritty work of the legislative process and the most time-consuming. My involvement, however, was not confined to the narrow technical legal field. My long commitment in politics made it almost inevitable that I should get involved in political issues apart from my function as a law officer.

As a law officer, I conceived it to be my duty to follow the traditional line of being available to explain the legal implications involved. This I sought to do without recourse to political points. Walter Elliot was kind enough to say in the Scottish Grand Committee that they looked on me as the *amicus curiae* of the whole committee on whom they

110

could rely when any legal points were raised. However, as well as being a law officer, I was a politician who had been returned to Parliament on a political ticket. Accordingly, when issues arose which were political and not legal I felt fully entitled to play my full part as a member of the Government's ministerial team. Arthur Woodburn, who had become Secretary of State for Scotland, often asked me to wind up debates on Scottish affairs. Thus I found myself involved in debates on subjects such as housing, education, home affairs and even agriculture.

The Scottish team at that time was Arthur Woodburn (Secretary of State), Tom Fraser and JJ Robertson (Under-Secretaries of State), Jimmy Hoy (Parliamentary Private Secretary), Douglas Johnston (Solicitor-General), and myself (Lord Advocate). Jimmy Hoy was a first-class parliamentary private secretary. He had a great capacity for unearthing information which was invaluable to the Secretary of State. He and I became boon companions both inside and outside the House of Commons. We shared an interest in football and spent our Saturday afternoons during the season either at Easter Road or Tynecastle as guests of the respective clubs, Hibernians and Heart of Midlothian. In Harold Wilson's administrations in the 1960s he was a junior minister in the Department of Agriculture, and on his retirement from the House of Commons in 1970 he was created a life peer and spent several active years in the Lords before his untimely death. Douglas Johnston and I had a very harmonious association as law officers. We had been contemporaries at the Bar and advocate-deputes in George Thomson's tenure of office as Lord Advocate. He succeeded me as Solicitor-General when I was appointed Lord Advocate. He stepped outside of the confines of Scottish affairs when the Finance Bills were going through the Commons and acted as a support to Frank Soskice who was normally in charge of the legal aspects of those intricate measures. I have dealt elsewhere with Arthur Woodburn and Tom Fraser, and all in all we were a very happy team. This relationship extended into Hector McNeill's tenure of office as Secretary of State, during which Peggy Herbison replaced JJ Robertson as one

111

of the two Under-Secretaries of State. Peggy in her own quiet way was a most efficient minister who enjoyed the respect of the whole House. When she joined Arthur and Jimmy in retirement from the House of Commons in 1970 she slipped out of public political life, but her attributes were not forgotten and were further recognised by her being appointed Lord High Commissioner to the General Assembly of the Church of Scotland for 1970–71.

In my opinion Arthur Woodburn's true worth as Secretary of State was never properly recognised, and he was hard done by. Those of us who worked close to him can testify to that. He had a deep and abiding love for Scotland and his whole ambition was to do as much as he could for Scotland and the Scots. He spoke a number of languages and was thus much in demand for parliamentary delegations which were visiting foreign countries. He could use a typewriter with great effect. This he proved on one occasion when I was with him meeting a body of professional people in connection with an issue which had arisen under the National Health Service in Scotland – and it was he and not Nye Bevan who was the minister responsible for the National Health Service in Scotland, something which many people ignored at the time or have subsequently forgotten. When agreement was reached between the parties Arthur dashed out of the room into the ante-chamber where there was a typewriter and typed out the terms of the agreement which he brought back for signature there and then. He was not taking any chances about a change of heart. He made a number of innovations, the fruits of which were not reaped until after he had demitted office and for which he has never been given proper credit. If he had a weakness it was that he had never lost the mode of address which he had developed as a lecturer in the National Council of Labour colleges, over which he eventually presided, and he still tended to lecture rather than address his audience.

When some sections of the media in Scotland set out to attack the Government, the prime vehicle for the attack is the Secretary of State. The *Daily Herald* excepted, Labour

112

had not a supporter let alone a sympathiser among the media in Scotland at that time, and Arthur was the target. He had been forthright in his criticism of some of the nationalists who were finding sympathy if not favour in some branches of the media, and because of this criticism he was accused of scaremongering, particularly in his reference to some of the activists and the blowing-up of pillar boxes and the threatened attacks on bridges in the border area. Things reached a climax as a result of one of those freak situations which arise from time to time. Niall Macpherson, the National Liberal member for Dumfries, now Lord Drumalbyn, had obtained an adjournment debate and had chosen as his subject the claims of Scottish Nationalism. Unless the business for the day has been completed earlier, the adjournment of the House is moved at 10 p m and the adjournment debate takes place during the ensuing 30 minutes. The normal drill was that ten minutes were allotted to the member who initiated the debate, ten minutes for discussion by other members, and ten minutes for the Government minister who had to reply. Unfortunately, the day's business concluded at about 4 p m on that occasion, so that over six hours became available for that debate which turned into a full dress one. Niall Macpherson took advantage of this and the debate turned from what might have been only a very limited aspect of Scottish Nationalism into the whole broad question of separation for Scotland. Arthur Woodburn, who had prepared for a short ten minute reply, had to deal with a wide variety of points. When rising to reply after Niall Macpherson sat down, he had perforce to depart from his prepared brief and in doing so he gave vent to his fears and feelings about the possible activities which might take place. The debate heated up with many members taking part, and when I came to wind up I tried to get matters on to an even keel. I had the feeling, however, that the adverse sections of the media would not be interested in what I had to say but would concentrate on Arthur's attack on the Nats, and that is what happened. The criticism of Arthur intensified, and when the Government had to be reformed after the 1950 election Clem Attlee dropped him

113

as the Secretary of State for Scotland and replaced him with Hector McNeill.

I was always very friendly with Hector and we had a strong mutual regard for each other. We worked in complete harmony and accord when he assumed office. Accordingly, I want to make it perfectly plain that anything I am about to say is not intended to reflect on Hector's ability for the post, which in any event he demonstrated in no small way during his short tenure of office. I do know that Hector would have been happy to remain at the Foreign Office, where he had made a big impact, particularly in his confrontations with Molotov, and could have legitimately looked forward to succeeding Ernie Bevin as Foreign Secretary if and when the ailing Bevin went. What I am concerned with was Arthur's dismissal and the method of it. Attlee, for whom I have always otherwise had the deepest regard, seemed to pay heed to Arthur's critics both in the party and in the media and failed to consult Arthur's immediate colleagues on whose views he could place reliance. In particular I think that he should have consulted Tom Fraser and myself. We had both worked in very close co-operation with Arthur and I have reason to believe that the Prime Minister regarded us both with favour. We would have given a balanced picture and a reliable appraisal which would, I am sure, have countered much of the unfair criticism which had been levelled against Arthur. But Clem did not do so, and as far as I know, he did not consult any of Arthur's other close colleagues. He did offer another ministry outside the Cabinet which Arthur refused, preferring to go to the back benches where he could make speeches unfettered by front bench restrictions. Despite all this, his loyalty to the party never wavered – nor did his loyalty to Clement Attlee. When Hector became Secretary of State, as I have already indicated, Peggy Herbison took over from JJ Robertson as Under-Secretary of State, but otherwise the Scottish team remained the same, although Jimmy Hoy relinquished the personal appointment of Parliamentary Private Secretary to the Secretary of State.

Hector was a warmhearted, friendly man who had scant

regard for bureaucratic red tape. I recall one instance when civil servants almost blew a fuse at the way he settled an inter-departmental dispute. A Bill was about to be presented to Parliament which was basically a legal one. A dispute had arisen between the officials in St Andrew's House and those in the Lord Advocate's Department as to whether the Bill should be introduced by the Secretary of State supported by the Lord Advocate or by the Lord Advocate supported by the Secretary of State. After long periods of argument which had failed to achieve a result on this 'great' constitutional issue, it was decided by the respective officials that there should be a meeting which they and the ministers concerned should attend in order to get an authoritative decision. It was fixed for 2.30 pm in Hector's room at the House, and Hector and I had lunch in the Members' Dining Room before it. During lunch Hector said to me: 'What's this all about?' and I explained with a smile the 'great' constitutional issue which was causing such a deep divide between the two departments. Hector said: 'Does it matter a damn which way the Bill is presented? It's a legal Bill and you'll be doing all the work.' He left it at that. In due course we were sitting at the top of the table in his room when the contestants marched in and took their places on opposite sides of the table. Hector said, as if completely unaware of the vexatious issue: 'What's this all about?' The leader of the St Andrew's House team set out his case with all due solemnity. The leader of the team from my department equally solemnly proposed his alternative submission. When he had finished, Hector put his hand into his pocket, took out a coin and tossed it in the air, saying: 'Heads you present it, John, tails I do.' I could not follow the path of the coin because I was sitting transfixed watching the looks of utter amazement and disbelief on the faces of the contestants. The idea that this great and important issue which had kept arguments going for weeks on end should be decided so perfunctorily if decisively was too much for them. I had great difficulty in not laughing outright, but I'm sure that there must have been a broad grin on my face despite the fact that when my eyes alighted on the coin it was sitting with its tail up. So were the tails of the St Andrew's House representatives, even if they were still showing signs of shock at this desecration of established methods of solving inter-departmental disputes. My own officials were somewhat glum, but they apparently took some satisfaction in the fact they had been defeated not by superior arguments, but by the vagaries of a coin which I suspect they considered was kept in the pocket of the Secretary of State for just such emergencies. I feel that there is a moral somewhere in this story from which Government departments might benefit. There is one thing, however, of which I am sure. It is imperative that the Secretary of State and the Lord Advocate should work in close harmony and co-operation as a team. I was fortunate in having such a relationship with both Arthur Woodburn and Hector McNeill.

I had been introduced in the House of Commons in late October 1947. My sponsors were Geordie Buchanan and Willie Hannan, the Scottish Government Whip, with Davie Kirkwood looking on benevolently. In my youth I had been particularly friendly with Davie's son Willie, a loveable character, whose early death was a blow not only to his family but to all who were privileged to know him. I had also had a long friendship with Davie Junior, and Davie (Senior) had always taken a kindly interest in me. In fact, when my Uncle John died in May 1930 Davie wanted me to let my name go forward for nomination for the Shettleston by-election occasioned by my Uncle's death. I refused because I had just turned 22, which I considered to be excessively young, and I had just graduated LLB to tag on to the MA which I had acquired in 1928. My apprenticeship as a solicitor had another year to run, and I regarded it as sensible to have a qualification as a solicitor to fall back on, in case anything arose which prevented me from going to the Bar. Of course, there was no guarantee that I would be selected if I did allow my name to go forward, and John McGovern, who eventually got the seat, would always have been a strong contender whoever stood against him. Anyway seventeen years further on there was the young

116

literature sales boy in the House of Commons with Davie and Geordie as his colleagues.

My baptism of fire as Lord Advocate was during the committee stage of the Agriculture (Scotland) Bill (which became the Act of 1948). In my experience at the Bar one of the few subjects with which I never had to deal was agricultural law, but on the practical side I had always Arthur Woodburn or Tom Fraser to hold the fort. Tom was an amazing young man and a very loyal colleague and friend. He was a miner before entering Parliament and represented Hamilton which was then regarded as 'a miner's seat', yet by dint of application he had acquired an extensive and deep knowledge of a wide variety of subjects, and this, added to a keen mind, made him a formidable minister. Ex-miner though he was, he had gathered a remarkable knowledge of agriculture and had already won the respect of the industry. I anticipated that the real danger would come from a critical examination of the provisions of the Bill by James Scott Cumberland Reid, KC. Scott Reid was a man who had already many years of parliamentary experience behind him, and he had built up a very high reputation. He was a former Solicitor-General and Lord Advocate, and was now Dean of the Faculty of Advocates. On any score he was a formidable opponent for the fledgling Lord Advocate. Later on during this Labour administration, he was to be appointed as a Lord of Appeal in Ordinary in the House of Lords, although he had no judicial experience. Appointments direct to the supreme court in the land of persons with no judicial experience were not unknown, but they were usually the result of the Lord Advocate of the day getting the appointment. The justification for Reid's appointment was purely his reputation as a lawyer, and it was unique in that the appointment was made by the opposing party in Parliament. That justification was amply established in the years that followed when he became an outstanding leader of judicial opinion both in the Judicial Committee of the House of Lords and the Judicial Committee of the Privy Council, over both of which he presided for many years. This reflected great credit on his Scottish legal training, particularly as the esteem in

117

which he was held was as great in England as it was in Scotland.

However, back to my muttons in the form of the Agriculture Bill. While I had worked hard on my brief and considered that I had mastered the points raised by the amendments which had been tabled, I realised that there were also minefields in the shape of follow-up questions by the experts and – perhaps the most dangerous trap for all ministers – the daft-laddie questions from lay members. In the course of my homework I had come across a small Scottish textbook on agricultural law by an advocate by the name of James Scott Cumberland Reid; so I took it along with me to the Committee. In the Scottish Grand Committee the opposing parties were separated only by a narrow table, and so were very much closer to each other than the traditional two-swords' length on the floor of the House of Commons. I was sitting just opposite Scott Reid, and I placed the textbook on the table along with my papers. This was not done as a threat, but merely for convenience if it was required. So far as I remember it was never required. It was a good number of years since Reid had written it, and he may not have recognised it. The Bill went through without much controversy or legal dispute. Whether this was due to kindly tolerance for a fledgling Lord Advocate or to the fact that there were no real legal disputes I shall never know.

As Lord Advocate I was of course involved in UK Bills as well as Scottish ones. It would be tedious as well as space-devouring to recount them all. I have already recounted my personal interest in the Courts Martial Appeal Bill. In one of the other UK Bills I made the opening speech in introducing the Bill in the House of Commons. It was a Bill introducing some changes of a technical nature in the National Health Service. This was the only occasion on which I made the opening speech in a debate, my usual role being to wind it up. I made careful preparation for my opening speech on the second reading and sent a copy of it for comment to Nye Bevan who was the minister in charge of the Bill and who was going to wind up, something which

The Wheatley's grocers shop on Shettleston Road

With parents 1935

John Wheatley (uncle) at Ministry of Health 1924

Graduation MA 1928

With Nancy Nichol
(later Nancy Wheatley) 1935

In the Army, England 1943

The family at the time of the 1950 Election

Scottish Office ministers and civil servants 1948
(*by courtesy of The Scotsman Publications Ltd*)

Sir Compton Mackenzie's birthday celebration 1966
(*by courtesy of The Scotsman Publications Ltd*)

With Herbert Morrison and others 1949
(*by courtesy of Edinburgh Evening News*)

On the bench 1954 (*by courtesy of Drummond Young*)

Lord Justice Clerk 1972 (*by courtesy of The Scotsman Publications Ltd*)

Kathleen and Tam 26 December 1963 (*by courtesy of Jack Fisher*)

The grandchildren 1985

Receiving honorary degree of Doctor of the University of Stirling 1976

With Lady Wheatley
(*by courtesy of Duncan Dingsdale, The Glasgow Herald*)

he loved to do. He was arguably the best debater of his time. He had a great command of the English language and a remarkable facility for using words in a most unusual context which were so apposite that it made you wonder why they had never been used there before. Other speakers could use magnificent phrases but they somehow reeked of preparation under the midnight oil, but Nye's phrases rolled off his tongue like the rushing waters of his Welsh mountain streams. I did not always see eye to eye with him, but I could never disguise my admiration for the brilliant intellect and gifted tongue of this self-educated man from a Welsh valley. If it had not been that his judgment was at times suspect and was linked to an innate impetuosity there would have been nothing in public life beyond his reach and capabilities. He sent me back my draft without comment and I heaved a sigh of relief. I did not regard this as a sign that he was not interested. The Health Service was his pride and joy and he was interested in every aspect of it, but there was little of controversy in what I had prepared and controversy was food and drink to Nye. I opened the debate in the traditional manner explaining the contents of the Bill. I knew that I would not have the members of House rolling in the aisles with ecstasy at my presentation, and I was right. The first spokesman for the opposition was very polite and in equally traditional fashion he thanked me for my explanations which he confessed he might have to study, and proceeded to launch a critical attack on the operation of the Health Service. That was the last we heard of the Bill. The remainder of the debate was a free-for-all on the Health Service. I am sure that Nye had anticipated that the debate would take this course and was delighted that it had. He dearly loved a political rammy, and in his winding-up speech he waded into the critics of the Health Service with gusto. The Bill got a second reading on the basis of its contents and not on the contents of the debate.

As a law officer I had to attend the committee stages of a number of UK Bills, but the number of such appearances varied considerably according to the Scottish interests, albeit I had also to deal with points of general legal interest. The most taxing one from my point of view was the Gas Bill of 1947–48. There were 35 sittings of the committee, some of which were very protracted. For instance one of the sittings lasted continuously from 10.30 a m on 11 May 1948 to 12.08 p m on 13 May 1948 – 49 hours 38 minutes in all. That is not a record. In more recent times there have been Bills which have had over 50 sittings of the appropriate committee. What possibly did constitute a record in the Gas Bill was the fact that one of the committee sittings lasted for almost 50 hours continuously, and like many of my colleagues I was in attendance throughout. I pause there to make this comment. I cannot accept that when such long sittings take place the requisite attention can be paid by half-awake members to the issues which have to be determined. I know that it is easy to pose the problem and leave it to someone else to find the answer, but the sooner the parliamentarians find the answer the sooner this blot on the credibility of parliamentary procedure will be removed.

The two Scottish Bills with a specific legal connection with which I was principally involved were the Legal Aid and Solicitors (Scotland) Bill and the Criminal Justice (Scotland) Bill, both of which became Acts of 1949. The Legal Aid and Solicitors Bill must take pride of place. It was a hybrid Bill in two quite distinct but interrelated parts. In the first place it introduced legal aid and advice into Scotland on a broad and substantial scale. The old poor roll system, supported as it was by the voluntary services of counsel and solicitors, had filled a gap over the ages, but frankly it was woefully inadequate. The proposed Legal Aid Scheme was the outcome of the reports of the Rushcliffe and Cameron Committees which had been warmly accepted, although the resultant Bill was subjected to a rigorous opposition in some legal circles in Scotland which had an unwarranted political background. The second part of the bill related to a matter which would have been normally the subject of a private member's Bill, but which I managed to get tagged on to the official Government Bill for tactical reasons. For many years a leading Edinburgh Writer to the Signet, Sir Ernest Wedderburn, had been trying to get a Bill through Parliament

120

to set up a Law Society for the whole of Scotland. At an earlier stage he had enlisted the services of Lord Normand, a previous Lord President of the Court of Session and then a Lord of Appeal in the House of Lords, to introduce such a private member's Bill in the House of Lords. Lord Normand introduced the Bill but, alas, it suffered the fate of many private members' Bills and failed to get through the parliamentary process. I realised from my experience with the solicitors' branch of the profession that a legal aid system such as was being proposed could never function properly without a single Law Society representing all the solicitors in Scotland. I presented this submission to the Government's Legislation Committee and obtained authority to incorporate into the Legal Aid Bill as a second but independent part what was in effect the previously aborted Bill of Lord Normand. And so it came to pass that the Law Society of Scotland was born and I acted as midwife.

Unlike the position in England, where the legal aid proposals there received the complete support of both branches of the profession and the fullest co-operation in the preliminary discussions on the practical working of the scheme, the proposals for the Scottish scheme met a substantial amount of opposition from the profession, much of it politically motivated. For instance it was widely suggested that we were nationalising the legal profession. Anyone who took the trouble to examine the proposals would have seen immediately the arrant nonsense of such a suggestion. But no doubt the critics thought that if they used what they conceived to be the dirty word nationalisation that would be sufficient to muster opposition to the measure. Moreover, some critics came to me with suggestions that the Bill as drafted contained certain dangers to the profession. I sought to assure them that there was no such intention and that the Bill could not be so construed, but I gave an assurance that I would consider amendments for the committee stage which would remove the doubts beyond a peradventure and the pin-pricking scrutiny of the critics. Despite the fact that I indicated to the critics the amendments I proposed and received an assurance that they met their doubts, the criti-

121

cisms were publicly voiced again both in the Press and in the House of Commons where opposition members seized on these criticisms without knowing the whole background story, which I felt duty-bound to explain to the House. That quashed the opposition to the Bill in Parliament.

When I was appointed Lord Advocate, I gave the office of Lord Advocate's Solicitor to Hugh Eaton, WS, who had been appointed to that office by my predecessor. Unfortunately within one week Hugh Eaton was tragically killed in a railway crash, and I had to find a replacement. One of the functions of that office is to keep the Lord Advocate in touch with what is going on in the legal world, and in particular to keep him informed on the feelings of the solicitors' branch on current issues. In fact it had previously been the practice for the Lord Advocate to appoint the solicitor of his choice to be the Crown Agent during his tenure of office, but this was simply a sinecure which only required the incumbent to have a white evening dress tie which he could sport if he decided to honour the High Court of Justiciary or the Appeal Court with his presence. The real work was done by the officials in the Crown Office, and George Thomson put an end to that charade by appointing the senior official, Lionel Gordon, to be the Crown Agent, and the appointment has gone to an official ever since.

In the circumstances I appointed Thomas J Addly, SSC, to be the Lord Advocate's Solicitor. He was a respected member of the solicitors' branch of the profession with a long experience and a perceptive mind. In his early days before World War I he had been involved in the setting up of Lloyd George's insurance and health schemes as a member of the Edinburgh Committee, and a propos of the criticism of the legal aid scheme to which I have just alluded he told me of the violent opposition to those earlier schemes by leading members of the medical profession in Edinburgh, along similar lines to those with which I had been confronted. There had been a mass meeting of protest in the Usher Hall at which certain leading doctors had spoken vehemently against the proposals. Nevertheless when the lists for operating the scheme were opened, the names of

122

three of the speakers were among the first to be entered. 'And,' said Tom, 'I would not be surprised if history repeated itself here.' I did not consider it worth while checking to see if his prediction was correct. It may be that some of the critics did not enter the lists, but I know of many of them who did. In fact, I doubt if there were many, if any, law firms carrying on a court practice which did not have one or more members of the firm enrolled. I do not find this surprising, because not to enrol was closing the door on what could be a very lucrative source of income, and in many cases it has become the sheet anchor of the practice, particularly among the junior members of the profession. I remember telling them that while legal aid had been introduced primarily for the benefit of the public the profession would be inherent beneficiaries. In many cases, and not just to the younger members, the scheme has been a life-line. I told them that it was common sense that the scheme should be properly used and not abused, otherwise they would be killing a goose that was laying golden eggs. The Faculty of Advocates and the Law Society responded in an exemplary manner both in providing the personnel for the professional duties required by the scheme and in manning committees for its proper administration.

It seems to me that a thorough and continuous scrutiny of the scheme to eradicate any anomalies or faults resulting in financial loss to the scheme is a much more pragmatic and justifiable way of proceeding that the root and branch changes proposed in the Legal Aid (Scotland) Bill which recently went through Parliament. The avowed purpose of the change is to cut down the cost of legal aid which has escalated considerably in recent years. It is understandable that a government would wish to see if such expenditure can be justifiably pruned. How that should be done is a different matter.

The upsurge in crime and the consequential increase in prosecutions are the obvious basic causes of the increase in the cost of criminal legal aid. These are factors which are as likely to operate under the proposed new system as they operated in the system which is being replaced. The fixing of fees is already in the hands of the Secretary of State. The only ways in which substantial savings can be made are by drastic cuts in the fees payable to lawyers providing the professional services and by drastic cuts in the entitlement to legal aid.

The Bill has passed through its final parliamentary stages and will soon become law. The Bill, however, is not the last word since much of the detail has to be filled in by regulations which will be subject to the affirmative or negative Parliamentary resolution procedure. These are unsatisfactory procedures, in that the secondary legislation by statutory instruments cannot be amended; they can only be accepted as presented or rejected. Thus there is no room for constructive amendments or indeed for any amendment, thereby eliminating one of the great safeguards which feature so regularly and to great benefit in the primary legislation of Bills. In view of the fact that no criticism has been made of the administration of the old system, and since the rising costs have been basically due to wholly independent factors, it is difficult to see the justification for the setting up of an entirely new administration. This is compounded by the fact that no such change was then proposed in the English system of legal aid and advice when the basic factors are virtually the same. The legal bodies in Scotland at all levels were opposed to the Bill, but now that the proposed changes are about to become the law it behoves all concerned in and outside the legal aid system in Scotland to seek to secure that the system works for the best interests of those for whom the scheme was designed from the start, namely the members of the public. In view of my interest in initiating legal aid in Scotland I have all along been concerned to see that the system works properly and free from abuse, and I shall maintain that concern. All that was required was an in-depth enquiry to ascertain if there were any abuses or gaps in the system and, if any such were discovered, how to eliminate them. I hope that under the new structure this will not be lost sight of.

I found the Criminal Justice (Scotland) Bill, which became the Act of 1949, a very interesting and satisfactory piece of legislation to put through the House of Commons. We did

124

not have by way of preparation for the Bill a report such as the Thomson Committee Report which investigated in depth many important aspects of the criminal law and procedure, and made various innovative recommendations. This report provided the groundwork for the provisions of the Bill which became the Criminal Justice Act 1980. That Act introduced many reforms and innovations, most of which have been accepted though some have been controversial. It is a much more radical measure than was the 1949 Act, and a much more important milestone in the development of Scots criminal law and procedure. That is not to say that in its time the 1949 Act was not an important piece of legislation. It broadened the base of sentencing and removed the more archaic features of it. It made important changes in the provisions for the treatment of prisoners and the methods involved therein. I found this work both intriguing and rewarding, all the more so because it related to a branch of the law in which I had always been very much involved.

There was a Bill of permanent importance with which I had to deal and which had a significant bearing on the lives of judges and sheriffs. It was the Administration of Justice (Pensions) Bill which became the Act of 1950. *Inter alia* it introduced pensions for widows and children of deceased judges at the expense of the judge or sheriff surrendering part of the benefits to which he himself would be entitled. It provided substantial security for the widow and children when to obtain a corresponding cover privately would have cost a much more substantial sum. It unfortunately lead to the one passage at arms which I ever had with the late Lord Cooper, even from the days when I was a young counsel and he was a leader of the Bar. I had consulted him and asked him to obtain for me the views of the High Court judges on the proposals, which were only of interest to married judges. He duly did so, and in addressing the House I reported the judges' views. What I said was not accurately reported in one of the Scottish newspapers, and when I got back to Edinburgh on the Friday there was awaiting me a letter from Lord Cooper protesting about my misrepresenting the judges' views. I simply replied by sending him without comment a copy of the *Hansard* report of the proceedings in the House. We had a meeting later in the day by which time he had read *Hansard*. He immediately apologised and said: 'You very properly reported the views of the judges.' And then characteristically: 'What are we going to do about that newspaper?' I replied: 'Forget about it,' and we did. I was glad that there had been no occasion for us to have a quarrel because of the good relations which we had always enjoyed. At his funeral, his brother James told me that it was Lord Cooper's express wish that I should have one of the cords which lowered his coffin into the grave. I was greatly touched by this final token of friendship from one who had always been kind to me and whose name will be writ large in the annals of Scots law. I had then the great privilege of writing an appreciation of the man at the request of one of our leading newspapers, my only doubt being whether I could do justice to the task.

In those heady days when I was Lord Advocate life in Parliament was for me as enjoyable as it was hectic. It was a joy and delight for me to be a senior minister in a government which in its first term of office was effecting many radical changes which altered the whole social and personal lives of the people of the country. In some quarters the 'Welfare State' has become a term of cynical derision. This I can neither understand nor tolerate. The philosophy of the welfare state is one of which any Christian country could be proud, and to deride it and then to dismantle it is in my view an act of desecration.

My days were long and full. I was in my office in the Lord Advocate's Department by 9.00 a m and I was in the House of Commons until it rose, which normally was supposed to be at 10.30 p m, although it was often much later. The first hour and a half in the morning was usually spent in my office dealing with administrative matters and correspondence, interlaced with discussions with the parliamentary draftsmen on current and prospective bills. At 10.30 a m there were usually meetings of some kind or another. The committee stages of bills which were not being taken on the floor of the House were usually set for that

126

hour, as were meetings of government committees such as the Legislation Committee and the Future Legislation Committee. I was not a member of the Cabinet, but it was the practice for a minister to be called to attend Cabinet meetings for a particular matter concerning his department. In this way law officers were liable to be called to Cabinet meetings on such a basis on quite a number of occasions. In fact at one time I seemed to be attending the Cabinet at least during one of its twice-weekly meetings. This in itself was quite an experience. It gave me a closer insight into the qualities of the senior members of the Government. Sitting in committee with one's colleagues is one of the best ways of making a proper assessment of their qualities. I was particularly impressed with the sharpness of mind and the acuteness of apprehension of Clem Attlee and Stafford Cripps. One thing which I did learn was that you should only intervene if you have something constructive and worthwhile to say. This seemed to be recognised by most if not all of those attending.

I thoroughly enjoyed the cut and thrust of the debates in the Chamber. As I have already said, I was frequently called upon to wind up debates on various subjects relating to Scottish affairs. I thereby learned the art of listening to what was being said while making notes for my reply on other points.

As I have previously recorded, the committee stage of some Bills was sometimes taken on the floor of the House and not in a committee room upstairs. That could mean sitting very late and, as a law officer's assistance was liable to be required one of them had to be available. Law officers were supposed to be walking encyclopaedias of the law irrespective of the subject under discussion, a flattering if wholly unrealistic view. On one occasion I walked into the Chamber and sat down on the Front Bench to do my stint. I cannot remember what the subject-matter was but a junior minister was dealing with it. I had barely sat down when an opposition member who was a lawyer asked a question about what would happen to a legal matter which had been raised under the previous law which the current measure was superseding. The junior minister was thumbing feverishly through his brief looking for an answer, so I whispered to him: 'I think I know the answer. May I deal with it?' A look of relief came over his face and he replied in the affirmative. I rose and said: 'The honourable member will find that the situation is provided for in section 38(2) of the Interpretation Act 1889.' The honourable member thanked me and the matter was closed. I heard from behind me the words: 'Well done, John' and looked round to see Davie Kirkwood beaming at me. Clearly, in his book, the boy from Shettleston who had trotted by his house in St Mark's Street on his way to St Mark's School had passed his examination. I gave him a grateful nod and accepted the thanks of the junior minister without disclosing that I had required to deal with that subsection of the 1889 Act on the previous day in relation to another matter, and had not simply plucked it out of my storehouse of legal knowledge. The standing of lawyers in the House of Commons is not so high that a bonus of that nature can be dispensed with. It called to mind a western film *The Man Who Shot Liberty Vallance*, the concluding scene of which contained these words or words of like import and effect: 'When the truth interferes with a legend, forget about the truth.'

Looking back on those days it is interesting to note that Elwyn Jones, who was the Parliamentary Private Secretary to the English law officers, himself became Attorney-General in due course and then occupied with distinction the highest judicial position in England and Wales, that of Lord Chancellor; and the Treasury junior counsel who 'devilled up' opinions for the law officers ultimately became Lord Chief Justice Parker. The subsequent history of the senior members of that team is not without interest either. Hartley Shawcross became President of the Board of Trade in the 1950 Labour Government, but later dissociated himself from the Labour Party. Frank Soskice followed him as Attorney-General and in due course became Home Secretary in Harold Wilson's first administration. He subsequently went to the House of Lords where, despite failing health and physical disability, he carried on an active political career. Douglas Johnston
128

remained in the Commons until January 1961 when he was appointed a judge of the Court of Session by a Conservative government on the strength of his undoubted standing as a lawyer. He had served thirteen strenuous years in Parliament. His great courtesy and graciousness were carried forward from the High Court of Parliament to the Bench of the High Court in Scotland, and his recent death, following a short period of retirement from the Bench, was a great sorrow to those who were privileged to know him and especially to those who were privileged to work with him.

I found my work as Lord Advocate absorbing and fulfilling, and in retrospect I can say that of all the jobs I have had to do it was the one which I have most enjoyed doing although it had a close rival in my work as Lord Justice-Clerk. It had, however, one big drawback. Allied to my duties as a member of Parliament it of necessity encroached on the time which I had with the family. The five children, whose ages cover a twelve-year span, were growing up through their various stages, and the burden and responsibility of seeing them safely through these diverse stages fell squarely on Nancy's shoulders. The way in which she discharged her duties in giving the children all the care and attention which they required, in instilling in them a proper sense of values in this topsyturvy world, and in setting an example in kindness and charity, while looking after me with loving care and consideration merits the highest appreciation. She, however, simply dismisses all this with a wave of her hand and the rhetorical question: 'What is a wife and a mother for?' During all the years of our family life she has been the lynchpin. Over and above all this she carried out with the same selfless devotion the duties of an MP's wife which she did to the great acceptance of the people in the constituency, by whom she is greeted with affection to this day.

During my tenure of office as Lord Advocate I had a number of unusual experiences. I cannot recount them all, but here are a few of them. Before the advent of legal aid, the tradition of the Faculty of Advocates was that 'counsel for the poor' would be provided free of charge for people

129

of scant means who could not afford or even have recourse to the money which would normally be payable to counsel in fees. In furtherance of this young counsel for a period of three years after their call to the Bar were expected to make themselves available as counsel for the poor at criminal circuits. This applied especially to the normally busy Glasgow circuit, and names were sent through in advance of the circuit to enable solicitors to know which counsel were available to them. When I was appointed Lord Advocate I was only 39 years old and, I suppose, looked reasonably young. On a Saturday morning before a Glasgow circuit I went in to the Advocates' Library where I had not been for some time to look up an authority which was not available in the Crown Office. A new boy on the staff came up to this strange face and said: 'There's a Glasgow circuit a week on Tuesday, can I put your name down as being available as a counsel?' This, I thought, was carrying the Faculty tradition a bit far, but I did not want to embarrass the youngster so I said; 'I'm sorry, I shall be otherwise engaged and cannot go, but I have arranged for someone else to be there in my place.' All this was the truth but not the whole truth. For instance, I did not inform him that the 'someone else' was an advocate-depute. Anyway, he seemed to accept the explanation and went away having done his duty.

The next experience was probably unique. I have not done any research on the subject, but I wonder if it had ever happened before that a 'devil' had installed his 'devil-master' as Dean of the Faculty of Advocates. It came about through an unusual combination of circumstances. Meetings of the Faculty of Advocates are presided over by the Dean. If the Dean is not available the Vice-Dean presides. If both are not available the Lord Advocate presides. When Jock Cameron was elected Dean he could not install himself, and there was no Vice-Dean since that office also had to be filled. Accordingly, I had to preside over the Faculty meeting at which my devil-master was installed as Dean. I doubt if a more pleasurable duty could befall a devil.

Another strange experience which I imagine was unique was when as Lord Advocate I presided over a joint meeting of the English Bar Council and the Council of the Law Society of England. I am not a member of the English Bar and you may wonder what I was doing there at all. Again it was due to a most peculiar combination of circumstances, and it came to pass like this. We were in the process of preparing provisions relating to legal aid and advice for inclusion in the respective Bills for England and Wales and Scotland. I had been called to the Cabinet meeting in the morning on some other matters. I was there when the meeting ended, and as I walked out the Lord Chancellor, Lord Jowett, said to me: 'I have a meeting on legal aid with the Bar Council and the Council of the Law Society in my room in the House this afternoon and I would like you to come along. I know the broad principles involved, but you know the details and you can fill me in if necessary.' I could not quite understand why he wanted a Scottish law officer for this, but I thought it diplomatic to signify my assent. I duly turned up and walked into the room with the Lord Chancellor. He was wearing the court dress which he normally wore under his gown which was laid out for him along with his wig on a convenient table. We sat down at another table facing an impressive and fairly large audience headed by Maxwell Fyfe, KC, MP, and Manningham-Buller, KC, MP, for the Bar Council and the President of the Law Society. The Lord Chancellor had only said: 'Good afternoon, gentlemen,' when one of the attendants of the House dressed in traditional full evening dress came into the room, marched straight up to the Lord Chancellor and said: 'My Lord, your presence is required in the Chamber immediately.' His Lordship rose and was helped into his gown and wig. He then turned to me and said: 'Just carry on until I come back.' Fortunately I had been provided with an agenda and given a briefing before we came into the room, and so I just carried on. The meeting lasted for about two hours but the Chancellor never came back. I managed to carry on the meeting with acceptance, but this was mainly due to the co-operation of both branches of the profession. This was in complete contradistinction to my experience in Scotland. No attempt was made to raise political points, yet there were present the two MPs to whom I have referred who were likely to be the leading opposition spokesmen when the Bill came to the Commons. Only matters relevant to the proposals which had been outlined were discussed, and if it was an unusual experience for me it was certainly a most pleasant one.

Work was both hard and intense, but there were compensations. One notable one was when, as Lord Advocate and a Privy Councillor, I was deputed to go along with Secretary of State Arthur Woodburn to a Privy Council meeting with HM George VI at Balmoral Castle, where His Majesty was on holiday. The King's Private Secretary was to make up the quorum of Privy Councillors at the meeting which had been arranged for the evening. We had in consequence to stay the night as the guests of their Majesties, though not on the conditions usually associated colloquially with that term. This was quite a prospect, and when Nancy saw how I had as usual packed my overnight case she told me that it would never do. She said to me: 'There will be a valet there who will unpack your case and you're not going there with a case packed like that.' I scoffed at the idea of having a valet to do my unpacking, but she was adamant about it, and since she came from Tollcross and I came only from Shettleston I bowed to her superior knowledge of how royal establishments are run and let her repack the case in her inimitable way, which I have always admired but could never emulate.

Arthur and I arrived at Balmoral late in the afternoon, having narrowly missed a head-on collision with a bus on the horrific bend at the Devil's Elbow. We had been driving round the bend on the wrong side of the road, but fortunately the bus driver, because of the size of his vehicle, had found it desirable to take the broad side of the bend in order to negotiate it. The two vehicles, each on its wrong side of the road, narrowly missed one another. I was so relieved at our escape that I was almost, but not quite, prepared to accept our driver's assertion that his method of negotiating the Devil's Elbow was the correct one. Fortunately for us the drivers were two of a kind. On arrival

132

we were detained downstairs for a while during which introductions and greetings took place, but when I walked into my bedroom I could hardly believe my eyes. There was a valet unpacking my case! I realised that in certain social matters Tollcross had the edge on Shettleston. When he finished unpacking the valet asked me when I would like a call in the morning. When I replied that 7.15 would do me fine, he said apologetically: 'Could you make that 7.30 as I am in attendance on His Majesty from 7 to 7.30?' There was only one answer to that, when I was not only receiving the service of a valet, but also sharing one with the King.

After our Privy Council meeting with the King we dressed appropriately and went in for dinner. And what a delightful and informal meal that was. In addition to their Majesties, the only people present were Princess Margaret and a small number of the Royal Household who were in attendance. Princess Elizabeth and Prince Philip were living in the adjacent estate but joined the party later in the evening. Arthur sat next to the King on one side of the table and I sat between the Queen and Princess Margaret on the other side. There was a real family atmosphere about the meal, and the conversation ranged over a number of topics and flowed over and up and down the table. It was remarkable how quickly we were made to feel at home. There was a most delightful tailpiece to the meal. In due course, we adjourned to a room which had been laid out for a film show. Princess Elizabeth and Prince Philip joined us there, and in the seats behind those reserved for the house party were seated estate workers and their families who had been invited to attend. The film had been flown up from London in the King's Flight, and was to become one of the great box-office attractions, with a theme tune which became one of the most popular of modern times – *The Third Man*. The estate workers of Balmoral probably saw the film before the film buffs of the West End of London.

Every aspect of that visit was touched by the kindness of the royal couple. The visit, however, did not end the kindness. Two days after I returned home the postman handed in a package. It was a brace of pheasants from Balmoral with

133

a card conveying His Majesty's compliments. There seemed to be no end to the hospitality, and for me it was a most privileged and never-to-be-forgotten experience.

While I thoroughly enjoyed my work as Lord Advocate and recognise that job satisfaction has much to do with how a person performs his job, I realise that it is even more important that the way you do your job is satisfactory to those for whom you do it. I shall not attempt any self-assessment of my tenure of office, preferring to leave that to others. When Parliament was dissolved in 1950 leading to the General Election of that year, *The Scotsman* carried a critical review of the Labour Government's performance in Scotland and of the ministers involved. It was very complimentary of the work of the 'young' Lord Advocate, and that, coming from a newspaper which was not politically disposed to the Labour Party, was personally very satisfactory. In supplement to that, I have two letters which I received from two quite disparate sources. The first was from Lord Normand, who himself had been Lord Advocate in the early 1930s and later Lord President of the Court of Session and a Lord of Appeal in the House of Lords, which he still was when he wrote. In fact I received the letter during the 1951 General Election campaign and it was prompted by something which he had asked me to take up. In the course of the letter he wrote: 'I should like to add for my own part how much I appreciate and how grateful I am for your readiness on all occasions to receive any representations from me on questions touching Scots law and Scottish lawyers. It is a firm part of the Scottish legal tradition that the Lord Advocate and the Scottish judges in the Lords should maintain close and friendly relations on such matters, and may I say that you have worthily maintained that tradition.' The second was from Clem Attlee after he had laid down the reins of office following the General Election of 1951. On 3 December 1951 he wrote to me a letter which I greatly valued, not for its comparison, which I feel related to the political aspect of my work, but for its appreciation. It is reproduced on the opposite page.

Years later, after I had left Parliament and was on the

3. XII. 51

My dear Ihh

Owing to pressure of work, I
am only now writing to express
to all my colleagues my appreciation
of their service in our forward.
I am very grateful to you for
all you have done. You have
in fact been the first effective
Lord Advocate that Labour
has ever had.

Yours ever
Clem

Bench, I had a 'phone call from Walter Elliot, who was then Lord High Commissioner of the Church of Scotland. The General Assembly of the Church was taking place and the Attlees had been invited to stay at the Palace of Holy-roodhouse as the guests of the Lord High Commissioner. Walter explained that the Attlees, who had been attending a number of functions, were going to be left alone that afternoon and he wondered if Nancy and I would be good enough to entertain them during that period. We were naturally very happy to do so. I had always got on well with Clem, whose brevity of expression was often mistaken for taciturnity, but he would become quite loquacious if you turned the conversation over to his pet sport – cricket. Talking of his brevity of expression, I like the story of his reply to the newspaper reporter who, on the occasion of his 80th birthday, asked, 'What does it feel like to be an octogenarian?', only to receive the reply: 'Better than the alternative.' Anyway on that afternoon in Edinburgh, our boys had been outside in the garden playing cricket, and they bore the hallmarks of their activity when I brought them in to meet the famous people. It had been raining earlier that day and the boys had managed to get a fair amount of mud on to their clothes and limbs. Nancy was appalled when I presented them in this condition, but when I explained that it was due to the enthusiasm with which they played cricket Clem started to quiz them at length on their interest in the game. If I had stage-managed it I could not have presented them in better fashion and a most pleasant time was had by all.

After I had demitted office and found myself in opposition, life in Parliament was something of an anticlimax. Whereas I had been fully occupied almost every minute of the day and had been very much in the heart of things I now had a very limited range of responsibility. I attended the debates in the Chamber regularly, hoping to broaden my knowledge of subjects in which I might take an interest apart from Scottish affairs. So far as Scottish affairs were concerned, the Opposition was fully covered with two former Secretaries of State in Arthur Woodburn and Hector McNeill and two former Under-Secretaries of State in Tom Fraser and Peggy Herbison. While I was given a limited number of opportunities to speak on general issues, my principal responsibility was to sit in the House or in the Scottish Grand Committee to deal with any Scottish legal point should one arise. After some months of this I went to Clem Attlee and asked if I could leave the opposition front bench and go onto the back benches where I would have the opportunity and freedom to intervene on any subject I chose, whereas on the front bench I could only intervene and speak as the official representative of my party. Clem said 'No,' adding that he wanted me to remain on the front bench to deal with legal matters.

So I continued to sit in on debates even when I was given no opportunity to intervene. Some of the debates were interesting and educational, others frankly, were boring. However, even boring debates can bring about interesting experiences, although not frequently enough. During one boring debate I decided to leave the Chamber and go for a cup of tea. There are various exits from the Chamber, one of which is behind the Speaker's chair, and this is the one normally used by front benchers, which was the one which I took. Now there is a convention that when the Prime Minister and the Leader of the Opposition wish to have a meeting to discuss privately a matter of urgency, they agree to meet behind the Speaker's chair, which in practice means the corridor leading from the exit behind the chair. I walked into that corridor only to find Prime Minister Winston Churchill and Clem Attlee ahead of me walking arm in arm with their heads bowed and close to one another. I thought that they must be discussing some high-level matter of urgency and wondered whether I should return to the Chamber and leave by another exit. I decided against that because the exit and corridor were for common use and I had no intention of eavesdropping. I decided to hurry past as quickly as possible, which I sought to do. I had not taken into account that Winston was getting quite deaf, and, like many deaf people, he was inclined to talk in a voice much louder than normal. Accordingly, as I was passing I heard

137

him say to Clem something which I was not supposed to hear, but which I am now free from prosecution under the Official Secrets Act to make public. 'I am running it at —— on Wednesday of next week and take my tip – have a good bet on it.' I am not normally a betting man, and as I did not quite catch the name of the course and did not know 'it's' name I was not tempted to break my habit and make a kill. In any event, politically I was not inclined to have faith in Winnie's prognostications, but I don't know what Clem did. I am sure that many people outside of Parliament would find it difficult to believe that such a conversation could take place between two persons who had to be continually criticising each other across the floor of the House of Commons. However, such relationships are not uncommon, and they constitute one of the pleasant sides of life at Westminster.

In those days finances were very tight, particularly for those members who had to find living accommodation in London apart from their family home elsewhere. I had Scottish colleagues who, because of the price of meals in the dining-room and the expense of living in London, were obliged to bring 'pieces' with them, and these with a cup of tea in the tea-room constituted their meals during the long periods of incarceration in the Palace of Westminster. The parliamentary salary then, which was £1,000 per annum and carried none of the fringe benefits which exist today, was hopelessly inadequate, and while conditions have been considerably improved they still compare unfavourably with those in many other countries.

When I was offered a judgeship towards the end of 1953 I found myself in a dilemma. It was a very attractive offer of work in the field of law, but I was very much immersed in politics. I did not relish leaving the political scene, although the restrictions under which I was then labouring were proving something of a frustration. But there was a personal factor which turned out to be the determining one. I had been away from Nancy and the family quite a lot during the previous years – in the army, in Parliament, and with the personal calls on my time as MP when I was living

138

at home. Nancy had been left with the task of bringing up the children and seeing to their welfare in every respect. I realised that if I accepted the offer, our family life could resume a normal pattern and I would be at home to play my part in it. That eventually decided me, and, having made the decision, I went to see Clem Attlee to inform him of it. This I could do on the basis that we were Privy Councillors, because such offers are not supposed to be discussed or discussed publicly before the official announcement is made. Herbert Morrison, also a Privy Councillor, was there at the time, and both tried very hard to persuade me to remain a member of Parliament. Clem indicated that he had me very much in mind for office, other than that of Lord Advocate, when Labour next came into power. This was a very attractive and persuasive point. I never doubted that Clem would keep his word if he was in a position to do so, but political life is a fickle thing, as indeed is life itself, and if circumstances occasioned a change of leadership, there was no obligation on a successor to implement the promise. This was properly so, as each Prime Minister has to be free to make his own choices. But the family considerations were paramount and I told them so. I accordingly accepted the judgeship and thus brought to a close a chapter of my life which I had found absorbing, challenging and fulfilling, and one for which I shall always carry a fond recollection. I count myself a lucky man that in leaving such a life with all its attractions for me I went into another one which has provided me with so much job satisfaction and interest. It has also provided me with the time to devote myself to works of public nature which I thoroughly enjoyed and counted as scant repayment for all that Scotland has given me.

12 Life on the Bench

I was installed on the Bench with the judicial title of Lord Wheatley on 2 February 1954. Some people might see a significance in the fact that I was translated from the hurly-burly of political strife in the High Court of Parliament to the neutrality and serenity of the High Court Bench on the Feast of the Purification. The title of Lord which is given to the judges of the High Court in Scotland is a purely honorary one. They are Lords of Council and Session in their civil capacity and Lords Commissioners of Justiciary in the Criminal Courts, but as such they are not peers of the realm and are not entitled to sit in the House of Lords unless, of course, they are peers in their own right. Their wives are given the honorary title of Lady, but this was not always so. When elevated to the High Court Bench in Scotland a judge has to decide the name by which he shall be called judicially. In former days it was quite common for judges to forsake their own names and choose a territorial title, such as the name of their estate if they had one, or their place of birth. In modern times most judges take their own name, unless there already happens to be a judge with the same name or there has been recently a judge of the same name with whom the new judge does not wish to be confused. In such cases a territorial title is taken. For instance, recently we had three Johnstons on the High Court Bench at the same time but only one of them (Douglas) was Lord Johnston. The others, Alastair and RS, are Lord Dunpark and Lord Kincraig, respectively. In 1904 a Scottish judge, an upright and good-living man who was not a peer but who had taken a

140

territorial judicial title, went with his wife to England on holiday. While he had become Lord X she had remained Mrs Y, and when he signed the register at the hotel this upright man entered Lord X and Mrs Y. The receptionist noted this and drew it to the attention of the manager who politely told the eminent Scottish judge that his was not that type of hotel and requested them to leave forthwith. This came to the ears of King Edward VII, who understandably recognised the embarrassment which such a situation might cause, and decided that his Scottish High Court judges and their wives should not be exposed to such a humiliation. Accordingly, a Royal Warrant was issued on 3 February 1905 ordaining that a wife would bear the honorary title of Lady consistent with her husband's title.

The work in the Scottish courts is not compartmented as it is in other jurisdictions. The judges have to deal with any kind of case which can be competently brought before the Court of Session in civil matters or before the High Court of Justiciary in criminal matters. The Court is divided into two tiers – the Inner House and the Outer House. The Outer House consists of courts of first instance and the Inner House consists of two appeal courts which hear appeals from the Outer House and lower courts. The appeal courts are the First Division presided over by the Lord President of the Court of Session and the Second Division presided over by the Lord Justice-Clerk. In a country where the large majority of the natives are football-daft, this conjures up the idea that there exist two leagues with promotion and relegation for the judges according to the points which they have amassed during the previous legal year or season. This is a misapprehension, perhaps fortunately so. There are four judges in each Division, three being a quorum. In recent years, owing to the growth and pressure of work, it has become common for only three judges to sit in the Divisions, thus freeing two judges for Outer House work or criminal trials throughout the country, and incidentally saving the Treasury the expense of two more judges. Apart from the appointment to the two Chairs of Lord President and Lord Justice-Clerk, appointment to the Inner House, when a vacancy arises, is strictly by seniority from the Outer House. This means that the Division to which an Outer House judge goes is purely fortuitous. It was the tradition that the Lord Advocate had the right of refusal in respect of any judicial vacancy which occurred, and when the vacancy was in the office of Lord President or Lord Justice-Clerk the right was usually exercised. There was a slight hiccup in that cosy state of affairs when Lord Alness succeeded Lord Scott Dickson as Lord Justice-Clerk. He was not then the Lord Advocate, but he had been previously the occupant of that office and had moved on to become the Secretary for Scotland (as the office then was), so presumably the order of precedence in regard to the right of refusal was extended to the order of precedence among government ministers. However, the pattern was broken in 1970 when George Emslie was appointed from the Outer House to succeed Lord Clyde (*secundus*) as Lord President, and again in 1972 when I was appointed from the wing of the Second Division to be Lord Justice-Clerk in succession to Lord Grant whose tragic death in a motor accident cast a shadow over the whole Court. This new pattern was carried on when Donald Ross was appointed from the Outer House to succeed me when I retired as Lord Justice-Clerk in September 1985. It will be interesting to see if this new pattern is carried on, but credit must be given to the Lord Advocates who were prepared to forego the previous practice, and in particular Norman Wylie who twice within two years did so. I thus had the strange experience of twice being given judicial office by a Conservative administration despite my political history.

There is an appeal from the Divisions to the House of Lords in civil cases but no such appeal in criminal cases. This is perhaps fortunate in the sense that our criminal law and procedure are so different from the English system that it is better that it should remain wholly in Scottish hands even although there are criminal statutes, such as the Road Traffic Acts, which apply to both countries. In civil matters, the common law and statute law are closely identified in many fields in both countries, which presumably explains the apparent anomaly.

The fact that, in Scotland, High Court judges can be called upon to deal with any type of case, civil or criminal, makes life on the Bench more interesting even if more challenging. It also means that counsel do not go in for the intense form of specialisation which characterises other legal systems. Successful advocacy depends on two basic factors – knowledge of the relevant law and the presentation of the case which involves cool and accurate judgment. Specialisation may make instant appraisal of the relevant law more readily available, but once that appraisal has been achieved – even if only by the midnight oil – the presentation of the knowledge and the arguments that flow from it are what really count. From my experience as a junior counsel in the House of Lords, listening carefully but not having to argue the case, I found that good Scottish all-round counsel could be just as effective as the so-called specialists, in that they presented their arguments clearly and effectively, whereas some of the specialists got bogged down in the mire of their knowledge and their long-windedness in presenting their case. I am not making this a generalisation, and I merely use it to emphasise the point that once the law on the subject has been mastered it is the presentation which matters, and that just as the counsel who regards himself as a practical expert can get bogged down by his knowledge if he does not know how properly to use it, so a specialised lawyer can lose the place and the ear of the court by a lengthy but confused exposition of the law. I wish to make it clear that I am not being derogatory of 'specialist' counsel as a whole – I have listened to many of them who are first-class pleaders. I am only trying to make the point that specialisation does not necessarily produce a better advocate than general practice – it all comes down to the individual and his talents.

I spent over 31 years on the Bench before I retired, the first 10 years as a judge of first instance in the Outer House and as the presiding judge at criminal trials. The next nine years were spent as one of the appeal judges in the Second Division dealing with civil and criminal appeals, and criminal trials on circuit. The final $12\frac{1}{2}$ years were spent mostly in hearing both civil and criminal appeals as president of the

Second Division and presiding at criminal trials. My experience of criminal trials during this final period was confined to the first half of the period, during which I tried to get to every circuit town, particularly those which I had not visited previously such as Oban and Jedburgh. I had finally to give up going on circuit for a very practical reason. In the earlier periods going on circuit meant being away from Edinburgh for about a week on average. Even in Glasgow, which was the busiest court of all, a circuit rarely ran for more than two weeks, often less. In other circuit towns the sojourn was often for less than one week. In the later period, however, the increase in criminal trials was such that even in circuit towns other than Glasgow the duration of the circuit might be two weeks and sometimes more, while in Glasgow the average period had almost doubled. With my various other duties I felt that this would be taking me away from Edinburgh for excessively long periods and would create an unjustifiable unavailability for my work as chairman of an appeal court. I accordingly stopped going on circuit, but with 25 years or so of criminal trials behind me I felt that I was not lacking in experience of them, while criminal appeals kept me in touch with any new developments that had sprung up or had been conjured up. As time went on I realised that my decision had been the correct one, particularly as the volume of work kept increasing.

There was a great deal of preliminary work to be done daily before the cases set out for hearing were started. I had to deal with bail appeals from the lower courts, and also with cases which had been remitted to the High Court for sentence. In addition there were cases under the accelerated procedure of section 102 of the Criminal Procedure (Scotland) Act 1975 where the accused had intimated in writing his intention of pleading guilty and his desire to have the case disposed of forthwith. In order not to encroach on the scheduled work of the court I put the bail appeals out for half an hour before the normal starting time for the sitting of the civil courts, thinking that this would be to the general convenience. I regret to say that I seriously misjudged the situation. I had thought that the Bail Act of 1980, which abolished money bail to all intents would reduce the number of bail appeals, but exactly the opposite occurred. The number of appeals varied from day to day, but there could be as few as four or five and as many as sixteen to eighteen. Moreover, it was deemed to be a convenient court to hear applications for extension of time to lodge appeals in criminal cases where the statutory time for doing so had been exceeded. All this was time-consuming and defeating my purpose of not conflicting with the scheduled work of the civil courts.

In an endeavour to rationalise and to expedite matters both in bail appeals and in applications for bail in the courts of first instance I formulated guidelines which I hoped would clarify the general principles by which granting of bail would be determined. I submitted these to the Lord Justice-General, Lord Emslie, for his approval which was granted. As far as I could gather, the issue of the guidelines had the desired effect, if not the approval of some accused and their legal advisers. But the subjective test is not necessarily the most reliable one! I had usually at least one sentence to cope with each morning and sometimes more. I shall deal with sentencing separately, and for present purposes I shall confine myself to the observation that the time taken to dispose of a case dealing with sentence alone can vary quite considerably. The nature of the charge or charges may call for long and detailed explanations whereas in other cases the facts of the charge are so plain that they speak for themselves. That distinction is not necessarily carried into the speeches of counsel. Crown counsel are often overburdened with material and the question for them becomes how much is relevant and necessary and how much can be safely and properly left out. Defence counsel on the other hand are often left to make bricks without straw, but understandably feel that they have to say something on behalf of their client. Their problem then becomes how to soften the judge's heart without insulting his intelligence. If they would only keep in mind that the judge has been through it all himself in his earlier days a great deal of embarrassment would be avoided.

When I was sitting as a judge of first instance in the Outer House I seemed to get landed with cases which had a peculiar

145

twist and became newsworthy. I did not pick these cases. I never once sought to have a case allocated to me. They were doled out to me by the Keeper of the Rolls. Nor did I attempt to glamorise the facts; the facts spoke for themselves, but were often odd and sometimes of public interest. I might have known from the start what my fate would be because of the very first case with which I had to deal. A man of 82 was seeking a declarator of nullity of marriage in that when he and his wife were married a few years earlier he was physically capable of consummating the marriage whereas his wife who was 52 was not. While this seemed somewhat odd, there was evidence adduced and not contraverted to establish both of these contentions. Accordingly, despite the woman's opposition, I had to grant decree of nullity to the old man and give him the freedom to go looking for another bride, hopefully without a similar blemish.

In the civil courts, divorce cases, especially if they are based on adultery, are the prime target for the media. This is markedly so if they involve prominent people or the facts are bizarre. I propose to deal in a very limited way with the divorce cases I had to dispose of and then only to illustrate a point which I wish to make rather than to take the lid off the evidence. I shall accordingly start by recounting what was certainly the biggest – and I hope the only real gaffe which I perpetrated on the Bench. Thankfully it has never been reported until now. To set the scene I must describe the *dramatis personae,* the roles they played and the issue at stake. The person who initiates the action, in this case the husband, is called the pursuer. The wife was the defender. As the wife was alleged to have committed adultery with a named man, the pursuer's case (the summons) had to be served on that man to give him the opportunity of coming into the process to dispute the allegation. This he did by lodging a minute in the process, whereupon he became 'the Party Minuter' and was referred to as such. The alleged adultery was said to have taken place at the back of the common entry (the close) of a tenement property in Paisley. Although there was a shorthand writer to take down the notes of evidence, to be extended and provided to the judge

146

if required, I had taken my own notes of the evidence which I regarded as material in my note-book. The evidence was very clear to me and I decided to give judgment straight away after hearing the submissions of the various parties. This meant that I had to rely on my own notes. I do not write shorthand, but like many judges I have my own abbreviations. Thus I had 'P' for pursuer, 'D' for defender and 'PM' for the Party Minuter. There is normally no direct evidence of adultery unless the parties are caught *in flagrante delicto* as we used to say in Shettleston, in preference to the coarser 'being caught at it' which was commonly used in less refined parts of Glasgow. Accordingly, Scots law had devised the delicate test of proof of adultery as being the finding of facts, circumstances and qualifications relevant to infer that adultery had taken place at a specified time and at a specified spot by the parties named. When I came to give judgment I gave a summary of the evidence, indicated which parts of it I accepted and which witnesses I believed or disbelieved. I then proceeded to pronounce the archaic formula, having in mind the need to fill in the appropriate names, place and time. For this, of course, I had to depend on my notes with their abbreviations. What I said was this: 'I accordingly find facts, circumstances and qualifications relevant to infer that on [the stated date] in the back close of the tenement property at —— Paisley, the defender committed adultery with the Prime Minister, and I grant decree of divorce.' This was not long after I had left the parliamentary scene where for years the initials PM meant the Prime Minister and nobody else – hence the gaffe. I realised right away that I had made it and hastened to correct it, but the damage was done at least in the eyes of one person in court. As I was making the correction I spotted sitting in the court, Cyril Grobel, an old Mount St Mary's boy, who was a great friend of mine. He was a London solicitor who had been involved as a witness in another case, and who had wandered into my court, no doubt to run the rule over me in my new role. I was not allowed to forget that incident for a long time, as he often asked me to repeat it on our regular visits to the Mount.

My early years on the Bench were so close to my political existence that inevitably the shades of the latter were liable to intrude on the former. It is perhaps appropriate that at this point I should explain and emphasise that when a person goes on to the Bench he has to remain clear of politics and political controversy, and discharge his duties with complete impartiality in conformity with his judicial oath.

The pomp and circumstance which had at one time characterised the circuits of the High Court of Justiciary, with a parade of judges and court personnel in open horse-drawn carriages making their way to the court, had long since departed before I went on to the Bench. By that time only two of the ancient customs survived. The first was the presence of trumpeters who blew a fanfare for the opening of the court proceedings every morning of the circuit. Their only other duty was to be in attendance outside the court building for the arrival of the judge whom they preceded to the judge's private room. Their presence for the fanfare was not really necessary since they blew it off-stage and were never seen. If a fanfare was required or desired, the playing of a recording would have been just as effective. Their presence to lead the judge in procession into the court building was purely ceremonial since the presence of police officers to see the judge safely into the building was more reassuring. They were not full-time employees and were often secured from the orchestra of the Empire Theatre in Edinburgh. They went to every circuit town as long as the use of this ceremonial was preserved, but the practice has been dispensed with for many years now. The other surviving ceremonial in my time was restricted to two circuit towns, Aberdeen and Inverness, where there were still army depots. On the first morning of a circuit the judge had to inspect a guard of honour consisting of soldiers from the depot, and members of that guard were on patrol duty all the time the court was sitting. The inspection of the guard was an obvious feature for a photograph in the local newspaper. I went up to Aberdeen to carry through a circuit not long after I went on to the Bench. I had, of course, to inspect the guard of honour and the inevitable photograph in due course

148

appeared in the local press. It was in July, at the time of the Glasgow Fair, during a spell of very good weather. I expected the court to be empty because of the weather but to my surprise it was packed every day. The circuit lasted the full week, and on the final day after the business of the court was completed I carried out the last official duty by thanking the Lord Provost and magistrates of the city of Aberdeen for their characteristically generous hospitality to the court during the circuit. That having completed the business, I rose to be conducted off the Bench by the macer. At that point a member of the public, seated immediately behind the dock, stood up and called out in a loud voice: 'Can I ask a question, John?' No doubt he was an inveterate heckler at public meetings, and it might be assumed that in addressing me as 'John' he was an old Shettlestonian. I did not get time to ask because he was immediately descended upon by a battery of court officials and policemen, the members of the guard of honour on duty being outside. He was hustled out of the court while I left the Bench with as much dignity as I could muster in the circumstances. However, an enterprising reporter from one of the national newspapers ran out of the court after them, and when the would-be heckler was released the reporter asked the 64,000 dollar question: 'What was the question you wanted to ask?' The reply almost certainly indicated that he came from Shettleston and knew me although I did not recognise him. It was: 'Since when did John Wheatley need a bodyguard?'

In the days of capital punishment murder trials were much more dramatic and awesome affairs than they are today. The stakes were so high that every aspect of the trial took on a sharper edge. The examination and cross-examination of witnesses were more exacting. The public benches were usually packed, and the onlookers seldom left their places. When the speeches of counsel and the judge's charge to the jury were being delivered, intent attention was paid to them. When the jury retired to consider their verdict the onlookers remained where they were to make sure that they would have a seat when the verdict was returned. During this interval, when the judge was no longer on the Bench and

149

the court was no longer in session, loud chattering would develop as the pundits in the public benches discussed the likely outcome, but when the bell rang to indicate that the jury were ready to return to court with their verdict, the chattering ceased immediately. When the jury returned to the court and the judge had resumed his place on the Bench, the Clerk of Court faced the jury and asked the question: 'Ladies and gentlemen, who speaks for you?' the person whom the jury had elected foreman would reply: 'I do.' The Clerk of Court, then asked: 'Have you reached your verdict?' If the answer was in the affirmative, the next question was: 'What is your verdict?' At this point you could hear a pin drop. The foreman would then deliver the verdict. If it was 'guilty' cries of anguish would come from relatives and friends of the accused accompanied by comments among the spectators. These understandably human reactions disturbed the normal quiet and decorum of the court which was restored by a macer like Jimmy Turnbull calling out in a commanding voice: 'Silence in Court.' That was usually effective, but if it was not the judge would step in and remind the assembly that this was a court of law and not a theatre in that if silence was not observed the court would be cleared. If on the other hand the verdict was an acquittal by either Not Guilty or Not Proven, the reactions were different, but none the less vociferous. Cheers from friends of the accused, protests from friends of the victim or from the pundits who had wrongly forecast the verdict. That however, did not conclude the proceedings. The jury had still to be asked by the Clerk of Court if the verdict was unanimous or by a majority, but if the answer was that it was by a majority, the majority was neither asked for nor disclosed. The Clerk then read aloud the verdict he had recorded in the official record and asked the foreman if that properly represented their verdict. If the answer was in the affirmative, the advocate-depute would move for sentence and then came the most awesome part of the proceedings. It fell to the judge to pronounce the sentence of death. Originally the words of the death sentence were in archiac form and related to more than the order for execution. For instance, among other

150

things it ordained that the accused's assets should be escheat (i e forfeit) to the Crown. But archaic forms of punishment such as escheat, attainder, corruption of blood, outlawry and fugitation were abolished by the Criminal Justice (Scotland) Act 1949. Even in its curtailed form the death sentence was a grim one to have to pronounce. 'AB, pannel [the accused], in respect of the verdict of murder just received the sentence of the Court is that you be taken from this place to the Prison of ____, therein to be detained till the ____ day of ____, and upon that day within the said Prison of ____ between the hours of eight and ten o'clock forenoon you suffer death by hanging; which is pronounced for doom.' As he pronounced the words 'which is pronounced for doom', the judge held the three-cornered black cap over his head. He had to do so because the cap would not with certainty balance on top of his wig, and the risk of it falling off at that dire moment could not be taken.

In my view this was the most disagreeable task which a judge was called upon to perform and I had to do it on several occasions. In fact the last two persons who were hanged in Scotland for murder were sentenced to death by me. I have always been an abolitionist, a fact which did not make my task any easier, and I was glad to see capital punishment abolished. But then a judge has to administer the law as it is, not as he would personally like it to be. The alternative would be judicial anarchy.

Three clear Sundays had to elapse between the date of the pronouncement of the death sentence and the date of execution. This was presumably to give the condemned man time to make his peace with his Maker, but it also gave the Secretary of State time to consider, after receiving such appropriate advice as he thought fit, whether the law should take its course or he should advise the monarch to grant a reprieve. There was one notorious occasion when the judge who had been provided with a copy of the death sentence misread the date of execution and ordered the unfortunate pannel to be hanged on 29 December instead of 27 December. By the time the Clerk of Court had drawn the judge's attention to the mistake the unfortunate man was on

151

his way down to the cells. Rather stupefied, through not knowing what was going on, he was returned to the dock. The judge gave him a most profuse apology and told him that he would be hanged not on 29 December as pronounced originally but on the 27 December, thus lopping two days off the poor fellow's life expectancy. I doubt if the apology was gratefully received, but all ended well since the man was reprieved in due course. It was only the death sentence which was reprieved, and when that was done a sentence of life imprisonment had to be substituted.

The merits and demerits of the issue of capital punishment have been canvassed backwards and forwards inside and outside of Parliament and I do not wish to go over them again. There was, however, one aspect of the system as operated in Scotland (and in England and Wales) which I have always regarded as an objectionable one from the human point of view. It was the final step in the procedure. Up to that point various people in differing capacities were involved in the legal machine which produced the sentence of death and its ultimate execution. The prosecutor had sought to obtain a conviction on the evidence adduced and had to move for sentence. The judge had to guide the jury on the law and focus the jurors' attention on the relevant issues. The jurors had to determine their verdict in conformity with the oath which they had taken, that they would truth say and no truth conceal so far as they were to pass on the assize. The witnesses might have had to give evidence which led to a conviction. If it did the judge had perforce to pass the sentence, but this was not necessarily the final say. If the law said that the sentence had to be carried out the public executioner had to do the job he was paid to do. (Incidentally, as Lord Advocate I saw the list of applicants for a vacant post of public executioner and was surprised at the large number of applicants.) If an appeal had been unsuccessfully taken, the appeal judges collectively would only be doing the job which they were appointed to do. All these people were simply cogs in a big legal machine and no single one was solely responsible for the ultimate result. That lightened the burden of responsibility to a tremendous
152

degree. But when all that collective process was exhausted, the legal procedure called on one man to make the ultimate decision. Whether or not there was a petition for a reprieve, the Secretary of State had to decide whether he should advise the monarch to let the law take its course and the execution to take place or to exercise the royal prerogative and grant a reprieve. To help him in his decision-making he could get such advice or information from any source which he considered relevant and necessary. That having been said, he was not just a cog in a machine. He was very much an individual and a very lonely one at that. Having gathered all the information and advice, he had to go into a corner, mull over it all, and then make the personal decision – that person shall live or that person shall die on a given date. That, in my view, was a responsibility that should not be placed on the shoulders of any single individual in a civilised society.

Perhaps the most outstanding example of this was the case of Craig and Bentley in England. The younger boy who was 15 could not be sentenced to death but the older boy who was 18 could be and was. It was the young boy who killed the policeman victim, whereas the older one had egged him on. The Home Secretary at the time was David Maxwell-Fyfe, and his decision was that in the older boy's case the law should take its course. There was a public outcry at this decision and Maxwell-Fyfe, later Lord Chancellor Kilmuir, was pilloried. As an abolitionist I was sorry at the result, but I could not pass judgment on it as I was not in possession of *all* the facts and relevant information. Nor were the critics. But I was also sorry for the man whose ministerial duties forced him to make a decision in those difficult circumstances, and, knowing the man, I was sure that he would carry out his responsibilities conscientiously and reach what he conceived to be the proper answer. I met him in the House of Commons one day and expressed these views to him. I felt sorry for him because of the personal abuse to which he was being submitted, and thought it only but right to let him know that there were some people who understood what was involved and sympathised with him

153

in the situation in which he found himself. He seemed deeply appreciative of my action, while I recognised how easy it is to be the critic and how difficult it is to be the one who has to make the decision.

The Bentley case no doubt had the effect of causing Parliament to pass section 5(2) of the Homicide Act of 1957, whereby in the case of any murder which fell into the category of capital murder as defined in the section the only person who could be convicted of such a murder was one who by his own acting had caused the death of the victim or who himself had used force on the victim in the course or furtherance of an attack on him. Capital murder still carried the death penalty while the penalty for non-capital murder was life imprisonment. Not only was there this distinction depending on the nature of the participation in the offence but a further distinction was drawn between the types of murder which attracted the death penalty and those which did not. The fact that the law of concert or association could be invoked in a non-capital murder case but not in a capital murder case seemed to me to be a recipe for confusion. I said as much to some of my judicial colleagues and opined that it would fall to one of us to try and explain all this to a jury. That was probably enough to secure that I would be the unfortunate judge to be called upon to do so, which I was obliged to do in the case of *HM Advocate v Miller and Denovan* (1960, unreported). I did this in as clear a manner as I could, but when both were convicted, one of capital murder and the other of murder, in accordance with the direction I had given to the jury in the event of findings of guilt being made, there was the inevitable appeal. My directions in law to the jury came under attack but the Court of Appeal rejected the criticisms and described the directions as a model of clarity. This unfortunate and misguided distinction in the law of murder was short-lived since it disappeared with the passing of the Murder (Abolition of the Death Penalty) Act 1965.

The two types of case in which the public and the media have taken the deepest interest are probably murder cases and divorce cases. The interest in murder cases has dwindled in recent years for two reasons. In the first place the abolition of capital punishment has taken a great deal of the tension out of murder trials. Secondly, most murder cases in Scotland are barely distinguishable from serious assault cases except that the consequences are different. That is often due to something quite apart from the actings of the accused. The path of the implement causing the injury can be fortuitous, in that one-eighth of an inch deviation in the trajectory is the difference between death and serious injury; the proximity of the assault to a hospital where immediate surgical treatment can be given to the victim, or the skill of the surgeon providing the treatment can result in life being saved when otherwise death would occur. In these circumstances such common types of murder case lose much of their news-worthiness and, accordingly, much of their public interest.

Divorce cases can be sensational, depending on the people concerned, salacious for those who have a penchant for salacity, and piquant, because of the circumstances. On the other hand, they can be drab, uninteresting and run-of-the-mill. The fact that the evidence in a divorce case cannot be reported in the media is an obstacle to a large spread of sensational copy, but in some of the newspapers that is compensated for by the space made available for other forms of salacious titillation. Since the judgment can be reported, the media can reproduce extracts from it, including the references by the judge to passages in the evidence. Whether the extracts properly reflect the purport of the evidence may depend on the context in which the passage was made and the fullness of the extract, and on this topic generally and its associated problems I shall have something more to say later. There is no doubt, however, that murder cases and divorce cases can bring out the baser aspects of human nature.

In my early days at the Bar divorce was divorce and was seriously regarded in view of the status of marriage and the consequences of its dissolution, particularly in regard to family life. It's Rake's Progress from the grounds on which divorce could then be granted to the standards required to establish grounds for the present do-it-yourself application to the court as a sort of Crown Post Office has played a major part in the break-up of family life and the problems of single-parent families which beset society in our country today. The facility with which marriage problems are solved by easy divorce has provided a ready-made solution for domestic disputes, and eliminates in many cases the incentive to make the marriage work. For centuries in Scotland there were only two grounds for divorce, adultery and desertion. This reflected the public attitude over centuries to the sanctity of marriage and to the limited grounds on which it could be dissolved. I remember when incompatibility of temperament became a standard ground of divorce in the United States in the early decades of this century, that concept became very much the subject of derision in this country. It was said to be reflective of the laissez-faire attitude of Hollywood to moral standards and obnoxious to the hard-headed commonsense of our people who considered that husband and wife cannot be said to be incompatible so long as the husband has an income and the wife is patable. In the space of forty years the whole law of divorce has been revolutionised to a point where almost anything goes.

The old law persisted until 1938 when insanity, cruelty and sodomy (or bestiality) were added to the list, and the period of desertion was reduced from four to three years. By the Divorce (Scotland) Act 1976 the whole law of divorce was radically altered. Only one ground of divorce now exists, but it is so widely based as to include nearly everything for its establishment. The sole ground is that the marriage has irretrievably broken down, but all the previous grounds and a lot more can be used as evidence to establish that. These new provisions are a reflection of the attitudes which society is prepared to accept today. In the eyes of some it would appear to be unseemly to base the dissolution of a marriage on the ground of adultery, cruelty or desertion, or even bestiality when a phrase such as 'the marriage has irretrievably broken down' is available, even if the evidence to establish it is based on adultery, cruelty, desertion or bestiality. Moreover, it is now offensive to speak of the person who has brought about the breakdown by such conduct as the guilty party or to refer to the victim of such

156

conduct as the innocent party. Such pseudo-sensitivity seems to me to reflect the mentality of the people who have brought about this so-called enlightened legislation. But there is much more to it than that. Most of the divorces are undefended. Divorce can now proceed on the basis of a summons and the affidavit evidence of the pursuer and a supporting corroborating witness. If the affidavits *ex facie* contain sufficient evidence to satisfy legal requirements divorce can be granted without the judge seeing the witnesses and testing the accuracy and validity of the affidavit evidence. Anyone with any experience of the old system when proof had to be led before a judge knows that the credibility, reliability and truthfulness of witnesses could be assessed by the judge and the acceptability of the evidence tested by him asking questions which had not been asked by counsel. In many cases it transpired that the evidence of the supporting witness was largely, if not wholly, hearsay and incompetent. That danger is more likely to occur when it is simply incorporated in an affidavit which the pursuer's solicitor can attest. There is, moreover, a further and most objectionable factor introduced by the 1976 Act. There is a presumption that the marriage has irretrievably broken down in certain specified circumstances. Accordingly all that has to be proved is that the specified circumstances appertain. These are: 1) that there has been no cohabitation for a continuous period of two years after the date of the marriage and immediately preceding the bringing of the action and the defender consents to the divorce; and 2) that there has been no cohabitation between the parties at any time during a continuous period of five years after the date of the marriage and immediately preceding the bringing of the action. In such circumstances the defender's consent to divorce is not required. I can understand, even if I do not approve of, the reasoning underlying the first set of circumstances, but in my opinion the second set of circumstances is contrary to justice and equity and the general principles of the law of contract — and entry into marriage is entry into a contract which is bilaterally binding as long as it persists. Parliament has decreed, and it is now the law, that a spouse who has

157

been wholly responsible for the break-up of the marriage by, for example, going off to live in adultery with a third party or who has driven the other spouse out of the family home by cruel conduct, or who has deliberately broken up the family home, can, after the expiry of five years, obtain a divorce from a wholly innocent spouse even against that spouse's wishes, because of the statutory presumption.

I know of no other instance where one party to a contract can get a legal annulment of that contract even where the other, and – may I dare to say? – the innocent party wishes the contract to persist. In my view this is yet another example – enacted by Parliament and not the result of legal process – of the loosening of ethical standards and the acceptance of a laissez-faire morality. This is destroying the concept of marriage, often in the face of marriage vows solemnly undertaken, with the resultant breaking up of homes and family life. This in turn, is in my view the cause of so much delinquency and social problems among young people in our present society. Experience of divorce cases has shown that in many instances, a wife, despite the abominable treatment at the hands of her husband which caused her to leave him, has demonstrated a long-suffering patience and a lingering hope that one day they would be reunited. That attitude, difficult to understand by people not so afflicted, was summed up in the answer which was often given to the question why a wife tolerated such conduct but said she wanted her husband back: 'You see, sir, he's my man.' This attitude of mind kept manifesting itself in cases of divorce on the ground of cruelty to explain why the wife kept living with a husband who was subjecting her to the most constant physical abuse until the point was reached when she could bear it no longer.

Another factor which made many wives hang on to a marriage despite physical abuse or infidelity was the desire to keep the family together in the interests of the children of the marriage. One of the most striking examples of this 'he's my man' attitude, which could have been amusing if it had not been so tragic in its innate simplicity, was the case of a wife who was seeking divorce on the ground that her

158

husband was living in adultery with another woman. This was before the present Act came into operation, and the action was undefended. The evidence adduced to me was woefully insufficient and when I suggested that I should continue the case to allow further evidence to be led I was informed that there was no further evidence available. I could scarcely believe this because the address at which the husband was living with the other woman in Craigmillar, Edinburgh, was just round the corner from the house in which the pursuer herself was living. I knew this because the area was part of my old constituency when I was in Parliament, and I thought that it was most unlikely that such a cohabitation could be taking place without it being notorious in the locality. The poor wife had only given formal evidence and I asked her to go back into the witness box in order to find out whether she could suggest some further source of evidence. Trying a shot in the dark I asked her if she had any personal knowledge of her husband living with this other woman. She replied that she had. I asked her to explain how she had come by that knowledge and out came the most extraordinary explanation. 'A couple of weeks or so after he left me, he called at my house and told me that he had obtained a job at the potato howking [lifting]. It meant an early start and he had to be up at six o'clock in the morning. He said to me: "That lazy bitch I am living with will never get up and get me my breakfast to put me out in time. Here's a key to the house. You were always a good riser. Would you come round and waken me and make my breakfast?" ' In response to some further questions which I put to her she said that she had agreed to do as requested and had carried out her undertaking during the two weeks that the job had lasted. She felt that she had to do it because it was part of a wife's duties to make her husband's breakfast and put him out in the morning. Most important of all she said that when she went into the house each morning her husband was lying in bed with this other woman. That was sufficient, in the light of the other evidence of an admission by the husband to a neighbour, to let the wife get the divorce which she was seeking. I make no

159

attempt to psychoanalyse the attitude of mind which leads a wife to do things like that, but I know from my court experiences that this was not an isolated case. What I can analyse is the conduct of that poor woman's legal advisers who had found it impossible to obtain the compelling evidence which was so readily available and thereby put the unfortunate woman's chances of a divorce in jeopardy.

I know that I had the reputation of being a difficult judge in divorce cases and the reason for that was said to be obvious. I can place my hand on my heart and avow that I never put any difficulty in the way of a divorce if there was sufficient evidence to warrant it. What I did insist on was that there was at least the minimum of evidence which the law required before decree of divorce was granted. This insistence did not go down well in certain quarters where the 1976 Act had been anticipated and the view was being taken that the fact that a divorce had been applied for was sufficient to indicate that the marriage had broken down, in which case it was silly to insist on the standards of yesteryear. I took the view that as long as the law of yesteryear prevailed the standards of that law prevailed and should be enforced. Counsel would come into court, lead their wholly inadequate evidence and then say to me with an appealing look: 'That's my evidence, my Lord.' When I replied: 'Do you want me to give my decision on that evidence or do you wish a continuation to lead further and sufficient evidence?' the continuation was always sought, albeit counsel would leave the court with his or her instructing solicitor growling at the intransigence of the judge.

In my time on the Bench so many divorce cases, defended and undefended, passed through my hands that not many of them stand out in my memory. That is perhaps because the evidence tended to be of the same pattern according to the ground on which the action was based. Undoubtedly the most interesting case in this field with which I had to deal took place in 1958, just four years after I went on to the Bench. A husband sued his wife for divorce on the ground of her adultery, the allegation being that she had given birth to a child although the husband did not have access to her

160

during the fourteen months prior to the child's birth. The wife did not dispute this, but averred that the child had been conceived by artificial insemination by a donor (AID) which she maintained was not adultery. This was a point which had never been decided in Scotland or in Britain, although it had been considered in some other countries. There were, however, some English cases not exactly in point, containing considerations which I found helpful. I could get no assistance from the sources to which I usually had resort, namely the Scottish Institutional Writers, but they had never been called upon to consider such a problem, living as they did in the uncomplicated days before science started to innovate on nature. In the result, I decided that AID was not adultery, and as the case was never appealed the soundness of that decision was never tested. My decision was simply that the defence of AID was not irrelevant, as the husband had maintained, but it was for the wife to prove it. The wife refused to supply evidence to support her claim, and decree of divorce was granted. I thoroughly enjoyed the challenge because it meant working everything out for myself, and basing the result as best I could on principles and not on what some other judges said in other cases not exactly in point. I shall always regard *McLennan v McLennan,* 1958 SC 105 as the most interesting civil case I was called upon to decide. It is probably academic now, in view of the widening of the law and the general test under the provisions of the Divorce Act 1976, but I took much comfort in the fact that, following my decision when the question of reform of the law on the subject was debated in the House of Lords, the Lord Chancellor, Lord Kilmuir, said that while the Government took the traditional attitude of neutrality in such matters he had been much impressed by my judgment.

The fact that the reporting of the evidence in divorce cases has been banned by statute since 1926 has been a frustration to elements in the media, particularly certain reporters and critics. They have accordingly to rely on the delivered judgment of the presiding judge for such of the facts as he has deemed necessary to refer to in explanation of the matters on which his judgment is founded. Experienced and responsible court reporters know how to summarise the judge's opinion and take extracts from it without interfering with the balance of it. Responsible critics take the trouble to find out what the judge was called upon to decide and the factors which he had to take into account and observe in arriving at his decision. Not all critics, however, observe these rules. I do not suggest for a moment that there should be any censorship on the report or in the criticism of a judge's opinion, but I do say that critics should know what a judge is called upon to do before calling in question what he has done. This was very prominently displayed in a divorce case which I had to decide. There was quite an interesting point of law in the case to which I shall make reference later but it has been completely overlooked and ignored. The facts in the case had no greater interest than those in many other divorce cases based on adultery, as this one was, but the persons involved were good copy for the media and the facts took on correspondingly greater interest. To me, however, this was just another case to which the usual rules applied.

The husband was seeking divorce from his wife on the grounds of her alleged adultery. I have to draw attention once more to the fact that, since it is rarely that a party accused of adultery is caught *in flagrante delecto*, proof has to be found in the inference from facts accepted as proved. Facts, of course, are usually disputed, and the judge has to make up his mind which witnesses who are in dispute on the facts should be accepted as truthful and reliable. This is particularly important in the case of the parties themselves who usually give differing versions of the material facts in issue. In view of the possibility of an appeal against his decision, the judge has to state his reasons for accepting or rejecting or impugning the evidence of a witness, particularly in the case of a party to the action. Where adultery is alleged to have been committed by the defender, the character, and in particular the moral character, of the defender may be of importance in relation to the question of what inference should be drawn from a certain situation. Moreover, there is an old brocard in Scots law in relation to inferences of adultery. In the days when the classics were regarded as the

162

foundation of a good education in Scotland, the jurists found that things could be more delicately put in Latin than in the rougher Anglo-Saxon. The brocard runs thus: *Solus cum sola in loco suspectu non praesumitur pater noster dicere* – A man alone with a woman in a suspected place is not presumed to be saying his prayers. However, lest this should appear to smack of sex discrimination, there is the provision in the Interpretation Act which paraphrased provides, not inaptly here, that unless the context otherwise requires, the male is presumed to embrace the female. In this particular case, the wife's moral character had been put in issue by the husband who alleged her infidelity with different men. All but one of these alleged instances had taken place before an occasion when the parties spent a night together in the husband's flat in circumstances from which I inferred that condonation or forgiveness of any previous adultery by the wife had taken place. That only left for consideration a subsequent incident on which the whole decision turned, and the vital question was whether the inference of adultery could be drawn from the suspicious circumstances of that incident. There was an interesting point of law to be considered stemming from an earlier reported case where it was stated that when a man and a women engage in a situation which is capable of a guilty or an innocent interpretation, the moral characters of the parties may be of crucial importance. It was in that context that I had to make a finding of the wife's character and to give my reasons for it. There were critics who suggested that I had gone out of my way deliberately and unnecessarily to blacken the woman's character and I trust that I have nailed that one. I wonder if the same outcry would have been made if the woman had been plain Mary Smith. Certainly the same judgment would have been issued if the circumstances had been the same.

I have dealt with this at some length because judges while in office cannot reply to criticism of their conduct in the exercise of their duties when such criticism is publicly made in the media, even when the criticism is ill-conceived and ill-founded and proceeds from an obvious lack of knowledge of what is required of the judge in formulating his opinion.

Members of the legal profession, writing in legal journals or in the press, regularly criticise judgments which have been delivered and they are no respecters of persons. Of course they are perfectly entitled to do so, even though the judges cannot go into the columns of the press or legal journals to reply, and can only hope that the point will rise again in some other case and be dealt with in the only medium available, namely the official judgment. This pastime is becoming more and more popular, but in my view, since the obvious contradictor is precluded from replying, there is a responsibility on the critics to see that the complaint which is the basis of the criticism is factually or legally well founded.

The circumstances attaching to divorce cases are usually mundane and lacking in press publicity value, but some are bizarre and I had my fair share of the latter. In delivering judgment the judge has to deal with such extraordinary circumstances as the evidence has produced, but he is not looking for headlines. That, however, is the joyous field of the gentlemen of the press. In one of my cases I held that the adultery took place in that the guilty parties had inter-course in a pigsty. The quite delicate headlines in the press, 'Love in a Pigsty', have remained with me ever since then. I have always had kindly treatment from the press. In 1964 I was the guest of honour at the annual dinner of the National Union of Journalists in Glasgow. I was presented with a large diploma to recognise the occasion and given a copy of the laureation. It was in very generous terms and I was re-reading it with great pleasure when I noticed the date, which I am sure had no significance – 1 April 1964.

In recent times everything connected with sex has to be given polite and inoffensive terms and so in the context of adultery lust has become love and fornication has become making love. Undefended divorces, which were very much of a pattern, were usually boring and dull, but occasionally a bit of light relief emerged to preserve the judge's sanity. One such occasion took place during an undefended divorce action at the instance of the wife on the ground of cruelty. She gave the full catalogue of assaults and then counsel put her mother into the witness box to provide the necessary corroboration. She was a formidable looking woman, the archetype of mothers-in-law so beloved of comedians. She gave what was presented regularly as corroborative evidence in undefended divorces by repeating what her daughter had told her about the incidents. Fortunately she was able to give some valid evidence about admissions made by the husband in conversation with her. Having elicited the tale of repeated cruelty, counsel in a somewhat pontifical manner said to her: 'Then, madam, in your considered opinion, could your daughter, without danger to her life, limb or health resume cohabitation with her spouse?' The old lady looked some-what blank at this mouthful and I thought to myself, sonny boy, if you are expecting an answer to that you have some hope, when suddenly she leant forward in the witness box, glowered at counsel and barked out: 'Never on your nelly, mister. . . .' That was an emphatic answer however incompetent much of her other evidence.

Work on the Bench was not confined to the broad distinction between civil and criminal cases. Within these two broad branches there was an infinite variety of work. A new dimension to my judicial work was introduced after I was given a life peerage in 1970. This not only entitled me to sit in the House of Lords but as the holder of high judicial office I was entitled to sit in appeals to the Judicial Committee of the House of Lords, if requested to do so. As I had been made a Privy Counsellor on my appointment as Lord Advocate in 1947, I was also entitled to sit in the Judicial Committee of the Privy Council if called upon, and I sat on both these bodies. Lord Emslie, the Lord President of the Court of Session, had also been made a life peer and a Privy Councillor, and he too has sat on these committess on occasions, but the growing volume of work in the Scottish courts, both criminal and civil, became so demanding on our time that we had to refuse requests to go to London since our first commitments were to our own courts.

The qualification to sit in the Judicial Committee of the House of Lords led me into another somewhat unusual experience. It has long been a matter of comment that the permanent membership of that Committee is such that in civil appeals from Scotland you can never have more than two out of the five law lords, which is the usual number composing the court, who are Scottish judges. Of the nine Lords of Appeal who are appointed to sit regularly on appeals only two are Scottish judges. As I have already mentioned, however, any peer who holds or has held high judicial office is entitled to sit in the Judicial Committee. On one occasion I was asked to sit in an appeal from the English Court of Appeal, and three of the five judges sitting were Scottish, Lord Kilbrandon and Lord Fraser of Tullybelton being the other two. The tables had been turned. Moreover, as I was senior to all the other judges in terms of date of appointment as a peer, I had to sit on the immediate right of the chair which was occupied by Lord Simon of Glaisdale. The English counsel in the case were obviously confused by the intrusion of so many Scotsmen in their midst, as was evident by the way that the opening counsel scratched away, somewhat unsuccessfully, to put a label on the new faces (Ian Fraser having been just recently appointed), and the confusion was somewhat increased as Lord Simon kept refer-ring to me as the Lord Justice-Clerk. However, all finished up with the judges being unanimous in their decision. This was perhaps just as well. I wonder what would have hap-pened if there had been the not unknown result of 3:2 division, with three Scottish judges on one side and two English judges on the other – and that on English soil.

There is a feature of our Scottish procedure which enables us to have a halfway house to the House of Lords appeal procedure in civil cases and a full appeal procedure beyond the normal Court of Criminal Appeal in criminal cases. Our courts are restricted by decisions of higher courts which are binding on them and higher courts can overturn decisions of lower courts. As I have already mentioned, in civil cases but not in criminal ones, there is an appeal from the Court of Appeal in Scotland to the House of Lords. In both civil and criminal cases it is possible for us to convene a Fuller Court to consider a previous decision of a Scottish Appeal Court. Thus a court of five judges can be convened to reconsider a decision of three judges, a court of seven judges to reconsider a decision of three or five judges, and a Fuller Court (traditionally thirteen when that was the full complement of judges) to reconsider a decision of seven judges or less. This is a very useful expedient in criminal cases where there is no appeal to the House of Lords, and any alteration in the law might otherwise be available only through legislation, often long delayed. Two comparatively recent examples of the use of this power radically to alter aspects of the criminal law established by earlier decisions of the Criminal Appeal Court are *Lambie v HM Advocate* (1973 JC 53) and *Brennan v HM Advocate* (1977 JC 38). In *Lambie* the law relating to certain special defences was completely revised and altered by a court of five judges, and the earlier cases which had laid the foundation for the wrong approach were overruled. In *Brennan* a court of seven judges reviewed and revised the law in relation to 1) insanity at the time of the offence, and 2) diminished responsibility, when the condition on which such defences were based had been self-induced through the deliberate and voluntary consumption of alcohol or drugs. In doing so the court overruled two previous decisions which in effect had allowed a defence of such a nature to go to the jury, and specifically held that a condition so induced constituted no defence on either of the foregoing grounds. *Lambie* set the ball rolling and since then there have been a number of Fuller Court hearings to clear up the criminal law both in evidence and procedure where errors had crept in on the authority of cases which had to be overruled. Fundamental principles have replaced artificial concepts and the law and procedure have been placed on a surer and more consistent basis. I have found at Commonwealth Law Conferences that many of the Commonwealth countries are intrigued by this procedure of Fuller Courts being used to review, and if need be revise, the law where it has gone wrong through the instrumentality of previous decisions which are found to be of doubtful or indeed of no validity.

I have a postscript to write about this procedure. When a Fuller Court is convened it is normally composed of senior judges, including the Lord Justice-General/Lord President and the Lord Justice-Clerk. If the judges are unanimous it is sometimes agreed that there should be an opinion of the court rather than individual opinions. A member of the court – usually one of the two most senior judges – is chosen to write that judgment. The composer circulates a draft of the opinion to the other judges for comments or proposed amendments. If there are any of these, they are discussed and a final agreed opinion is issued in this form: 'The opinion of the court delivered by Lord X.' There are some critics within the profession who simply refer to the opinion as the opinion of Lord X, thereby giving the impression that it is the opinion of a single judge. It lends force to the criticism when the impression is given that what are being attacked are the views of one judge, whereas the collective views of all the senior judges who sat on the case might be thought to be more difficult to assail. This tactic is all the more obnoxious when the criticism is contained in a non-legal journal, whose readers may not all be aware of the procedure and the weight of opinion under attack.

The responsibility for the clearing up and the tidying up of the law in recent years reflects great credit on Lord Emslie, the Lord Justice-General, who, either by himself initiating such references to a Fuller Court or sanctioning requests for such references, has enabled substantial and beneficial changes to be made. While on the subject of the Lord Justice-General, who functions as head of the court in criminal matters while at the same time functioning as head of the court in civil matters under the title of Lord President of the Court of Session, I would like to put the following on record. In the eighteen years I spent on the Bench before I became Lord Justice-Clerk, I had no idea of the extent or the intensity of the administrative work which is laid on the shoulders of the Lord Justice-General/Lord President of the Court of Session. During my tenure of office as Lord Justice-Clerk, Lord Emslie consulted me on matters connected with the running of the courts and this gave me an insight – albeit only a partial one – into the scope and volume of the work with which he had to deal. If I started to catalogue that work

168

I would have come to a sudden halt, conscious of the fact that I was missing out more than I was putting in, so I shall not start. This was all over and above the work which he had to put in and the responsibilities he had to carry while sitting in the chair as President of the First Division Appeal Court. I have had the experience over a period of 13 years of occupying the 'chair' in an appeal court and I have some appreciation of what it involves. How George Emslie managed to fulfil his duties in both spheres I have difficulty in imagining, but I have seen the results and can vouch for the efficiency and acceptability of his labours.

When lay people see a judge walking away from court at 4 pm, they must be thinking: 'That's the life of Reilly.' Little do they know that he still has a great deal of work, and often the most difficult part of his work, to do at home. In Scotland we go in for written judgments (it is called taking the case to avizandum) on a much larger scale than is done in other jurisdictions where *ex tempore,* ie immediate, judgments find more favour. If judgments are short and uncomplicated I personally consider that *ex tempore* judgments can meet the requirements. However, if they are difficult and complicated I consider that it is desirable that they should be taken to avizandum. I am often asked how I did the judgments which I had taken to avizandum. It is a matter of personal choice, and I take the view that if it is a long or difficult one it is better to work it out in manuscript and have a fair copy typed from that rather than to dictate it on to a tape. That way it is easier to stop and think, or check back on what you have already written, and to take up the thread again after such interruptions have been concluded. This homework can take up most of the evenings and can often stretch into the wee sma' hours, and also into the weekends.

The civil courts have long vacations during Easter and summer recesses and do not sit on Mondays, but the criminal courts have no closed periods. In the more leisurely times this made life much easier for judges, but with the recent large increases in the number of criminal trials and criminal appeals these vacation periods have been considerably eroded by the number of trials which have to be arranged in Edinburgh and in the extended number of circuit towns, and criminal appeal courts which have had to be held during these erstwhile vacation periods. A vacation court sits regularly during the vacations to deal with urgent civil business, which means that judges, apart from the Lord President and the Lord Justice-Clerk, have to take their turn to be on duty. Moreover, there are always sittings of the High Court in Edinburgh to deal with cases remitted there for sentence and these cannot always be manned by the vacation judge because of the pressure of civil work in the vacation court. Like so many things, vacations for judges are not what they used to be. As for the 'free Mondays' they are more apparent than real. Apart from being useful in helping to keep the judge up to date with his homework they are convenient times for judges who have undertaken public or semi-public work to arrange meetings of the organisations or committees in which they are involved. Historically Scottish judges have a fine record in this field of public duty. This leads me inevitably to consider my own involvement in such activities.

13 Extramural activities

Lest it be thought that my keen interest in politics and the law limited my activities to these spheres, I must make it clear that my interests were spread over widely diverse fields. This provided me with mental recreation away from the confines of my normal work. In the case of a judge it enables him to see the problems of life and of current society on a much broader canvas than can be portrayed in a court room. There is a misconception in many quarters that judges live in ivory towers and are completely divorced from the realities of life that surround them. That may be due to inept remarks passed by a judge on an isolated occasion which is then regarded as typical of all judges. Nigh on fifty years ago when I was a young counsel a story was current regarding a sheriff whose court was in a working-class area in the West of Scotland. He was hearing an action for damages arising out of a motor accident, and a witness was asserting that not only had he seen the accident take place but that it had taken place at one o'clock. The sheriff asked him how he knew that it was just one o'clock and received the reply, 'Because I was going home for my dinner.' 'Nonsense man,' said the sheriff, 'no-one ever has dinner till after seven o'clock in the evening.' From such remarks general opinions of judges can be formed. Certainly experience in the criminal courts must give a judge an insight into certain aspects of life in the community, but there are many other aspects of life and its problems, and it is the connection with these other communal activities which opens fully the doors of experience.

In my time I have had a fair diversity of such activities,

171

and they can be conveniently grouped into the following categories with which I shall deal in turn. They are: 1) chairmanship or membership of government-appointed inquiries; 2) semi-public activities through association with organisations in the field of social care and public interest; and 3) personal recreation, such as playing golf and watching soccer, the latter of which saw me involved in some further spin-off activities. Golf and soccer inevitably lead to stories, and some of these I shall recount later. While I shall deal with the instances under these heads, several were taking place contemporaneously.

1 Government-appointed inquiries

The first calls made on me in this field were made shortly after I resumed practice on my return to the Bar when the war had ended. I was asked to take over the chairmanship of the Scottish Nurses' Salaries Committee, a departmental committee consisting of representatives of the employers, who were local authorities, on the one side, and representatives of the nursing profession in different grades and in different sectors, on the other, with an independent chairman. I found this to be an interesting post and one which I felt could be rewarding. There were two things which I considered to be of importance in relation to the work. The first was that I found that the leader of the employers' group always wanted to see what the counterpart body in England was doing before he would commit himself to anything. This I found to be unacceptable. The second was that the practice had been to settle the salaries at the top level first and make the way down through the differentials. In the result there was not much left for those at the bottom of the scale such as the student nurses. In certain quarters the shadow of Florence Nightingale seemed to loom over the thinking – nursing was a dedicated service which should not be sullied by mundane disputes on such matters as salaries and conditions of service. The spirit of dedication still permeates so many of our nurses at all levels, but there is no reason why in this day and age such dedication should be
172

exploited to the extent of denying them fair standards of remuneration and conditions of service. So I decided that we would reach our decisions on our own deliberations without waiting to see what happened in England, and on that basis we set about devising our own salary structure starting at the bottom and working our way up through the differentials. That, hopefully, would secure that the lowest paid would get a merited award and the higher grades would get differential awards based on that. I also wanted to set up a Nurses' Charter dealing with conditions and hours of service. This could only operate when there were sufficient nurses to operate it, and this created a vicious circle, because recruitment was only likely to be successful in the numbers required if the Charter conditions were implemented and adequate salaries provided. We were working hard on this when I had to resign on being appointed Solicitor-General in March 1947. In any event, the committee came to an end with the introduction of the National Health Service which had to have its own structure with different employers. I had likewise to resign my chairmanship of the committee to inquire into the production of milk in Scotland, to which I had also been appointed. My parliamentary and ministerial duties precluded me from undertaking any such committee work, and I had several years away from it until I left Parliament.

Early in the 1960s, I undertook the chairmanship of a governmental inquiry into the teaching profession in Scotland. I was a bit doubtful at first as to what the committee might achieve because most of the members were representative of different and often conflicting interests in the field of education. However, at our first meeting I reminded the members that we were functioning in a semi-judicial capacity and not as a house of representatives, and they responded magnificently throughout the whole work of the committee. In the end we produced a unanimous report, the recommendations of which were accepted by the Government and resulted in the Teaching Council (Scotland) Act 1965 being enacted whereby the General Teaching Council for Scotland was established – something which the teachers

173

had been anxious to achieve for a very long time and without which they had felt that they were in an inferior position to other professional bodies which already had established councils.

In 1964, I was appointed a member of the Royal Commission on the Penal System in England and Wales under the chairmanship of Lord Amery who, as Heathcoate Amery, had been Minister of Transport and Chancellor of Exchequer in Conservative governments. I was the only non-English (or Welsh) member of the Commission, but I found myself playing a very full part in its deliberations. So much so that when Lord Amery was unable to attend meetings he asked me to take the chair. I found that at least some of my colleagues were very interested in and intrigued by various aspects of the Scottish penal system which I brought to their notice. I, in turn, received ample compensation from the insight which I obtained into the English system and by a visit to the United States to see how the various forms of penal system operated in certain selected states and in the federal jurisdiction. Unfortunately, this Royal Commission came to an abrupt halt in 1966 without reporting, although much work had been done. In fact some of the branches into which the work had been divided were completed. The Commission was composed of people representing a variety of disciplines and experiences, and a division arose not so much in my opinion from irreconcilable views as from irreconcilable personalities. This produced an *impasse* in the drawing together of the different aspects of our work for the purposes of a report, and this was reported to the Home Secretary, Roy Jenkins. Owing to government changes, he was the third Home Secretary during the two years of the Commission's existence, the other two being Reginald Maudling and Frank Soskice, and he decided without any full consultation with the members that the Commission should be disbanded. The work which had been done was not wasted, however, as arrangements were made for our papers to be passed over to the Criminal Law Revision Committee for their use. From my own personal viewpoint I had learned much and experienced a great deal. A study

174

of the penal systems of other countries is not a proselytizing exercise but is one where consideration should be given to the question of whether certain aspects of the other systems could, with profit be grafted into one's own system. It is a two-way exercise which can be mutually beneficial.

I had just been severed from a connection with one Royal Commission when I became involved with another. In 1966, I was appointed Chairman of the Royal Commission on Local Government in Scotland. This was a challenging but absorbing remit on which three years of hard work and careful thought were spent. Changes in local government structure have tended to follow a 40-year cycle in Scotland, and the fundamental changes which were recommended were not likely to meet with universal approval. Radical changes, however necessary, seldom are, human nature being what it is. The tendency to judge proposals by subjective rather than objective criteria is very strong. Yet our report in 1969 both in its major recommendations, which were unanimous, and in the modifications thereof in structural details as suggested by a minority of our members formed the basis of the Local Government (Scotland) Act 1973 on which the new and existing system of local government in Scotland is founded. There is much which could be written on it — and much has — but this is not the vehicle for such an exercise. There is, however, one thing which I feel compelled to say. Some of the criticisms of the report seemed to suggest that we had just plucked our recommendations out of thin air without regard to local interests. I have to put on record that we reached our conclusions only after careful study of all the evidence, written and oral, before us, and all the submissions made by interested parties, as well as the product of the careful and detailed research by our Intelligence Unit, all of which were made public along with our report. In particular we published the criteria on which we determined the areas of the different authorities, these criteria having been derived from careful research by the Unit. By custom the report of a Royal Commission is referred to by the name of its chairman and certain people have talked about the recommendations of the Wheatley

175

Report as if they were things which I had devised out of my own mind.

The Commission was a broadly based body, but we worked as a unit. We were unanimous in our view that a completely new structure of local government was called for and that it should be a two-tier structure of regional and district authorities with appropriate functions being allotted to each. There were, of course, minority views on such matters as the need for all-purpose island authorities, the boundary lines of authorities and the allocation of functions. Minority reports can be healthy things, provided they are based on solid foundations. They can indicate that matters have been thoroughly considered before decisions have been made and that members had an independence of mind. Moreover, they give greater strength to the other matters on which there were unanimous views, rather than weaken the recommendations as a whole. In our case, some of the recommendations in the minority reports, such as the need for all-purpose island authorities, appealed to the Government when the Bill was being prepared, and Parliament endorsed that view. There was complete harmony among the members during the long hours of our three years' deliberations and visits to local authorities at home and abroad. The intrusion into private time was increased by the large amount of homework which was entailed. One of the important things which in my opinion we did, and which I regret to say has received little, if any, notice in the corridors of power, was to formulate what we conceived to be a philosophy of the role of local government in the scheme of things. In Scotland local government, like Topsy, had 'just growed', and had developed piecemeal and without pattern, so that the old system was punctuated by anomalies and inaccuracies. I regret to say that in recent years the role which we had unanimously envisaged for local government in the scheme of things has been badly eroded and the concept of local democracy as its base has been badly dented.

I found the work of the Royal Commission interesting, educational and rewarding. Moreover, it provided me with an experience which I consider worthy of recounting, not because of the personal pleasure which it afforded me but because of the insight which it gave me into the way in which Her Majesty the Queen carries out her duties, many of which are wholly unknown to her subjects, whose knowledge of her duties and responsibilities is confined to the coverage which her public appearances are given by the media.

Shortly after the Report of the Royal Commission was issued I received an information from Buckingham Palace that Her Majesty was pleased to grant me an audience to discuss the Report. That audience duly took place, and for almost an hour the Queen quizzed me in detail about various aspects of our Report and our recommendations. What particularly impressed me was her detailed knowledge of the Report and its recommendations, which betokened several hours of careful study devoted to them. If it is thought that her interest in such matters is a pure formality, my experience provided the complete contradiction.

In February 1971, I was asked by the Home Secretary and the Secretary of State for Scotland to conduct a one-man Inquiry into Crowd Safety at Sports Grounds. This was prompted by the Ibrox disaster at the beginning of that year, and I restricted my inquiry primarily into the problems at soccer grounds. However, because of the potential identity of problems at rugby union and rugby league grounds, I included them as well. My lifelong interest in soccer made an interesting task that much more interesting. The only assurance which I could give when I undertook the inquiry was that there would be no minority reports or reservations. I am glad to say that my report, which recommended the licensing of these grounds by the appropriate local authority, was accepted by the Government and translated into legislation in the form of the Safety of Sports Grounds Act 1975.

2 Semi-public activities

In 1956, shortly after I went on to the Bench, I accepted the office of Chairman of the Executive Committee of the Royal Scottish Society for the Prevention of Cruelty to Children, and occupied that office for the next 23 years. I thoroughly enjoyed those years with the RSSPCC. The work was very worthwhile and of great social importance. The members of the various committees who gave their services voluntarily were drawn from every part of the country and from practically every walk of life. They were charming people who worked unsparingly for the Society. The members of the staff – both in the field and on the administrative side – were imbued with the same spirit, and the work which they did was tremendous. During my time we were very fortunate in having consecutively as General Secretary two such dedicated people as Claude Cumming-Forsyth (1934–1968) and Arthur Wood (1969– to date), both of whom had their public service recognised in Honours lists. The Society celebrated its centenary in 1984 and Brian Ashley has written a comprehensive history of its work. I can best illustrate the efforts put in by the members of the Society and the staff by setting out briefly the task (which hangs round the necks of all charitable bodies) of finding the money to keep the work going. Even with the changing value of money and ever-increasing costs, the rise in expenditure has been phenomenal. In 1956 the expenditure of the Society was £59,000. In 1979 it was £685,000 and in 1984 it was £951,000. The largest item of expenditure is the salaries of our operators in the field, the inspectors and (women) visitors, who carry out the work for which the Society exists – the *prevention* of cruelty to children. Their efforts, the goodwill which the Society has engendered in the public eye and the public support which all this has created, have seen the Society through these gigantic problems.

In 1968, I was appointed as a Privy Council nominee for membership of the University Court of the new University of Stirling and was elected to be the first Chairman of that body. I occupied that position for the next eight years and had then to retire under the provisions of the University's Charter. The history of the foundation and growth of that university, its development, its troubles and its triumphs over adversities, merit a book on its own, and the demands

178

of space in this book are such that I must confine myself to a few generalisations. To make a tribute inadequately is perhaps worse than making no tribute at all, and on that basis I must ask my many friends at Stirling University to excuse my seemingly short reference to my connection with it. It was a great privilege and a great experience to be so closely involved in the establishment of an entirely new university in Scotland for the first time in centuries. We started in a single building called Pathfoot, which housed everything – lecture rooms, administrative offices, the lot. We had 150 students. Plans for the physical and academic development and the building-up of relationships had to be made and put into operation and these matters were all spearheaded by the Principal. We were fortunate in four of the key positions in the university. The first Chancellor was Lord Robbins who was a giant of a man physically and mentally, with a great track record in public service and a noted educationalist. The Principal and Vice-Chancellor was Dr Tom Cotterill, whose energy and drive in the tasks which had to be faced during those early formative years produced excellent results. Together with the trauma of the incidents which occurred during the visits of Her Majesty the Queen to the university, which received widespread publicity in the media, these labours undoubtedly played a major role in his early and tragic death. Perhaps we ought to have realised that the complexity and burden of the responsibilities which he took upon himself were too much for one man and we should have insisted on some of these being taken off his shoulders. He was such an enthusiast and so dedicated to his job that it was difficult to put an effective brake on his activities. The first Secretary was Harry Donnelly who came from the Education Department in St Andrew's House and was eminently equipped for the job. Bob Bomont was the Finance Officer and his clearheadedness and ability to get directly to the kernel of a problem proved to be of great value both in those early and difficult days and in the later periods which brought problems of their own. In due course he became Secretary of the university, a post which he still holds.

The plan was to make Stirling a campus university and a more beautiful site for one would be difficult to find. I thought that my official duties would require my attendance at the university only for meetings of the Court and, in due course, graduations. How wrong I was, but may I say what a pleasure it was to journey through from Edinburgh if only to see that wonderful setting and enjoy the company of the friends I made, particularly during those early and thrilling days. The calls on my time were greatly increased by unfortunate incidents. Harry Donnelly died early on and the position of Secretary had to be filled. I had to preside over the Selection Committee and this meant meetings. Then there were the unfortunate incidents during the Queen's visit which occasioned the need for further meetings to consider matters arising therefrom, such as disciplinary measures. I took no part in the disciplinary trials since I had to preside over any appeals which resulted, and which in fact I did. We had had relatively little student trouble before this, but the incident was stage-managed, and not solely from within the university. I am glad to say that the university has overcome the unfavourable publicity which resulted. Its academic progress and achievements evidence this. A successor had to be found for Tom Cotterill and again I was Chairman of the Selection Committee. With all the advertising for the post that had to take place, with the consequential vetting of applications and subsequent interviews with selected applicants, a great deal of time was consumed. To suit everyone's convenience these meetings took place in the evenings, which meant I had to motor through to Stirling after a full day in court and usually was lucky if I managed to get home much before midnight – to open my court bag and read what papers I required to read for my following day's work. It was all worthwhile since it was important to get the right person for the post. This we did in appointing Dr William Cramond as the new Principal. He is a man of wide experience and distinction who slotted into the position quietly and efficiently in a remarkably short space of time. This transition was made easier by the splendid work done during the interregnum by Professor Fred Holliday and
180

Professor Jim Trainer who undertook the role of Acting Principal in turn. They were not content simply to carry out a holding operation, but advanced the development of the university through difficult times with marked success. Bill Cramond carried on this good work, and ere long he had brought serenity and prosperity to the university despite the financial restrictions which have become a feature of modern university life.

During all these extramural activities I was determined that they should not trespass on my judicial duties, from which I sought absence only on rare occasions and then only in an emergency. I found time for these other affairs in what was euphemistically called my spare time. The selection process had to be gone through again when the replacement for Harry Donnelly retired as University Secretary and Bob Bomont was appointed. I have nothing but the happiest memories of my association with Stirling University. The work was interesting and absorbing. I made many good friends among the members of the Court and members of the academic and administrative staff. I have a lasting memento of that association in the honorary degree of Doctor of the University which was conferred on me on my retirement in 1976, something which sits comfortably with the honorary degree of Doctor of Laws which my own University of Glasgow conferred upon me in 1964.

When I was appointed Lord Justice-Clerk in 1972 I found that I had to undertake more committee responsibilities by virtue of my new office. I was Chairman of the Secretary of State's Advisory Committee on Justice of the Peace, whose principal work was in connection with the District Courts which were set up to replace the old JP and Police Courts. I was also Chairman of the Sir James Duncan Trust, founded by the former MP to give awards to members of the public who had given assistance to the police in the exercise of their duties. This was a very commendable public-spirited gesture to encourage a much-needed but seldom implemented activity in our society today. I also became a Commissioner of Queen Victoria School, Dunblane. While each of these commitments was in itself not too onerous, collectively they

181

occupied a great deal of my time. I am not suggesting that I was overworked. I always made my judicial duties the first priority and as long as I did not allow meetings to clash with that work it was simply a matter of finding time. When you are busy you have to find ways and means of getting through your work quickly. And when you find yourself voluntarily taking on more work, it is clear that you know that you can find the time for it.

When soccer players won the right to have freedom of contract it was found necessary to set up an independent tribunal to determine the compensation to be paid in those instances where the clubs could not agree on a figure for a transfer fee. I was asked by the Scottish Football League to act as the independent chairman of the tribunal which determines disputes of that nature when both are Scottish clubs and to be Scotland's representative on an international tribunal which determines disputes between clubs in different parts of the United Kingdom. To one who spent quite a number of years at the Bar with experience of how reparation actions for personal injury are settled, the way that a player's talents and potential keep expanding or retracting according to whether the evaluation comes from the selling or the buying club causes me no surprise. An independent and objective assessment is called for and that is why the tribunal is there.

I then agreed to be Chairman of the Hampden Appeal, instituted by Queen's Park FC, to ingather funds to enable alterations and improvements to be made to bring up to the standards for which modern conditions and safety requirements call, the ground which for so long has been recognised as Scotland's national stadium. The response to the appeal has been very satisfactory and the planning has been such that a changeover to an all-seated, covered stadium will one day be achieved. Major alterations and improvements have in fact already taken place.

For years I have been a trustee of the Catholic Radio and TV Centre at Hatch End in Middlesex, and although the trustees require to meet only once a year, urgent matters arise from time to time which call for visits to Hatch End.

182

The original Director there was my old class-mate at St Aloysius College, Father Agnellus Andrew, OFM, who created and developed the Centre, and was the embodiment of the Centre until he was obliged to retire on his appointment as a Bishop with special duties in the field of communication at the Vatican. I was also involved in the field of communications for a short period when I was the Scottish Catholic representative on the Central Religious Advisory Committee on Broadcasting under the chairmanship of Dr Runcie, then Bishop of St Albans. Unfortunately for me the meetings of this committee took place on a Wednesday in London, and I did not feel justified in repeatedly asking time off from my judicial duties to attend these mid-week meetings. I was accordingly obliged to tender my resignation, which I did with great regret as the work seemed to me to be both interesting and worthwhile.

While I was still Chairman of the Executive Committee of the RSSPCC, I was asked to become Honorary President of Age Concern (Scotland), a position which I still hold. This is an enthusiastic organisation doing a splendid job of work for the older generations of our community, and it has brought me back into participation in problems which exercised me considerably when I was a Member of Parliament.

My association with these various bodies and activities has provided abundant evidence of the great amount of voluntary work undertaken by people in Scotland through different organisations. It is heart-warming to see the concern which these people have for others, be they young or old, or in between, who are in need of help or support in some shape or another. It is a pleasure to be associated with them. I have also become associated recently with two projects for the mentally handicapped and I am very impressed with the care and patience which characterise the people who are associated with this particular social problem. Most of my connections have been related to people and their problems, and not with buildings, but for some years now I have been a trustee of the Scottish Churches Architectural Heritage Trust. This has been set up to provide financial support to

183

churches of all denominations for the repair and preservation of churches with an architectural heritage. The executive work of the Trust is carried out by the Council, of which the trustees are members, but the trustees have the overall responsibility for the administration of the Trust and its funds. So far a substantial number of grants have been made to churches of different denominations, but, as in the case of so many charitable bodies at the present time, the inflow of money is limited and the competition for it is keen. This spread of interests makes life much more interesting and it is a positive antidote to stagnation in one's later years.

There were many compensations attached to the duties which were undertaken. For instance, the trustees of the Catholic Radio and TV Centre at Hatch End are the Metropolitan Archbishops of Scotland, England and Wales (and this has included two Cardinals) and three laymen of whom I am one. It was a great pleasure not only to meet but to work with such eminent churchman. I have had a long personal friendship with Cardinal Gray since his episcopal ordination in 1951 as the Archbishop of St Andrews and Edinburgh. He became an outstanding figure not only in his own church but in the communal life of Scotland. He was created Cardinal Priest in 1969, the final accolade in his priestly career. He played a leading part in the bringing together of churches and his efforts in ecumenism were fully reciprocated by leading churchmen in other denominations. The greatest personal satisfaction which he must have obtained was from playing host to Pope John Paul II when he made his historic visit to Scotland, and in arranging meetings between the Pope and leading figures in other churches in Christian fellowship. The advance in ecumenism in Scotland is something which has afforded me the greatest degree of satisfaction and pleasure. Cardinal Gray and I usually travelled together to London for meetings of trustees at Hatch End. This companionship was simply an extension of the personal companionship which we enjoyed over the years, and found expression in such things as pouring out tea for the old folk at their annual Christmas party in the Cathedral Hall, or in cross-talk at Catholic dinners where it

184

seemed inevitable that I should have to propose the toast of the Hierarchy and the Clergy and he should reply. It happened so often that I suggested to him that it would be a pleasant novelty if we reversed the roles, since he could give a much more illuminating insight into the Hierarchy and Clergy and I had sufficient experience to present a plea in mitigation in reply. We marched along together for many years and we both retired in 1985.

The Commissioners of Queen Victoria School were an interesting mixture. The Acting Chairman of the Board was the General Officer Commanding Scottish Command for the time being, and there was a substantial number of former high-ranking officers in the different services, some of whom had been GOC Scottish Command in their day. The lay members came from the fields of education, business and administration, thus constituting a wide body of experience and my association with them was as beneficial as it was enjoyable.

The people whom I met and worked with in the other spheres of activity were from many different walks of life, but they had one thing in common – a strong streak of public-spiritedness which had to find expression in some form of good work. Despite misconceptions in some quarters that membership of such bodies bring financial rewards, it cannot be stressed too emphatically that these people give their services voluntarily, and are often out-of-pocket in the process. The spread of friendship which all this engendered has made life that much more pleasurable for me, as have the many contacts which I have made in the legal profession, with my colleagues as a judge and in my political career. As I have been penning these words I have been asked, and have agreed, to act as President of the Scottish Council for the International Year of Shelter for the Homeless, which is a United Nations Year in 1987. It is comforting to think that at 78 one is still regarded as being in circulation.

I trust that I have not given the impression that life for me was all work and no play. Since I was a boy I have always had time for good holidays and pleasurable recreations, as I hope I can now demonstrate.

3 Holidays and recreations

As a boy, I spent a good deal of my school holidays in Comrie. My parents usually took us for a summer holiday during July or August. Our venue was usually one of the Clyde resorts and we normally rented a house for the period. This involved taking bed and table linen and cutlery as well as the usual paraphernalia, necessitating the use of that essential piece of family equipment, a hamper. As we did not have a car, public transport had to be used to get to the railway terminus or to one of the steamers which plied the Clyde resorts. The old Glasgow tramways were just the thing for this. Each route had a different colour of tramcar, green, blue, white, red or yellow, and so was instantly identifiable from afar. The green tramcars which passed through Shettleston took you to all the main stations and many of them went past the Broomielaw where some of the steamers had their starting-points. Others started from Gourock or Wemyss Bay or Craigendoran which involved a train journey. The hamper could be placed on the tram driver's platform thereby preventing it from being an obstruction to passengers.

I know of no finer sailing area than the Firth of Clyde and our destination was always one of the watering places, some reachable by train, others by boat: The three railway companies, the Caledonian, the North British and the Glasgow and South Western, had their own boats, each recognisable by its individual colour of funnel. The competition for passengers resulted in exciting races for piers such as Dunoon. This caused great excitement among the passengers who vociferously urged their own steamer to greater efforts. The steamers and the piers bore evidence of this competition, because the former were often driven too fast for the delicate manoeuvre required to take the latter in safety. The fares on the steamers were cheap and the sail 'doon the watter' was one of the highlights of the holiday. Alas, one by one these old steamers, each with its own attractive name, have disappeared from the scene, and I feel that I share with many other people the hope that one day we shall see their modern counterparts gracing the waters of the Firth of Clyde. In the meantime all that we have are nostalgic memories of the *Lord of the Isles* and *Jeanie Deans* and all the other characters, which are brought back to life when we see the wonderful collection of models kept by Canon Sidney McEwan in his house in Dunoon.

In my boyhood I had several very pleasant holidays in Ireland, the south of England and in France to which I was taken by my Uncle John and Aunt Mary as a companion for my cousin John Patrick. After our marriage, North Berwick was a convenient and favourite stand-by. The children loved it, and there was always plenty for them to do. It was also convenient for me when I was at the Bar and when I was Lord Advocate because I could always nip into Edinburgh at short notice if required. We interspersed our visits to North Berwick with holidays in other parts of Scotland such as Barra, the island of Seil, Ballater, Crail and Crieff. The peace and tranquillity of Barra, its lovely beaches, one of which we often had to ourselves, and the friendliness of the people made our holiday there a perfect one. The holiday on a farm on Seil was made memorable by one factor in particular. A little tongue of the Atlantic makes its way inland to form the island and it becomes so narrow that it is crossed by a humpbacked bridge over which we regularly passed. When our youngest child, Michael, who was just over five years old, went back to school he kept boasting to his classmates that during the holidays he had crossed the Atlantic 48 times!

We had many happy family holidays, but inevitably these had to come to an end as the children grew up and left the nest. Nonetheless on different occasions we had Kathleen, John, Patrick and Michael with us when we went on holiday, if they had not arranged to go on a type of holiday suitable for young and energetic adolescents but wholly unsuitable for ageing geriatrics. On such occasions, however, Nancy and I still played tennis with whoever came along with us with progressive lack of success. Tony joined the Society of Jesus immediately after leaving school and his holidays with us terminated. Ironically, this opened up new holidays for

187

Nancy and me, taking us to places where otherwise we might never have been. For instance, when he was a student at Fordham University we went to New York to visit him. We spent a week in New York itself where Tony joined us daily and conducted us around. As the university was on vacation, he had ample free time to do so, except for one day in the week when he regularly visited a school in the outskirts of Harlem and taught black and Puerto Rican children English and civics, and engaged them in discussions on current affairs. We spent a few days with Mr and Mrs Carey, friends of Kathleen and Tam, in Washington DC, and then went for a week to colonial Williamsburg where Tony joined us. This is a most interesting town. It is steeped in the history of the American Revolution and the characters associated with it. Beginning in 1927 it has been restored, mainly at the expense of John D Rockfeller Jr, to what it was like at that historic time. The various trades which operated then are reproduced and the costumes and clothing of those days are worn by the inhabitants. Thousands of visitors flock to it, and while cynics might accuse it of being a gimmick, we found it full of interest and legitimate history. One of the most satisfying features is that motor-cars are banned within the city limits. Free buses circle the town at regular intervals, and there is a peace and tranquillity which is a joy to people whose lives are lived in the jungle of modern traffic. When we left Williamsburg, Tony had to return to Fordham, and we made for Alexandria, outside Washington DC, to spend a few days with old friends T J and Margaret Gragg. We first met them when T J was the Colonel Commandant of the US base at Kirknewton outside of Edinburgh in the 1960s. They are a delightful couple who had charmed many Edinburgh people with their friendliness and hospitality during their stay here. Indeed T J had won an award presented by the US authorities to the officer I/C the unit based in other countries which had established the best relations with the local community. This may have been a public relations exercise, but the award mirrored the personal character and activities of T J and his helpmate Margaret who, despite crippling disabilities which were an

188

aftermath of a severe attack of polio, was a charming hostess full of vitality, and a dear friend of ours.

We were to travel from Williamsburg to Alexandria by Greyhound Bus, and when we discovered at the bus terminus that the journey would last several hours without any break for refreshment Nancy asked me to go to the sweet counter to get some biscuits for the journey. When I enquired what kind of biscuit she suggested something like Jacob's chocolate biscuits. I doubted if they had heard of such 'cookies' in Williamsburg but manfully I tried. I went to the sweet counter, behind which was a lady who looked as if she had come out of a book or a film. She was of average height but of comely build. She had deep brown skin, flashing eyes, beautiful white teeth and a radiant smile. When I tentatively asked if she had any chocolate cookies, she beamed at me and said in a southern drawl: 'Honey child, I'se the only chocolate thing left here.' I was sure that she spotted a rookie and was putting on an act, so I muttered a polite thank you, to receive the inevitable 'You're welcome,' and returned to Nancy to report failure. We spent a few very happy days with T J and Margaret and their sons Jim and Charlie and a housekeeper who hailed from Bathgate. She had been their housekeeper at Kirknewton and had gone with them when they returned to the States. We left Alexandria and made for Long Island where we spent a final week. Tony was within a reasonable distance, and as he had obtained the use of an old dilapidated car he spent most of the time with us.

In due course Tony went to Mexico to undergo a course in theology as part of his vocational training. Inevitably we landed in Mexico City to spend some time with him. Mexico is a land of amazing inconsistencies and contradictions standing virtually side by side. Space does not permit me to write all that I might about that unfortunate land – unfortunate at least for such a large percentage of the population. We decided that we all needed a restful holiday, and as Tony had acquired the use of a car, we set out to Acapulco, taking a Jesuit colleague of Tony with us. We rented a flat for a week, and during that time we lazed a lot and bathed a lot. It was very interesting but it was impossible not to be

189

thinking constantly of the comparison of this holiday playground with the stark poverty which we had seen elsewhere
in Mexico. On the way home from Mexico we made a
diversion to San Francisco which Nancy was anxious to see.
I had been there during my visit to the States in connection
with the Royal Commission on the penal system in England
and Wales and liked it. We stayed in Redwood City on the
outskirts of San Francisco as the guests of Eddie and Helen
Cody and enjoyed touring Northern California with them.
Of the limited number of cities which I have visited in the
States, San Francisco is the one in which I could have lived.

Now that Tony is back in Britain, and has been stationed
in London, Liverpool and now Manchester, the incentive to
extend our holiday travels to places where he is located
has waned. Instead we seek more leisurely yet interesting
holidays such as sailing down the Rhine and the Danube.
Both the sailing and the intermediate stops at places of great
interest provide a restful and yet interesting holiday for
people of our age and we have enjoyed such a holiday in
the past two years.

Holidays naturally make one think of recreations.
Although soccer and golf were my favourite sports, tennis
and swimming were our holiday recreations. This was not
because we were exceptionally proficient at them but because
we could all indulge in them together. At school I played
both soccer and rugby but when I left school I opted for
soccer. My first team was the Shettleston Guild of Youth
team for which I elected to play rather than join the soccer
section of the Glasgow University Sports Club. Just as I
chose to carry out my political activities locally in Shettleston
rather than at the university, so I decided to engage in
my sporting activities locally. Had I wanted to follow my
football career further afield I think that I would have sought
entry to one of the junior sides of Queen's Park FC, the
team for which as a boy I had a great liking, no doubt
hoping that I would make my way up to the senior side.
My interest in Queen's Park has persisted and I felt honoured
when I was asked to propose the health of the Club at its
Centenary dinner. In due course I signed for Shettleston

190

Celtic, one of the two junior clubs in Shettleston at the time, the other one being Shettleston FC, for whom I would have sooner played but was not asked to do so at that time. I played several seasons for Shettleston Celtic with some measure of success in goal scoring while at the same time managing to graduate MA, LLB at the university. My success at goal scoring, while playing as a half-back in the days before the elastic phrase mid-field player was devised, stemmed from a certain proficiency which I had acquired through practice in what are now called dead-ball situations. I had also acquired a technique for penalty kicks which proved productive in results. Shettleston Celtic eventually folded up, which was not surprising since it had been living on a shoestring for a long time. When this happened Shettleston FC asked me to sign and I agreed. This afforded me great pleasure, because when I decided to confine my football to my immediate locality I had hoped that one day I would play for 'the Town'. This I proceeded to do, but alas for only one season. During that season I managed to maintain my goal-scoring efforts from free kicks and penalty kicks and I was asked to re-sign for the following season but I had perforce to refuse. The reason was that I was due to be called to the Bar. That meant that I had to move to Edinburgh and stay there. Then there was always the chance of injury, which might not only affect my playing fitness but could affect temporarily any practice at the Bar which I was trying to develop. So reluctantly I said no, but I have retained a keen interest in the Club from afar and have been its Honorary President for several years.

I have kept my interest in the game alive as a spectator. For many years my old friend and parliamentary colleague the late Jimmy Hoy, who was MP for Leith and then became a life peer, joined me in regular attendance at Easter Road and Tynecastle on alternate Saturday afternoons watching the fortunes and misfortunes of the Hibernians and Heart of Midlothian. The Scottish Football Association and the Scottish Football League have been very kind over the years in having me as their guest at their games and it is these to which I now normally give my attention. For nigh on eight years I have not gone to a club match in Edinburgh or elsewhere. My interest in the game has not been confined to spectating in my later years, as is evidenced by my involvement in safety in sports grounds, the compensation tribunals and the Hampden Appeal to which I have already referred.

I was only false to my allegiance to soccer once. St Mungo's Academy in Glasgow, which in my schooldays at St Aloysius College was the only other Catholic secondary school in the area, had changed from soccer to rugby as the school game. Some former pupils of the Academy wished to form a FP Rugby XV, but not having played rugby themselves they had to start from scratch. Someone who knew that I had played rugby at Mount St Mary's asked me if I would join them as a guest player. This was after I had been called to the Bar, but despite the reasons which had decided me to give up playing junior football I succumbed and agreed. I was beginning to feel the lack of intense physical exercise and decided to take the risk. It was surprising how quickly the lads took to the game and what was lacking in finesse was compensated for by enthusiasm. I spent two seasons with them and enjoyed every minute of the time. I only gave up because I was getting married before the next season began. In the two seasons I played I escaped injury with the exception of a slight concussion on one occasion but I felt that to carry on in the face of the impending nuptials might be tempting providence. This defection to rugby had an amusing outcome. Several years later I was through in Glasgow opening a fete for a charity and as I was walking round after the official opening I was introduced to a very attractive young lady. She greeted me thus: 'I have been dying to meet you. I have your photograph over my bed.' I was beginning to realise how film stars must feel when they meet their public, but when she spoke again she brought me back down to earth with a bang. 'You see, it's a photograph of the St Mungo's FP Rugby XV and my husband was in the team along with you.' This naturally takes me to stories of football and golf.

4 Tales of football and golf

Football stories are legion and one could fill a book with them. Accordingly, I must of necessity be selective. Freed from the call of rugby duty I was able to resume my attendance at senior soccer matches. A number of my contemporaries at St Aloysius College were in the habit of congregating at the old half-time board on the west terracing at Celtic Park, and I knew that I could meet them there any time Celtic were playing at home. As I was by this time reasonably well established in my practice at the Bar and was usually engaged in one or more undefended divorce actions on the Saturday morning, I could only get to a match at Celtic Park if I made my way hurriedly from court in Edinburgh to the Park via Waverley and Queen Street stations and a taxi to the ground. On one occasion, Celtic were playing Queen's Park, the two clubs which shared my affection at that time. I had been held up in court and when I reached the ground the game had started. From there on the story belongs to my old friend and classmate Brian Maguire. This is how he related it to me. 'Queen's had made a very clever move which almost resulted in a goal. I applauded the effort, whereupon one of the Celtic faithful with a green and white scarf round his neck glowered at me for what he obviously regarded as an act of near treason. "What are you clapping that lot for?" quoth he. "Look here, my man," I said, "I, too, am a Celtic supporter, but I always appreciate good football and if I see good football I applaud it, no matter from what source it comes." Feeling rather smug, I turned round and saw you just arriving – sporting a bowler hat, wearing a black jacket and waistcoat with black striped trousers, and carrying a rolled umbrella in one hand and a briefcase in the other, exactly as the up-and-coming advocate should be dressed, but also the cartoonist's concept of the traditional Queen's Park supporter. I greeted you and you returned the greeting. Whereupon the representative of the faithful snorted and said to me, "And I suppose he's a bloody Celtic supporter too."'

The strongest argument against the highly desirable all-seated stadium is the fact that the wit of the terraces might be lost to football. Perhaps the cream of the stories is the one told to me by a Partick Thistle director. On a very wet day the rain had washed out the whitewash markings on the pitch at Firhill and resort had to be made to the use of sawdust for marking the lines. Shades of my young days! Thistle had a player who sported the modern hairstyle of some footballers – hair down to his shoulders. This is only an apparent handicap if the player breaks sweat. The player was having a bad game and when going for a long pass he slipped and his hair fell among the sawdust. He stood up and started to shake his head vigorously in order to dislodge the sawdust. At this point one of the long-suffering Thistle supporters who was standing in the enclosure directly below the director's box, turned round and shouted up to the directors: 'Take him off – he's split his heid.' *Sic transit gloria mundi* – Firhill style!

Bigotry in football is a deplorable thing, but it can have its lighter sides. Celtic had strong Catholic and Irish connections in its origin as a club but never had any religious disqualification in their signing of players. They signed a young Protestant who had great footballing potential. In due course he made the first team and played in his first match which was away from home. He had a very good game and Celtic won. When he came into the dressing room after the game, he slumped down on the bench, the picture of dejection. Jimmy McGrory, Celtic's star centre forward, who was a kindly soul, sat down beside him, put his arm round his shoulders and said: 'What's wrong son?' 'It's that crowd,' came the reply. 'They got me down. They kept calling me a Papist bastard.' Jimmy said consolingly: 'Don't let that worry you. I'm called that nearly every time we play away from home and I don't let it worry me.' The youngster was not to be consoled for he replied: 'It's all right for you, Jimmy, but you are one.'

Lest it be thought from what I have written about my own football days that I was something special I must recount this incident. In the 1929 Parliamentary Election at the age of twenty-one, I was addressing an open-air meeting in

194

Parkhead in support of my Uncle John's candidature. The election agent, John Oliver, was mooching around the back of the crowd to get the reactions. He heard one man say to his mate: 'Is that young Wheatley that plays for the Chips?' (The Chips was the local pet name for Shettleston Celtic.) 'Aye.' 'Well he's a bloody sight better speaker than he is a fitba' player!'

I got a great deal of satisfaction out of golf which I took up after I left school. I was a member of Sandyhills Golf Club in Shettleston, and played there regularly until I went through to the Bar in Edinburgh. I had a regular four-ball match on a Saturday morning – a fact which I did not disclose to the football clubs for which I played in the afternoon. I never felt that the morning exercise ever affected my physical condition for the afternoon game. In Edinburgh I became a member of the Royal Burgess Club at Barnton, and later I also joined Dalmahoy. I did so because a great friend of mine was a member there and as we played a lot together I did not like going too often as his guest. His name was Bernard McAllister, known affectionately by all and sundry as 'Wee Mac', a man of sterling character, sincerity, simplicity and good humour, with a most infectious chuckle. He may not have been the world's best golfer but he was arguably the world's most enthusiastic one. He kept his golfing gear in the boot of his car against the chance of getting a few holes wherever he might be. On one occasion on his way back to Edinburgh from a business trip in the North of Scotland he made a diversion to Dalmahoy for a few holes before darkness fell. So great was his haste that he did not go into the club-house to change, but changed in his car and made his way direct to the first tee with his clubs at the alert. He confessed to being a bit nonplussed at the smiles on the faces of the people whom he passed. On reaching the first tee a fellow-member said to him: 'Are you going out to play, Mac?' He replied that he was and asked the interrogator if he wanted to join him. 'No, I just want to watch you' was the reply. This puzzled him even more, but he proceeded to indulge in a few practice swings before driving off. It was only when he was engaged in this exercise

195

that he realised that he was still wearing his bowler hat! When he had to give up golf through ill health I resigned from Dalmahoy. Golf was never quite the same without him, but he fought his illness with that patience and tranquillity of purpose which characterised his whole life right up until his death.

In due course I joined Kilspindie, a delightful little course in Aberlady, near Gullane, while still retaining my membership of the Royal Burgess. By this time I was on the Bench and my name was on the waiting list for Muirfield. When my turn came for admission there, I became a member of the club whose course many of the top golfers regard as the finest one of all. Being a member of three clubs seemed somewhat superfluous so I resigned from the Royal Burgess.

I have never played in club competitions at Muirfield. I confined my activities to matches such as our own Bench and Bar foursomes, and Bench and Bar contests with the English Bench and Bar, which is an annual event played in alternate years at Muirfield and Woking, with the North of Ireland Bench and Bar played in alternate years at Muirfield and Portrush (now alas in abeyance), and a fleeting contest with the Southern Ireland Bench and Bar played at Gullane No 1 and Portmarnoch in successive years. There is also an annual match between the Bench and Bar and the WS Society at Muirfield which I played in regularly until recently. A standard game at Muirfield is a two-ball foursome, a form of game which I originally detested but which I came to like and enjoy. On one occasion I won our own Bench and Bar foursomes, and I did so with Willie Fleming as my partner. He was called to the Bar four years before I was born, and I was a judge at the time we forged our way to the final and victory. He was a dear old fellow and even at his age – he was born in 1880 and was at least eighty at the time – he was an excellent foursome partner. He could not hit his drives very far, but he was always straight – thereby giving support to the doubtfully understood advice of an old caddy to an English visitor: 'The secret of Muirfield is – keep the ba' on the clippit bit.' His short game was incredibly good, and his putting was deadly. His eyesight
196

was not too good and I remember that at one hole (the 14th) when he had to play a shot to the green, he could not see the flag and asked his caddy for a line. 'Do you see that big white house on the hill? – that's your line.' Willie, who kept a record of the result of every match he played, knew the course and distances like the back of his hand. He selected a club, lined himself up on the white house and played his pitch, leaving the ball nine inches from the hole. That left me with my favourite – and best – stroke, and we won the hole and eventually the match.

If we found four judges who were free on a Monday, a judge's four-ball match was arranged. During one such match in which I was partnered by Lord Johnston against Lord Justice-Clerk Thomson and Lord Mackintosh, we witnessed what was possibly the most amazing feat ever carried out on any golf course, let alone on the tigerish Muirfield. We had reached the twelfth tee and were preparing to drive off when a four-ball match came up the long fifth hole which runs parallel but in the opposite direction to the twelfth. The four players had each played their second shots and their balls were strung across the fairway about 80 yards from the green. In accordance with convention we waited until they had played their third shots before driving off. The convention is not so much a matter of good manners as a recognition of the waywardness of some drivers, a category which does not exclude judges. Anyway the first player pitched up and his ball went into the hole. The second followed suit. The third was somewhat over-enthusiastic because his ball hit the pin and bounced a couple of yards to the side instead of going into the hole. The fourth, however, restored normality for his pitch went into the hole. I realise that this sounds incredible, because the odds against it happening must be astronomical, but I give my solemn assurance that this happened. Alas, the other three judicial witnesses are now dead, and, apart from the performers if they are still alive, I am the only person who can vouch the occurrence.

Golf is a more satisfactory game than tennis for an ageing parent. Father can teach his sons the rudiments of tennis, but within a few years they have sprouted to the six-foot stage

197

and blast the ball past their decrepit tutor to his increasing discomfiture. At golf your game is regulated not by your opponent but by your own ability or inability and the hazards of the course. That makes it easier to take on your sons as the years roll by, and so I gave up tennis in favour of golf exclusively.

14 Reflections

On re-reading what I put down on paper from my recollections of events without the benefit of contemporaneous notes I began to reflect on some of the topics with which I had dealt in perhaps too sketchy a fashion. In particular, I felt that while I had touched on certain legal matters in the course of my historical review of events, it might be appropriate to devote a chapter to my reflections as a judge on various aspects of the law and its administration.

1 Politician and judge

I suppose that some people may wonder how a person who has lived such a political life can exercise that impartiality and objectivity which is required as a judge. It is basically a matter of mental self-discipline. As I have said on many occasions, the judge has to administer the law as it is, not as he would like it to be. This is what his judicial oath requires him to do and what common sense dictates. I have never allowed my personal or political views to interfere with or affect my legal judgments. I can illustrate that by reference to two occasions when a Labour-controlled local authority came before my Division of the Court charged with contempt of court in that they had failed to obtemper an order of the court.

What had happened was this. Parliament had passed legislation which required local authorities with responsibility for housing to carry out certain administrative duties, and which had given to the Secretary of State power to order the authorities to carry out these duties if they had failed to do so. The Secretary of State, with the authority of the Act of Parliament behind him, came to court and obtained an order from the court instructing the local authority to perform their statutory duty within a prescribed time. The local authority failed to do so and this was reported to the court by the Secretary of State. We properly refused to allow the justification for the Act of Parliament to be discussed, since it was not suggested that it was *ultra vires* and the justification for it was for Parliament to decide not the court. Accordingly, the only question was the nature of the penalty which was to be imposed and in each case we imposed a substantial fine. In imposing these fines, I pointed out that the court was not passing judgment on the merits or demerits of the Act but was affirming and asserting the authority of the court. We imposed the sentence for the deliberate flouting of that authority.

Without appearing to be complacent, I do not consider that there is anything basically wrong with the law of Scotland and its administration which calls for radical surgery. Any imperfections are of a procedural nature which, with one or two exceptions, could be remedied by the court without resort to legislation. After more than 53 years in the law and over 31 of them on the Bench there are naturally a number of things which one might or might not want to see changed. In my view most of these are in the realm of criminal law, and as there are usually strongly opposing views on proposals for change in this sphere it is better that changes should be preceded by an investigation in depth by an official and responsible committee of inquiry, such as the Thomson Committee which preceded the Criminal Justice Act 1980. Many of the provisions of that Act stemmed from the recommendations of that Committee.

2 Capital punishment

From time to time the issue of capital punishment being restored arises, and it is perhaps of interest to draw attention to significant situations which existed between the third and the fifth decades of this century. From the end of July 1928 to mid-December 1945 no one was hanged in Scotland. From the end of July 1934 until 26 June 1944 there was only one verdict of guilty of murder returned in 76 murder trials in Scotland and that one was quashed on appeal. There were numerous cases where the charge of murder was disposed of on a defence of insanity at the time of the offence or insanity in bar of trial (that the accused was insane and unfit to plead). Moreover, many of the murder charges were disposed of on a plea or verdict of culpable homicide. The most significant of the figures is the one which shows that in the years between 1934 and 1945 there was only one jury verdict of murder and that one had to be quashed. I realise that individual views on capital punishment may be changed by circumstances, but it is not unreasonable to assume that during that period juries were averse to returning a verdict which would carry with it the sentence of death. While such an attitude might change it is at least equally possible that it might not, but the figures are interesting, relating as they do to part of a period when gang warfare and the use of an open razor as a weapon were prevalent.

My personal experience of such cases was that, because of the aversion to the death penalty, juries looked sympathetically at any alternative verdict which was left open to them on the facts. The principal alternative was a verdict of culpable homicide on diminished responsibility or provocation. Such qualified defences were bolstered up by opinion evidence on the subject by alienists and psychiatrists whose sympathetic approach often bordered on the absurd, but which was gratefully scooped up by jurors of a similar mind. This was particularly obvious when the defence of diminished responsibility was raised. The matter was compounded by the fact that the doctors took a different view from the lawyers on what constitutes insanity and diminished responsibility. Clearly it was the legal view which had to prevail in a criminal trial, but many of the doctors were not prepared to cede that. In any event, some of their theories advanced as opinions could not hold water in the eyes of lawyers, and I have heard the most unbelievable theories

201

propounded. However, when the unbelievable is believed in a criminal trial it is evidence which can be proceeded upon, and that is what happened. I am not suggesting that there were not any perfectly legitimate defences, supported by appropriate evidence, but there were far too many of the other kind. I leave the matter there for the readers to formulate their own opinions.

3 Corporal punishment

The other vexed question which raises its head from time to time is the matter of corporal punishment. The demand for its restoration is usually refuelled when there has been an upsurge of crimes of violence with or without sexual overtones. The abolition of whipping for such offences goes back for well over 100 years so far as adults are concerned, and it is usually adults who are involved in such crimes. By the Act of 25 Victoria chapter 18, section 2, the power to order whipping of offenders, apart from children, was almost abrogated in 1862. It was provided that no offender above 16 years of age should be whipped for theft or for crimes committed against person or property. Section 2 of the English Criminal Justice Act 1948, which was applied to Scotland by section 81 of that Act, provided that 'no person shall be sentenced by a court to whipping; and as far as any enactment confers power on a court to pass a sentence of whipping it shall cease to have effect.' This comprehended offenders under 16 years of age and so the birch disappeared. The history of these Acts should be borne in mind when restoration of corporal punishment is being considered. It is much more difficult to unscramble eggs than to scramble them.

4 Verdicts in criminal cases

I consider that the time has come for the figures of a majority verdict in a criminal trial to be announced in open court. I see no compelling justification for the retention of the existing system of non-disclosure. The change would eliminate any chance of a mistaken or an invalid verdict being announced since it would disclose *ex facie* any such error. Our system of two forms of acquittal verdict, not guilty and not proven, results in three possible verdicts being left open to the jury, and contains the seeds of mistake or misapprehension. That leads to the vexed question of the justification for the retention of two forms of acquittal verdict. There might be an ancillary argument on which verdict should go if acquittal could only be by one verdict, but that, in my opinion, causes no real problem. The difficulty in getting people to accept the logical argument lies basically in sentiment which overrides logic. The fact that the not proven verdict is ours and nobody else's seems to outweigh all other considerations. It sits uneasily beside the fundamental concept of the presumption of innocence.

Hume on Crimes, 11. 422, deals with the history and introduction of the not proven verdict which to my mind establishes quite clearly that it was the product of a procedure which was instituted towards the end of the seventeenth century 'when the fashion was introduced of giving special interlocutors of relevancy on the libel, which naturally gave occasion to a corresponding change in the style also of the verdict.' The jury were called upon to give a verdict on whether the facts in the special interlocutor were proved and this led to 'proven' or 'not proven'. Thus the not proven verdict was born. Prior to this, 'not proven' was not one of the alternative verdicts which were in use, and now that the procedure which gave rise to it has long ceased to operate, the justification for its retention only exists in sentiment or in nostalgia. There is another account of how the not proven verdict came into existence. It is to the following effect. In the time of the Covenanters religious and political views were thought to influence jurors more than the evidence adduced in court. Jurors were unwilling to find one of their own persuasion guilty or one of the opposite persuasion not guilty. Accordingly, the Lord Advocate, Sir George Mackenzie, devised the procedure of setting out in the dittay (the charge) all the points upon which the prosecution relied for a conviction, and the jury's function was to find these points proven or not proven. If they were not proven the prosecution fell. If they were found to be proven it was for the judge to decide whether they constituted the charge as a matter of law. This removed from the jury the responsibility of finding the accused guilty and appeased consciences. Perhaps these were just two different ways of explaining the same innovation. On any view the need for the expedient has long since passed.

Hume a little later on says: 'Not uncommonly the phrase "not proven" has been used to mark a deficiency only of lawful evidence to convict the pannel; and that of "not guilty" to convey the jury's opinion of his innocence of the charge.' There was a time when this formula was adopted by judges and given to the jury in presenting them with the different forms of verdict open to them, but that practice has shaded off considerably in recent times. *Hume* just records this as a matter of practice but he does not give any expression of approval or disapproval of it; nor does he seek any justification for it. With all due respect to those who wish to see it retained, I feel that the logical argument must prevail against it. The presumption of innocence which means that an accused is held to be innocent until proved guilty, and the requirement that the prosecutor has to prove his case beyond reasonable doubt combine to establish that if there is a reasonable doubt about the prosecution case which has the effect of holding that it has not been proved, then the accused is deemed to be innocent and so not guilty would be the correct verdict.

If there is no place in our present system for the non proven verdict it should disappear. There are defence lawyers who consider that if that were done accused persons would lose an advantage, namely an escape for jurors who have doubts about the accused's guilt but are unwilling to give him a certificate of innocence. If jurors are paying heed to the proper directions which a judge should give, they have to consider whether any doubts they have are real doubts and not, for example, just prejudices, and if they are real whether they are reasonable in all the circumstances of the case. If they are, they should acquit on a not guilty basis; if they are not they should convict on a guilty verdict. In recent times, the late Lord Justice-General Cooper, Lord Cameron and I have queried the justification for the not proven verdict. The only logical argument to support its retention is that it should constitute the one form of acquittal verdict, but in competition 'not guilty' would seem to have the prior claim. Not only was it the original verdict, but it is consistent with the presumption-of-innocence concept.

Sentimental adherence to the not proven verdict can only be at the expense of the standing of Scots law which would be seen to be clinging to something which is indefensible in logic and a relict of a procedure long since abandoned. I trust, therefore, that sooner rather than later, this anomaly which Sir Walter Scott once referred to as 'that bastard verdict, not proven,' will be removed from our criminal law.

5 Legal aid

I have already expressed my views on the changes currently being made in the administration of legal aid. Whatever the system may be, I share with many people the desire to see that it is run properly and is not made the subject of abuse at the expense of the public purse. There is in my view one glaring flaw in the system being operated at present and which is liable to occur in any other system unless checked. It is a situation where more fees can be paid to lawyers for inefficiency than would be paid for efficiency. Let me table a case in point. It is in the civil sphere and I choose it because it most easily demonstrates the flaw. In civil cases a party has to present his case in written pleadings. If the pleadings are lacking in specification or do not reveal a case or a defence in law, the other side can take a plea to the specification or to the relevancy of the pleadings. If such a plea is successful then technically the pursuer's action could be dismissed or the defences could be held to be irrelevant. In practice, however, it usually follows that the unsuccessful party asks to be allowed to lodge a Minute of Amendment to cure the defects in the pleadings. If this is allowed, it is usually on the basis of expenses thereby caused being paid to the other side. It is not unknown for this to happen more than once, and if the unsuccessful party is legally aided, the counsel and solicitor can be paid fees for preparing the necessary amendments and for the further appearances in court to get the defects and deficiencies rectified. One cannot generalise on this because the defects may be due to negligence, or inefficiency, both of which are blameworthy, or to an obscurity in the law which has to be clarified by the court, where the blameworthiness may be slight or even nonexistent. Only the judge dealing with the case is in a position to know whether it falls within one or the other category, and the extent of the fault if it exists.

Accordingly, I suggest that statutory power should be given to the judge to order that in respect of matters in the process where expense has been unnecessarily incurred through the negligence, carelessness or inefficiency of the lawyers acting on behalf of a legally assisted person, no fees will be paid to the lawyers out of the Legal Aid Fund in respect of the expense caused by such additional procedure. I see no justification for a premium being put on efficiency and a bonus being placed on inefficiency. The circumstances can be so varied that I do not see anyone being in a better position to determine such matters than the judge who is dealing with the case. The same policy should be operated in criminal cases. I realise that it is more difficult to identify deliberate or culpable wasting of time by various devices so that trials are unnecessarily prolonged, but that does happen. On the other hand, care has to be exercised to see that a legitimate handling of the defence is not circumscribed by the threat of loss of fees. Again, only the judge can determine whether there have been deliberate and contrived delays in the trial which were quite unnecessary for the proper promotion of the defence, and I would suggest that the judge should be given the statutory power to curtail fees out of the Legal Aid Fund in respect of deliberate and unnecessary delays occasioned by the way that the defence has been carried out.

6 Procedure for change

The law is an on-going process, and the law and its procedures must be fashioned to meet the needs of the times. The machinery is there for this to be monitored – the Law Commission, the Rules Councils for the Court of Session and the Sheriff Court, *ad hoc* committees to consider and report on specific matters, and Royal Commissions for wider and more fundamental problems. In view of the alarming growth of criminal cases and the problems arising therefrom, I suggest that there should be set up a standing Criminal Law Revision Committee. This should be broadly based, and so would be more objective and authoritative than some of the groups which have sprung up during the past few years, which may savour of self-interest, and appear to be lacking in independence and objectivity.

7 Sentencing policy

Sentencing policy was a subject in which I was deeply involved, particularly during my years as Lord Justice-Clerk. Both in presiding over the Court of Criminal Appeal and in dealing with so many cases which found their way to the High Court for sentence, I had to play a significant role in the formulation of sentencing policy. The Criminal Appeal Court is in a particularly strong position to establish a sentencing policy, especially in a period of escalating crime, when serious offences, hitherto rare, become so common as to constitute a social crisis. As the two Divisions of the Appeal Court sit alternately on criminal appeals it is manifestly desirable that they should follow and appear to follow the same lines. I am happy to say that on this, both the Divisions in my time were on the same wavelength.

There are various factors which, so far as relevant, should be taken into account in deciding the appropriate disposal of any particular case. The factors which are usually cited are the punitive element, the individual and the general deterrent elements, the retributive element, the reformative element, and the elements of public safety and public interest.

The degree to which any one of these factors will play a part will depend on the circumstances of the particular case, but in my experience the major clash tended to be between the public interest and the public safety on the one hand and the interests of the accused on the other. This can lead to strong emotive arguments on either side. The judge is there to take a dispassionate view and decide which (and to what extent) competing submissions should prevail.

This was most strongly impressed upon me during my sojourn to the United States when I was visiting the penal establishments as a member of the Royal Commission on Penal Reform. A party of us were visiting a very modern Federal prison to which had been sent some of the worst prisoners from outmoded prisons which had been closed down. Everything was ultra-modern with closed circuit television and electronics allowing two men in a control room to do work which previously occupied the personal attention of a substantial number of staff. There was, however, a strange atmosphere about the place which some of us put down to the impersonal nature of the gadgets by which the place was run and the lack of proper human relationships. I happened to be leading the party at the time and I asked the warden if we could have a private session with a dozen of the worst cases. He was very reluctant to agree because of the records of the men, and one of the commissioners was a lady, but with her help I managed to persuade him to let us have our way. I felt that if we had a bodyguard of prison officers we would never get anywhere with the prisoners. It was arranged that we should have a one hour's session with them, but in the result we had two and a half hours, and at that we had to put on the closure. I appreciate that it could be said that any escape from the normal routine would be a relief to prisoners who would have an incentive to prolong the discussions, but the discussions were so absorbing that it was the interest taken in the topics which prolonged the proceedings and nothing else.

I asked them to give their views on this ultra-modern prison, how it was run, and the régime in general. Of the twelve prisoners, eleven were very intelligent and articulate. The crimes of which they were convicted included murder, rape, dope peddling, armed robbery and stealing motor-cars. In modern America, a motor-car is just about as necessary for survival as the horse was in the Old West, and stealing a car today is looked upon with the same severity as stealing a horse was in years past. What came through from their contribution was that our surmise was correct − that in the midst of all the modern equipment human relationships had been badly dented. The point of the story however is this. The leader of the prisoners in their criticism was a tall good-looking young man of distinctly Italian appearance, who had acted as our waiter at lunchtime. Our intelligence was that he had been convicted for a fourth time for pushing drugs, that he was associated with the Mafia, that he had been sentenced to 30 years' imprisonment, and that because of the nature of the offence and its threat to society there would be no question of parole being granted. After re-counting a number of criticisms about the régime this man said to us: 'I am in here for 30 years. I am 26 years of age. I know that there is no parole for me. They have devised a programme to train me for my release into society when I am 56, and they are surprised that I am unwilling to co-operate in what I regard as a wholly unrealistic situation.'

That epitomises the stark nature of the problem, looked at from the prisoner's point of view; but the other side of the coin has to be looked at. It is even more stark. The traffic in drugs, especially hard drugs, is perhaps the biggest social problem in the United States. Apart from the effects of these drugs on human lives and the consequential degradation, despair, misery and injury, often fatal, to health, this pernicious traffic is at the root of so much crime in that country, just as it is becoming in this country. Serious crimes are motivated and committed in order to obtain the wherewithal to acquire drugs. Other serious crimes are committed by people acting under the influence of such drugs.

I cannot leave the story of that meeting without an interesting epilogue. At the end of our discussions, I thanked the prisoners for giving us their time and for the contributions which they had made to the proceedings. As we rose to leave the room, the leader to whom I have referred asked if he could say a few words. I indicated my assent, whereupon he said, and I repeat his words verbatim because they were etched on my memory: 'Sir, on behalf of my colleagues and myself, I would like to thank you and your colleagues for coming here to talk to us. Among us we have collectively first-hand experience of many of the prisons in this country, but you are the first set of people who thought it worthwhile to come and ask us for our views on the system – and you crossed the Atlantic to do it.' It all sounded so civilised, yet, having regard to his background and record, it was quite clear that there was at least the distinct danger that on his release, whenever it took place, he would be back among his 'colleagues' in the Mafia, peddling drugs on a scale consistent with the activities of that organisation. So which interest should prevail?

The same problem kept cropping up before me in court, particularly during my tenure of office as Lord Justice-Clerk, and it was not confined to drug cases. When a case comes to the High Court it is there because of the seriousness of the offence or offences or the significant nature of the accused's previous convictions, or a combination of both. A wider range of sentences is more readily available in the lower courts than it is in the High Court, and yet people keep urging the High Court in a serious case to adopt a form of disposal which might be appropriate in the lower courts in respect of a much lesser offence, but which would be wholly inappropriate for the type of offence for which the accused has to be sentenced.

To provide examples of this, I have in mind two cases where the accused had pled guilty to culpable homicide on a charge of murder. The Crown had accepted a plea of guilty to the lesser offence on the basis that there had been an element of provocation on the part of the deceased. In each case there was room for doubt whether there had been provocation as the law interprets that term, but as the Crown had accepted the reduced plea the case had to proceed on that basis. This meant that the sentence to be imposed had

210

to be altered from the mandatory one of life imprisonment to such determinate disposal as the judge might determine. In both cases, on the strength of a recommendation made by the social worker in a social enquiry report that the court should place the accused on probation, defence counsel urged me to adopt that form of disposal in view of the provocation alleged. Now in each case the killing was a brutal and deliberate one. The element of provocation had already been taken into account by the Crown reducing the charge from murder to culpable homicide, but I was being asked to make a further reduction on the sentence on the same ground, and for the same reasons. Even the previous clean record of the accused could not wipe out the callous and brutal killing of a woman in the prime of life. Much was made of the recommendation for probation by the social worker, although I had previously made it clear from the bench that it was no part of a social worker's duty in submitting a social enquiry report to recommend a form of disposal to the court. A social enquiry report can be helpful to the court at any level to set out the factual background and history of an accused person, but it is for the judge and the judge alone to determine the matter of disposal. The judge has to take into account all the relevant factors. Many of the recommendations are made on the basis of what would be best for the accused – rather like a doctor prescribing a remedy for a patient – without any regard to the nature of the offence. What is relevant is for the social worker to say, as many of the experienced ones now do, that if the court is considering a certain form of disposal the accused is a suitable subject for it.

At a meeting which took place some years ago at the request of senior social workers, the then three senior judges, Lord Emslie, Lord Cameron and I, explained and laid down the foregoing principles regarding the contents of social enquiry reports for the benefit of the courts, but although this was acknowledged by the senior social workers present, the same format of a recommendation on disposal continues to appear in many reports. As in the two cases I have mentioned above, I have had occasion to point out in court the disadvantages which such wholly inappropriate recommendations, and pleas by counsel in further support of them, can produce. The relatives and friends of the accused can be led into hoping that such a disposal is at least a likelihood if not a certainty, only to have their hopes dashed by a judge who takes a realistic view of the circumstances, not the least being the nature of the crime. I do not wish to appear to be inhibiting people from putting forward anything which is relevant to the mitigation of sentence. I am merely pointing out that the introduction of unrealistic submissions does not advance the plea in mitigation and may lead to unnecessary disappointments.

This leads me to consider the factors to be taken into account. So far as the punitive element of punishment is concerned, it is only extremists who say that it should not be a factor at all – a view which runs contrary to an otherwise general view that it is right when people break the law or the rules that they should be punished. The offenders usually accept that, the only issue being the form and extent of the punishment. Even being taken away from family and home is in itself a punishment to anyone with sensitivity. I have often referred to general and individual deterrents and the difficulty of assessing how successful the general deterrent is. Statistics can be produced to establish that a general deterrent has not succeeded by reference to subsequent offences, but it is difficult if not impossible to get figures of those who have been deterred. One thing is clear to me.

In considering the deterrent factor one has also to have in mind the factor which in my book counts for a great deal – the protection of decent law-abiding people and their families, who are entitled to look to the courts to adopt justifiable measures to protect the law-abiding from the law breakers. A form of crime may become so rife in a country or in a community that people go about their normal pursuits in fear and trepidation of becoming the latest victims of the wrongdoers. In that situation, I consider that the judges are entitled to sound the warning that in order to call a halt to that form of crime severe sentences will be imposed on persons who commit it, and to follow this through by imposing such sentences if the warning is disregarded. I know that if I cite examples I shall be accused in certain quarters of being emotive, but what I have to say is based not on emotion but on years of experience on the bench. People find all kinds of explanations for crime and its current increase, but in my experience, so far as serious crime is concerned, there are the following root causes: drink, an obsession with sex, a desire to get easy money quickly, and drugs. There are all kinds of excuses put forward in mitigation of serious crimes, but there is usually one or more of these factors in the background of the actual offence, over and above conditions which are common to all citizens in the same circumstances as the accused, most of whom are able to cope without breaking the law. In many of the cases of serious assault right up to murder there has been a background history of excessive drinking and now drugs. Often the difference between murder and serious assault, where knives or similar implements are used, is the result of factors with which the accused has had nothing to do. I have already referred to them, but for present purposes I must repeat them. They are the trajectory of the wound and its proximity – even to an eighth of an inch – to a vital part of the body, the proximity of the locus of the assault to a hospital where the victim can get early surgical attention, and the skill of a surgeon. The reckless criminality of the aggressor is just the same in both cases, and this has to be borne in mind in determining the appropriate sentence.

There seems to be a view taken by a growing number of men that females are fair game for sexual intercourse, and so, when the females are not co-operative they are forced to submit to the man's sexual demands. I wonder to what extent this view stems from television and films. There is much talk at the present time about the effect of violence shown on television, but there is another evil influence stemming from the media. Time after time on television you find the macho 'hero' meeting a girl for the first time and before you know where they are they are in bed together. If this was essential to the plot it might be argued that such a scene was defensible, but in virtually every case, the bed

213

scene is entirely gratuitous and is introduced simply to add salacity to the proceedings. This alone might cause young males to think that this is the natural outcome of a casual meeting, just as so many newspapers, hoping to win the circulation battle by printing nude pictures, provide the sumulus to embark on sexual escapades. One of the most terrible features of the increase in sexual assaults is the number of such assaults which are being perpetrated on young children, and it is only the fortunate ones who are not subjected to further vicious assaults or even fatal ones. This is not a problem which relates only to females. Young boys are subjected to such treatment by deviant males, and many parents are afraid to let their children out of their sight because of the danger. Going to and coming back from school are periods of great concern to parents, and the protection of the public must obviously play an important part in determining the appropriate sentence in such cases.

In some of these sexually-deviant cases, I have been informed by doctors that there is no known cure. This means that however long a sentence is imposed, the deviant is entitled to be set free as soon as his stated period of incarceration, less remission, has been served. It also means that such a person is knowingly let loose on society, and people, young and old, are put at risk. It seems to me that for the proper protection of the public, and indeed in some cases in the interests of the offender, the appropriate disposal is a sentence of life imprisonment, it being made clear to him that this means he will be detained until such time as the authorities are satisfied that he is sufficiently cured to allow him to be released without posing a danger to society. This would involve co-operation by the offender in any remedial treatment being provided to him, and would hopefully inspire such co-operation.

It is frequently represented in court, no doubt with the intention of having the period of incarceration cut down, that sexual offenders (and particularly those who offend against children) are subjected to harassment and physical violence at the hands of other prisoners. However reprehensible criminal conduct may be, the punishment should

214

be determined and carried out by the properly constituted authorities, not by fellow prisoners. Deviant offenders should probably be housed in a special type of institution where both the appropriate type of punishment and the appropriate remedial treatment should be provided.

Another aspect of this form of crime which almost baffles comprehension is the number of old women who are the victims of attacks, often by young men. Old women living alone are exposed to the danger of men getting access to their homes on some pretext or other and then to assaults in order to extract information on where money or valuables are to be found, coupled with threats of further visits and further assaults if the police are informed. Then, almost unbelievably, there are occasions when very old women are the victims of a rape or some other form of sexual assault irrespective of their ages. I had a case where an old woman of 84 was such a victim and other cases where the victims were in the upper seventies. Probably the most lasting damage is to their minds. They live thereafter in a constant state of dread. Every time there is a knock on their door they panic, and the previous experience is vividly brought back into their minds.

Such dastardly crimes obviously warrant severe punishment, and if warnings that severe punishment will be imposed on persons resorting to that form of criminal conduct are ignored it may well call for a stepping-up of sentences to drive home the message that the courts are not kidding. If women cannot feel at peace in their own homes, and women and children cannot go about without the fear of a sexual attack, there is a cancer in our society in the eradication of which the law must play its full part.

The upsurge in armed robbery and other forms of hold-up, and the development of the drug-pushing trade have the same common root: the desire for quick, easy and lucrative financial returns. Particularly in cases of pushing drugs, people have become involved who have no previous criminal record. They have been induced to go into crime by the greed for easy money. They are an integral part of the big money business in drugs which is proving such a menace in our society. The lesson from the United States and other countries is clear. The big shots at the top often manage to keep themselves clear of detection one way or another, but if you can cut off those who are the actual dealers in the chain of distribution you are effectively cutting off the trade. In my view, if the big shots are caught exceedingly long sentences are justified, and if the dealers are caught their indispensable part in this pernicious traffic warrants substantial sentences, both as a punishment and as a deterrent, individual and general.

Armed robberies have become commonplace, and the lure of substantial money hauls is attracting small-time crooks and persons who have never been in trouble before, as well as hardened criminals. It has to be made plain by stiff sentences that those who venture into this form of crime are in a game in which the stakes are high on both sides. Moreover, inexperienced criminals tend to panic more in a crisis than the hardened professionals, and firearms, particularly sawn-off shotguns, in the hands of a panic-stricken individual are potentially lethal. Here again substantial sentences may be called for, even in the case of a first offender.

These various types of cases underline the extent to which our prison system is inadequate and the need for more varied penal institutions so that people who have offended against the law in many differing ways are not housed in the one institution and subjected substantially to the same régime. Apart from new prisons to solve the overcrowding problems the need for diversification of penal institutions is clear. I appreciate that in competition with so many other things required in our society, such as hospitals, schools and social services, additional facilities for people who have broken the law do not have a high priority in the public mind, but such changes are manifestly required.

I resent the lobbies which, instead of clamouring for such diversification, call upon the judges to cut down long sentences in order to ease the burden of overcrowded prisons. The answer to the problem of overcrowded and inadequate prisons lies in the building of more purpose-built prisons and not in interfering with the proper instruments of the
216

administration of justice. In our way of life, it is judges and judges alone who determine the appropriate sentences. This may be qualified to a certain extent by restrictions laid down by parliament. There may be sentences prescribed by law with no discretion left to the judge. Or limits may be set on the term of imprisonment to be imposed (the 'max-min' system). Subject to that, however, judges should not be dictated to by politicians on the subject of sentencing in an attempt to find a solution to a problem that they themselves should be solving. The contrary view is the first step in undermining the impartiality of the judiciary and the freedom of judges from political pressure. The contrary view is a characteristic of a totalitarian state and not of a democracy.

I agree, however, with the suggestion that there should be restrictions on sending people to prison for short periods for minor offences. Many more alternatives are available. Cluttering up prisons with short-term prisoners only magnifies the problems of the prison authorities. The trauma of being in prison for the first time may have a deterrent effect on some first offenders but the minor recidivists can 'do it on their ear'.

8 Attempts to defeat justice

There is one further matter to which I feel that I must allude. The administration of justice is being fettered, and has been fettered for some time now, by the difficulty in getting appropriate evidence into court. For various reasons witnesses are unwilling either to come forward or to adhere to their statements if they are obliged to go into the witness-box. The unwillingness of witnesses to come forward at all to give evidence of an occurrence which happened in their presence would appear to be due to an alarming and widespread incidence of myopia, and when their eyesight has been good enough to permit them to make a statement relevant to the offence, a serious attack of amnesia is liable to set in by the time they have entered the witness-box. The absence of evidence from such people often results in a prosecution failing. The myopia may be self-induced. The amnesia is often explained away by allegations that threats have been made and the fear of reprisals. If it is established that such witnesses have admittedly lied in giving evidence, they can be dealt with at the end of the trial by the judge on the ground of contempt of court through prevarication. If the witness does not admit having lied in his or her evidence but the prosecutor considers that he has evidence to establish that the witness had lied, then a charge of perjury can be brought in a separate prosecution. By such conduct a serious blow to the administration of justice has been struck, and, depending on the circumstances, a very substantial sentence may be called for. If, on the other hand, the reluctance of the witness to tell the truth is said to be the result of threats to him or his family, a serious problem is posed for the judge. The threats may be real or fictitious, the latter being quite easy to conjure up. If this succeeds the whole case may collapse.

This means that the administration of justice is being determined not by the normal processes of the law and by the duly authorised authorities, but by thugs who utter such threats to save their own skins or the skins of their friends. It is the duty of people who are genuinely subjected to such threats to report the matter to the police and seek protection. If they ignore this duty and deliberately go into the witness-box and commit perjury they must accept the consequences. These may have to be severe in the interest of the proper administration of justice. This should be made clear and carried into practice if the warning is ignored. Manifestly if the people who utter such threats are brought to book the punishment imposed should be commensurate to the damage done or sought to be done to the administration of justice and should reflect to a high degree both the punitive and the deterrent elements.

9 The criminal

The actions of professional criminals provide an interesting study. The prospective gains are so large that people from all walks of life are being attracted into high-return crime. When that form of crime has severe antisocial effects these gamblers must be taught that if the stakes are high the losses must be made to outweigh the gains. Carefully prepared plans are as essential to many of these large coups as the careful execution of the plans, which often call for a high degree of self-discipline. An example of this was exposed during the Shettleston bank robbery to which I have already referred. The accused McKay and Gray, had seduced a young bank clerk who was a frequenter of Gray's betting shop, and persuaded him to bring the keys of the bank outside for a sufficient period to enable impressions of them to be made before returning them to their normal place. This was done, and, despite one misfire, duplicate keys for the front door and the safe were obtained. The information on which the crooks were proceeding was that the best time to rob the bank was the eve of the last day of the month when some £40,000 would be in the safe for paying out teachers' salaries on the following day. When the duplicate keys were obtained, it was decided to carry out a dummy run one night in the middle of the month to make sure that the keys worked. When the robbers got into the bank and opened the safe they found money in it which they took out and counted. It amounted to £16,000. They then put the money back into the safe, locked it and left the premises, closing the front door behind them. They returned on the eve of the end of the month, went through the same procedure up to the point of counting the money. When they discovered that the money amounted to almost £40,000 they took it away, locking the front door behind them.

All the risks which attended that operation were present on the previous occasion when £16,000 was there for the taking, but they spurned what must have been a great temptation and took all the risks again for the greater haul. The stolen money was never recovered. Dandy McKay

219

disappeared to the United States where he had facial plastic surgery. Gray was tried and convicted of the charge, having been involved both in the plotting of the crime and in its execution. McKay left the States and went to live in Killiney, a suburb of Dublin, where he was arrested, extradited and brought to trial in Glasgow a year after the trial of Gray had taken place. He had been the mastermind of the operation but had taken no part in its execution. Fortunately in the interests of justice he involved himself in the pay-off to one of the participants, and that, plus an overheard telephone conversation between him and the young bank clerk who had confessed to the police, was sufficient to implicate him. His counsel, Harold Leslie, told me later that when he was down in the cells interviewing McKay while the jury were considering their verdict, with a view to obtaining material relevant to a plea in mitigation in the event of a conviction, McKay said to him: 'Of course, they will convict me. If I get less than ten years I'll be lucky. If I get more than ten years it will be a liberty. If I get ten years it will just be about right.' Need I say? He was convicted and he got ten years.

Although I spent over 31 years on the Bench and had to deal with many accused persons, I have no recollection of ever having to deal with the same person twice – with but one exception, and that was Alexander Gray over whose trial in the Shettleston bank robbery I presided, and who later appeared before me for sentence after pleading guilty to another and lesser offence.

During that 31 years I had to deal with a large variety of cases and a large number of accused. The issue of guilt or innocence is a matter for the jury and not for the judge. It is but natural for a judge to have some view on what the verdict might be or should be. While I appreciate that there have been cases where it has been established on appeal that a jury's verdict cannot stand or subsequent events have established that it was wrong, I am only concerned in what I am about to say with cases in which I personally presided and not cases in general. I have no recollection of ever feeling that the jury had convicted a man whom I thought should have been acquitted on the evidence. On the other hand, on a number of occasions I have felt that an accused had been acquitted when on the evidence he should have been convicted. However, as I have said, that was the jury's function and not mine and it was their view which decided the case. Mistakes are liable to be made either way, but if they are to occur, it is better that they should not be made so that an innocent man is convicted.

10 A final thought

With the general lowering of standards in our society today, it is imperative that standards in the administration of justice should be maintained by all who are involved in it. Once standards are allowed to slip, the rot sets in and a general decline results. In Scotland we are the inheritors of a great legal tradition. It behoves us to see that the standards on which that tradition is based are not eroded. If on occasions I may have appeared over-strict, it was simply because I felt that standards were not being preserved. There is no point in telling a witness to take his hands out of his pockets when giving evidence if the counsel who is asking him the questions is allowed to keep his hands in his pockets. Indeed, there is more excuse for the witness who may be in strange surroundings and has thrust his hands into his pockets to make him feel at ease. That is only a minor example and it is cited to direct attention to the areas where the need to maintain standards is most important. It may be a benefit to a young counsel to correct him early rather than allow him to carry on bad habits. An experienced counsel, that is one experienced in bad habits, should not expect the same gentle treatment. Judges are responsible for the running of their courts and this entails seeing that the appropriate standards are preserved.

Epilogue

Looking back down through the arches of the years, would I have wanted things to be different? In general the answer is 'No', although there are some aspects which I would have liked to be different. I am not referring to my unrealised ambitions to be a 'tottie' boy or a barber's soap boy or a Scottish soccer internationalist. I must consider the more fundamental aspects of my life. I have been most fortunate in that I have enjoyed to a marked degree the work that I have had to carry out in various spheres. However, that was achieved at the expense of the time I had available with the family, and that is something which I wish could have been different. Perhaps it was not possible having regard to the way things fell for me. Perhaps the way in which Nancy coped made me oblivious to the responsibilities I was laying on her shoulders. The fact that there were accordingly no crises was perhaps an opiate. If Clem Attlee had agreed to my leaving the opposition front bench for the back benches to let me have greater freedom to cultivate other political subjects and intervene more often in the parliamentary debates in opposition, I might have spent the rest of my life in politics, providing of course I continued to be returned as an MP. What that may have had in store for me is imponderable. What I know is, it would have prevented me from having the career which I have had as a judge, something which gave me great job satisfaction and which in retirement I have sorely missed.

In honesty I must ask myself the question: with all that has come my way, have the principles and philosophy which motivated me in my early days altered or wavered? The honest answer to that honest question is 'No'. There may have been occasions when I have found myself in disagreement with the way people have sought to apply the principles and the philosophy. That did not mean that the principles and philosophy were wrong. It was the abuse of them that was wrong. I hope that the basic sense of values and priorities which were inculcated in me when I was young are still with me.

And so, may I repeat what may appear to be a recurrent theme? I have been fortunate and I have been blessed. Of course, there have been disappointments in that some things have not turned out as I would have liked, but that is life, and both in my public and in my private life I have been compensated as well as any man could reasonably hope to be. *Deo gratias!*

Index

Index